THE KIDDS OF AMELIA, DINWIDDIE & NOTTOWAY COUNTIES, VIRGINIA, 1734 - 1853

Compiled by Reiley Kidd MD, William R. Kidd, and Sandra K. Kidd

Published by Lulu.com, Morrisville, North Carolina USA

The Kidds of Amelia, Dinwiddie & Nottoway Counties, Virginia, 1734-1853

Compiled by Reiley Kidd, MD, of Seattle, WA, William R. Kidd of Newport News, VA, and Sandra K. Kidd, of Decatur, GA

ISBN: 978-1-6780-9308-2 (paperback)

Published by Lulu.com

TABLE OF CONTENTS

This Table of Contents names most **but not all** of the 52 individuals who appear in this book.
Names not listed here may be found by browsing the book by the person's first name.
All individuals in this book are listed alphabetically by their first name. When two or more persons
share a given name, they are listed in chronological order (earlier individuals first).

INTRODUCTION

This book is a compilation of all the records mentioning the surname of Kidd that we were able to find in Amelia, Dinwiddie and Nottoway Counties, Virginia from 1734, when Amelia County was created, to 1853 (the last year whose records we have examined exhaustively).

We elected to combine these three counties into one book because most of our Kidds lived in the area where these counties converge, as seen in the figure below, and because many of them left records in two or sometimes all three of these counties in their lifetimes.

Figure: An 1895 map of the three-county area covered in this paper. Namozine Creek forms the boundary between Amelia and Dinwiddie counties; Ammon, the small community near which George4 Kidd settled by 1782, is in the SE corner of Amelia County, located in the area just above the "F" of Ford, in Dinwiddie County

We began the ambitious task of producing compilations like this for over twenty Virginia counties with several objectives:

1. To find virtually every existing record mentioning the surname of Kidd in these Virginia counties prior to 1850;
2. To analyze these records and ascertain (if possible) whether the individuals are descendants of the Thomas Kidd who arrived in the Virginia colony by 1648, and if so, their line of descent; and
3. To distinguish between proven, documented relationships and those which are widely shared and held to be accurate, but for which proof is minimal or non-existent.

THE RECORDS OF AMELIA, DINWIDDIE AND NOTTOWAY COUNTIES

Amelia County was formed in 1734 from Prince George and Brunswick counties. Its records are complete. Even the tithables lists (the colonial equivalent of the later personal property tax lists) are extant.

Dinwiddie County was formed in 1752 from Prince George County. A courthouse fire in 1835 destroyed many records up to that point, and General Sheridan's cavalry destroyed many of the remaining records during the latter days of the Civil War.[1] One lone Order Book for 1789 is all that has survived prior to 1835. Deed books are available from 1833 forward, and will books from 1830 forward. Fortunately for us, the Dinwiddie County Personal Property Tax Lists and Land Tax Lists, being state records, were stored elsewhere, and were not lost. These are available via Familysearch.org or the Library of Virginia.

Nottoway County was formed from the southern portion of Amelia County in 1788; prior to that it comprised Nottoway parish of Amelia County. Most of Nottoway County's courthouse records were destroyed or stolen by Union troops in 1865, during the final months of the Civil War.[2] Only a few volumes of deeds, orders and wills survived. Fortunately, as with Dinwiddie County, the Land Tax Lists and Personal Property Tax Lists were state, not county records; these were stored in Richmond, and survived the war.

A list of the sources used in the creation of this compilation are listed in <u>Appendix One</u>, found on page 125 and following.

SOME TIPS ON USING THIS BOOK

ABBREVIATIONS used in this book:

    LoV = Library of Virginia   *LTL(s) = Land Tax List(s)*
    MSX = Middlesex County   *PPTL(s) = Personal Property Tax List(s)*
    RK = Reiley Kidd, one of the authors of this compilation
    WRK = another of the authors of this compilation

---

[1] Jones, Richard L., *Dinwiddie County. Carrefour of the Commonwealth*, Whittet & Shepperson, Richmond, VA, 1976, p. 32., and p. 315. In fact, a smattering of other Dinwiddie County records prior to 1833 also survived (listed on page 315), including Chancery Order Book No. 1, 1832-1852, Record Book Circuit Court of Law & Chancery, 1819-1841, and miscellaneous unbound wills.

[2] This included all the deed books to that date; several deed books were later returned. When WRK, one of the contributors to this paper, visited the Nottoway Courthouse in December of 2002, the Circuit Court Clerk showed him a note in the back of one of the deed books from one of the Yankee soldiers written to "Johnny Reb", stating that they should thank him for returning what books he did.

Names in **<u>BOLD UNDERLINED FONT</u>** *have been added to the Family Tree that we are constructing on Ancestry.com, that includes all the DOCUMENTED descendants of Thomas1 Kidd of Middlesex County, Virginia. This tree can be found at:*
https://www.ancestry.com/family-tree/tree/37652986/family
You may have to copy this URL and paste it into your browser to reach this tree. Once there, be sure to look in the Media Gallery of these individuals, to see what documents and other sources have been added.

EXPLANATION OF THE GENERATIONAL NUMBERING SYSTEM WE USE

Before you get started, an explanation of the numbering system we have used in this book is in order: The number following an individual's name in this compilation indicates the number of generations relative to our common ancestor, Thomas1Kidd. Thus, for example, "George4 (Benjamin3, William2, Thomas1)" is short-hand for "George Kidd, 4 generations down from Thomas the immigrant, and the son of Benjamin3, grandson of William2, etc."
Again, the numbers used in this system refer to the generation of each named individual, *relative to Thomas1 Kidd*, the patriarch of our Kidd family.

Our Kidd ancestors favored several English given names, and repeated them in each generation; George, James, John, William and Benjamin were used in nearly every generation, in multiple branches of a family. In order to separate these individuals with shared names but in the same location and generation, we have arbitrarily listed them as James5a, James5b, etc.

AND NOW, TO THE KIDDS OF AMELIA, DINWIDDIE AND NOTTOWAY COUNTIES, VIRGINIA!

THE KIDDS OF AMELIA, DINWIDDIE
& NOTTOWAY COUNTIES, 1734-1853

The information here is freely shared with Kidd family researchers for their personal use. We ask that you credit this book or the KiddRoots.org website when using this information, and that you use it in its original form. Thank you.

PREFACE

It is our belief that most if not all of the Kidd males in this book are the descendants of Thomas Kidd, the immigrant who was in York County, Virginia by 1646 (hereafter referred to as **Thomas1**), through his son, William (**William2**), and through William's son, Benjamin Kidd (**Benjamin3**). We know that one, and most likely two of Benjamin's sons moved from Middlesex County, Virginia to Amelia County, arriving there by 1762. We know of no other Kidds from other lines arriving later, up to 1850, although one cannot be certain that this did not occur. Because of this geographical and temporal proximity, most if not all the Kidds listed here probably descend from one of these men. The results of the Kidd Y-DNA Project for the descendants of several of these individuals on this list support this hypothesis, but do not prove it.

Benjamin3 Kidd[3] of Middlesex County, Virginia died there in 1761. Shortly thereafter, two of his sons migrated south, and settled in the southeastern corner of Amelia County, VA, near Namozine Creek; their land was within a mile or two of the Dinwiddie County line, and just a few miles north of Nottoway County. The younger son, **Benjamin4 Jr.,** left little trace of his time there, and appears to have returned to Middlesex County. The older son, **George4 Kidd**, remained in Amelia County for the rest of his life. <u>He and his wife Elizabeth raised a large family, including 6 sons; they are the progenitors of the Amelia, Dinwiddie and Nottoway County Kidds, with many descendants scattered across the U.S. today.</u>

Colonial records are difficult to research, since few records have survived, and because most records that have survived relate to individuals with more education and wealth than our ancestors had. Research of this particular family is even more difficult, because they moved back and forth between Amelia County and the two adjacent counties, each just a few miles from where **George4 Kidd** settled in 1763. Two of these counties, Dinwiddie and Nottoway, are among the "burned records" counties, meaning that most early records have been destroyed or lost.[4]

Genealogical research in such situations is akin to working on a 1000-piece jigsaw puzzle in which many pieces are missing – regardless of how hard one works, the picture will never be complete, and some guesswork and imagination will be required.

We have tried to find as many of the "pieces" (the mentions of these ancestors in the historical records of the three counties, and elsewhere) as possible, in order to have the best chance of eventually coming up with a good "picture" of the individuals and their relationships to each other.

---

[3] In our compilations of records left by the Kidds of Virginia, we employ a numbering system to designate an individual's generation, relative to Thomas Kidd, the immigrant and patriarch of the Virginia Kidds. This number follows the individual's name, as in "Benjamin3 Kidd" here; this Benjamin Kidd was in generation three, and was the son of William2 Kidd, and grandson of Thomas1 Kidd, the immigrant.

[4] In Dinwiddie County, fires in 1831 and 1865 destroyed nearly all early records. In Nottoway, most courthouse records were destroyed in 1865, during the Civil War. A few volumes of deeds, wills and court orders have survived.

This compilation lists all historical mentions that we have found for every individual with the surname of Kidd in this 3-county area between 1734 and 1853. Within it, individuals are listed in alphabetical order, by their given name. Entries for each individual are arranged in chronological order. Where more than one person shares a given name, we've attempted to distinguish between them by factors such as varying amounts of land, slaves or other property; names of proven spouse or children; whether literate or not; etc. When that was not possible, we left the data elements under one name, while recognizing that those facts may represent different people. Finally, individuals sharing a particular given name are listed in relative chronological order (i.e., in the order in which they appear in the records).

This compilation of data has been contributed by several individuals,[5] all of whom trace their roots to the area around Namozine Creek. We are indebted to each of them.

ANN M. KIDD, the wife of James6a Kidd. See <u>Nancy M. Kidd</u>.

ARCHER/ARCHIBALD J. KIDD, the son of Jasper5 (George4, Benjamin3, William2, Thomas1) Kidd and his first wife, Susan/Susanna Powell Kidd[6]
Born abt. 1830,[7] in Dinwiddie County, VA[8]
Married (1) Dorothy Mingee on 1 August 1859 in Petersburg, Virginia; two children:
  1. James H. Kidd, born ~1865
  2. Richard E. Kidd, born ~1867
Married (2) Mary Ann Williams on 8 Sept 1868 in Greensville County, VA; three children:
  3. William Haley Kidd, born April 1870 in Brunswick County, VA
  4. John D. Kidd, born 12 August 1876 in Southampton County, VA
  5. Julia Elizabeth Kidd, born 26 August 1881 in Greensville County, VA
Date of death is unknown, but supposedly in Greensville County, VA
Ancestor of Rebecca Starr, one of the contributors to this compilation.

---

[5] Reiley Kidd, a descendant of George4 Kidd via his son, Lodowick; Troy Kidd, a descendant of the same George Kidd, via his son, James5a; William R. Kidd (WRK) of Newport News, Virginia, most likely a descendant of George4 Kidd via his eldest son, Benjamin5; the late Jane Andrews, whose husband Preston was a descendant of Thomas J. Kidd – Thomas J.s connection to George Kidd is unproven, and hypothetical at this time; and Rebecca Starr of England, a descendant of George4 Kidd via his grandson, Archer/Archibald Kidd.
 See <u>Appendix Two</u> on page 135 for an abbreviated Descendants Chart for George4 Kidd (male descendants only).

[6] From the 1868 (second) marriage record of Archer Kidd, which lists his place of birth, and names his parents.

[7] His DOB is very uncertain from the various records he left:
 1850 census listed as 20, makes birth year ca. 1830
 1859 marriage register listed as 31 makes birth year ca. 1828
 1861 Civil War CMSR listed as 31, makes birth year ca. 1830
 1868 marriage register listed as 42, makes birth year ca. 1826
 1870 census listed as 42, makes birth year ca. 1828

[8] Archer's 1859 marriage record lists his place of birth as Dinwiddie County, and that is a contemporaneous record, and thus more likely to be true. The death certificate of his son, William Haley Kidd, states that his father, Archie was born in Mecklenburg County, VA, and that Archer's wife was May (Mary) Williams, born in Brunswick County, VA. A copy of this death certificate was provided to me by his descendant, Rebecca Starr, July 2009. While this is not a primary source for Archer, I'm including it here for completeness.
 Mary's place of birth is uncertain - the 1870 census states she was born in NC.

1846 – Archer appears for the first time on the Dinwiddie County, VA Personal Property Tax List (Lewis P. Lanier's list), listed as **Archibald Kidd**. He was taxed for himself, no property and no horse or mules.

1848 – He appears again on the Dinwiddie PPTL, this time listed as **Archer Kidd**, along with a Francis Kidd, another newcomer to Dinwiddie County. Both have no slaves, horses, or other taxables.

1850 – On the federal census in the Northern District, Dinwiddie County, VA, p. 456, HH 338:
Kidd, Susan 52WF VA
   " , Francis 25WM laborer VA cannot read or write
   " , **Archer** 20WM laborer VA cannot read or write
[This Susan Kidd MAY be the same Susan Kidd who died in magisterial district #1, Dinwiddie County, VA in October 1859.[9]]

1859 – Dinwiddie County, VA Marriage Register: "This is to license and permit you to join together in the Holy State of Matrimony **Arch[d] J. Kidd** and Dorothy Pillian, and for so doing this shall be your warrant. Given under my hand this 30th July 1859.
C.A. Hargrave, clerk." [10]
The marriage occurred on August 1, 1859, in Petersburg. His name is spelled out as **Archibald J. Kidd**, single and age 31, born in Dinwiddie County; her name is the same as above, widowed and age 45, also born in Dinwiddie. Her parents are listed as John Mingee and Raney (from other records we know she was Louise Rainey) Crowder. His parents are listed as "Joseph" Kidd and Susan Powell. We think the father's name is a clerk's error, since the record otherwise perfectly matches our Archibald, son of JASPER Kidd and Susan Powell.[11]

1860 – We are unable to find him on the 1860 census, despite the marriage record above.

1862 – **Archer Kidd** enlisted in the Confederate army, along with his brother, Francis.[12] Both survived the war. He enlisted at Petersburg and then mustered in at Norfolk, VA 10 days later. He was in the Hargrave Blues, which was initially Company I of the 12th VA Infantry, a unit that was later reorganized into Co. K of the 9th VA Infantry.
Substantiating the view that Archer and Archibald were the same person, the single Civil

---

[9] from Ancestry's U.S. Federal Census Mortality Schedules, 1850-1880 database, for Dinwiddie County, VA in 1860, magisterial district #1, p. 193. It lists her as a pauper, and did not indicate her marital status; perhaps the person recording the information or reporting it didn't know her. This might also explain the large discrepancy in her age between the 1850 census and this record.

[10] Dinwiddie County, VA Marriage Register, 1850-1867, p. 60, viewed 6/29/2003 by WRK. Archer's age was listed as 31 and Dorothy's as 45. Rebecca Starr believes that Dorothy was Dorothy Mingee, b. abt. 1812, the daughter of John T. Mingee and Louise Rainey Crowder. She first married Wiley Pillion (or Pillian). Evidently he died, and she then married Archer Kidd. This explains the discrepancy in their ages.

[11] CURRENTLY MISSING THE CITATION FOR THIS ENTRY. One would think that it would be in Dinwiddie County Marriage Register, vol. 1, 1853-1861 (FHL #1929644, item 1) but it is not. Perhaps the page was inadvertently skipped during filming? The Dinwiddie County Court Clerk's office searched their records, without success. They suggest that this record may be in the Petersburg City Marriage Register.

[12] Kidd, Archer: (April 30, 1862), 2nd , Co. A; enlisted at Norfolk; hosp. Jan. 30 - Feb. 29, 1864 (measles) in Confederate States Hospital; present Oct. 1864.
Kidd, Francis: (April 30, 1862), 2nd , Co. A; enl. at Norfolk; present Oct. 62; deserted to the enemy; sent to Washington, D. C.

War file for them has an index card for each, referring to the other name; and the company
and regiment was identical for each name.

1868 – On Sept. 8, 1868, **Archer Kidd**, age 42, married Mary A. Williams (age not listed) in
Greensville County, VA. Archer was widowed at the time of this marriage, and Mary Ann's
marital status was "single." Both were residents of Greensville County at the time of their
marriage.[13] This marriage record lists his parents as **Jasper and Susan Kidd**, and his place
of birth as Dinwiddie County, VA. His occupation is listed as "miller." The space in the
record for the names of the bride's parents was left blank.

1870 – On federal census in Bellefield twp., Greensville County, VA, Poplar Mount P.O., p. 313,
HH 7/7:
Kidd, Archer 42MW farm laborer VA cannot read or write
   " , Mary A. 27FW keeping house NC
   " , James H. 5MW VA
   " , Richard E. 3MW VA
   " , William H. 1/12MW VA   born April

By 1880 – **Archer Kidd** is believed to have died in Greensville County, VA. His wife, Mary A.
Kidd, is listed as a widow at the time of the 1880 federal census.   She and their surviving
children are listed in Belfield district, ED 27, sheet 47C, p. 24, HH 450/464:
Kidd, Mary A. WF 38 <u>widowed</u> farm laborer VA VA VA
   " , James WM 12 S son farm laborer VA VA VA cannot read or write
   " , William WM 8 S son VA VA VA
   " , Jno. D. WM 3 S son VA VA VA
(They are evidently very poor, and live among other farm laborers.)

At this point, the date and place of his death remain a mystery.[14]

**<u>ASA KIDD</u>, the son of George5a (George4, Benjamin3, William2, Thomas1) Kidd of Amelia
County, VA[15],[16]
Born abt 1805 in Amelia County, VA
Married Jane C. Sutherland in 1825
Only two of their children (George F. and Virginia A.) are named in his will; no other
known children, to our knowledge.
Died testate in Dinwiddie County in 1864 or early 1865**

1825 – In a deed signed 3 November 1825, **Asa Kidd** of Amelia County for $393 sold to John H.
Brown of Petersburg, Virginia a parcel of land containing 65 ½ acres, adjoining George
Kidd, the estate of Archer Neal, Bolling's old mill pond, and John H. Brown. This land had
been purchased by said Kidd from Jack Neal. Asa signed this deed, and could write.[17]

---

[13] Virginia Marriage Index, p. 237, photocopy of index provided by WRK; supplemented by the actual entry in the
   Greensville County, VA Marriage Register for 1868, copies also supplied by WRK.
[14] No record of his death has been found in the Greensville County, Virginia Death Registers, 1853-1896, or elsewhere
   in Virginia.
[15] Rev. War pension application R-5907, pursued by Asa after George died.
[16] Amelia County, VA DB 34, p378.
[17] Amelia County, VA DB 27, pp. 420-422 (scanned images available).

On 17 November 1825, **Asa Kidd** of Amelia County, VA married Jane Sutherland, daughter of Kendall C. Sutherland, of Dinwiddie County, VA. [18]

1826-1855 – **Asa Kidd** appeared for the first time on the **Amelia** County, VA Personal Property Tax Lists by name (previously an unnamed tithable in his father's household) in 1826, taxed for 1 slave and 1 horse.
In 1827, **Asa Kidd** was taxed for 3 slaves & 1 horse.
In 1829, he was again taxed on 3 slaves & 1 horse.
He continued to be listed on the **Amelia** County, VA Personal Property Tax Lists until 1855, but not thereafter. (See 1855, below; in that year he sold his Amelia County land and relocated to Dinwiddie County.)

1826 – **Asa Kidd** served as a Constable in Amelia County, VA in 1826.[19]

1827-1833 – The Land Tax Lists (LTLs) of Amelia County indicate that **Asa Kidd** received 150 acres in Amelia County 19 miles SE of the Courthouse from George Kidd (his father) in 1827; the land on which George Kidd was taxed dropped from 422 acres to 272 acres in that year, and Asa appears on the 1827 LTL, taxed on this 150 acres, on Namozine Creek and adjoining George Kidd.[20]
He continues to be taxed on 150 acres annually through 1833.[21] (See 1834, below)

1830 – We are unable to find him on the federal census in Amelia County, VA, or elsewhere. He was probably in the household of his widowed father, George Kidd:
George Kidd: **1FWM 20-29** & 1 60-69; 1F<5 & 1 20-29. Eight slaves.

1833 – On 3 March 1833, John B. T. Brame and Mary his wife of Amelia County sold to **Asa Kidd** of the same place for $192.55 a parcel of land in Amelia County containing by estimation 43 acres, adjoining George Kidd and Neal's estate. This deed was recorded in the May 1833 County Court.[22]

1834 – On 19 April 1834, Alexander Allen and Martha his wife of Amelia County conveyed a parcel of land in Amelia County "on which Adams meeting house now stands, containing and laid out for one acre of land" to a group of Trustees of the Methodist Episcopal Church. The Trustees, listed by name, were Henry H. Southall, James Allen, **George Kidd**, William T. Green, William Coleman, William D. Southall, **Asa Kidd** and John Clay. The deed stipulates that the land is conveyed in Trust, with the understanding that the trustees "will erect or build, or cause to be built…a place of worship for the use of the members of the Methodist Episcopal Church" and that it remain in use for this purpose, in coordination with and ministers provided from this denomination.
The deed was proved in court and admitted to record in Amelia County Court on 26 June 1834.[23]

---

[18] Marriage announcement in "The Intelligencer and Petersburg Commercial Advertiser", November 22, 1825.

[19] Historical Notes on Amelia County, Virginia, pp. 490, 484.

[20] Amelia County, VA Land Tax Books, 1819-1841, on Microfilm #15, Library of Virginia, abstracted by William R. Kidd, November 2003.

[21] Ibid.

[22] Amelia County, VA Deed Book 31, pages 174-176, retrieved via familysearch.org from FHL #30444, images 104-105.

[23] Amelia County Deed book 31, pp. 400-402, photostatic copy obtained from the County Court Clerk's office, because the online images via familysearch.org were too faint to be interpreted, January 31, 2021.

Also in 1834, the amount of land that Asa Kidd was taxed for increased from 150 acres to 193 acres, reflecting the addition of 43 acres that he bought from John and Mary Brame in 1833.[24]

1835 – On 20 January 1835, John B. T. Brame and Mary his wife of Amelia County sold to **Asa Kidd** of the same place for $500 a tract of land in Amelia County containing by survey 232 acres, adjoining William Coleman, George Kidd, Asa Kidd, Alexander Allen, and Elizabeth G. Torborne. This deed was admitted to record in Amelia County Court on 12 February 1835.[25]

1835-1848 – The 1835 Amelia County **LTL** shows **Asa Kidd** taxed on 425 acres of land, reflecting the addition of the parcel he purchased from John and Mary Brame earlier this year. He continued to be taxed annually for 425 acres through 1848.[26]

1836-1851 – **Asa Kidd** served as a Justice of the Peace in 1836, 1837, 1839, 1841-1844, 1846, 1848, and 1851.[27]

1838 – On 15 December 1838, George Rowlett and Martha O. Rowlett his wife of Amelia County conveyed one acre of land lying on the Richmond Road in Amelia County to William D. Southall, Benjamin G. Jones, John S. Quarles, Mathew Turner, Matthew(?) Allen, **Asa Kidd**, and William T. Green, the Trustees of the Methodist Episcopal Church of America for the sum of $1. Much of this deed was indecipherable, due to fading, and we are unsure of the terms, and whether this was a sale of land, or a lease. Likely it was similar to the 1834 deed (see above) involving the Methodist Episcopal Church. The deed was recorded in Court on 24 January 1839.[28]

1840 – On the federal census in Amelia County, p 187:
Asa Kidd: 1 WM 5-9, 2 10-14, 1 15-19 & 1 30-39; 1F 10-14 & 1 30-39. Six slaves. Next door is his father George Kidd.

1848 – On 26 September 1848, Robert Cousins and Sarah his wife of Amelia County conveyed a 2-acre parcel of land in Trust for the sum of $1 to Watkins Turner, Robert Coleman, James Allen, **Asa Kidd**, Benjamin C. Jones, William D. Southall, James H. Clay, Armistead Coleman,& Richard E. Clay, trustees in Trust, for a house of worship, called Poplar Hill,[29] to be built, for the use of the members of the Methodist Episcopal Church South; and if the ME Church South should cease to occupy this land and hold services there, then the land

---

[24] Amelia County, VA Land Tax Books, 1819-1841, on Microfilm #15, Library of Virginia, abstracted by William R. Kidd, November 2003. Available upon request.

[25] Amelia County, VA Deed Book 32, page 111-112, retrieved via familysearch.org from FHL #30444, images 290-291.

[26] Amelia County, VA Land Tax Books, 1819-1841, on Microfilm #15, Library of Virginia, abstracted by William R. Kidd, November 2003. Available upon request.

[27] Historical Notes on Amelia County, Virginia, pp. 490, 484.

[28] Amelia County, VA Deed Book 34, pages 57-58, retrieved via familysearch.org from FHL #30445, images 298-299.

[29] The location of this church is depicted on the undated nineteenth century map of Amelia County found on the inside front cover of *Historical Notes on Amelia County, Virginia,* by Kathleen H. Hadfield and W. Cary McConnaughey, Amelia, VA, 1982. Namozine Creek forms the eastern boundary of Amelia County; look just 1 inch left of the first syllable of "Namozine," and you'll see it, on Willis Road, just below its intersection with Cousins Road.

was to revert to Robert Cousins or his legal representative.
Asa Kidd was a Justice of the Peace at the time of this record.[30]

1849 – The Amelia County LTL for 1849 lists **Asa Kidd** as being taxed on two separate moieties of land: 1) the 425 acres adjoining William Coleman & E. G. Torborne, 19 miles SE of the Courthouse (that he'd been taxed on since 1836); and 2) a new parcel of 272 acres, adjoining Sally Brown & others, also 19miles SE of the Courthouse. This is the land devised to him by his father, George4 Kidd, judging from a note in the margin.[31]

1850 – On the federal census in Amelia County, p. 58.
Asa Kidd 48MW farmer $3000 VA
Jane C. Kidd 42FW VA
Virginia A. Kidd 19FW VA
(no others)
The Slave Schedule for this census shows that he owned 12 slaves in 1850.
[His son George is living in Petersburg, VA, in the HH of his relative, George W. Southerland. See George Fendale Kidd in this document.]

1854 – On 7 November 1854, **Asa Kidd**, the executor of the estate of Patty Allen, deceased, acting in accordance with her last Will and Testament, sold at auction to the highest bidder a tract of land in Amelia County containing 383 acres and adjoining the lands adjoining the dower tract, N. C. Gregory, the estate of John Clay, deceased. Peter Cole of Amelia County was the highest bidder and purchased the land for $1187.30.
This deed was entered into record in County Court on 16 January 1835.[32]

1855 – On 18 January of this year, **Asa Kidd** and Jane C. Kidd his wife of Amelia County sold to George A. Cralle of Nottoway County for the sum of $3290 a tract of land in Amelia County containing 678 acres, adjoining the lands of James A. Coleman, Peter Cole, Jno. W. Coleman and William Brown. This deed was recorded in Court on 22 February 1855.[33] With this transaction he sold the Kidd family home at Ammon, a small community N. of Namozine Creek in the SE corner of Amelia County. This provides a connection with the earliest Amelia County VA Kidd, his grandfather, George4 Kidd of 1772 (see ff.) [34]

1855-1858 – **Asa Kidd** appears on the **Dinwiddie** County, VA Personal Property Tax Lists in these years.[35] After selling the family land in Amelia County, he moved to Dinwiddie County. We have not checked the Dinwiddie PPTLs beyond this date.

1856 – On 15 November 1856, **Asa Kidd**, acting as Executor of the estate of Patty Allen, deceased, sold to Edward A. Featherston for the sum of $1294.57 a parcel of land in Amelia County, bounded by the Namozine Road on the north, on the south by Wintercomack Creek, on the east by the lands of Robert Cousins, and on the west by the lands of Henry C. Gregory,

---

[30] Amelia County, VA Deed Book 37, pages 480-482, retrieved via familysearch.org from FHL #30447, images 273-274.

[31] Amelia County, VA Land Tax Books, 1819-1841, on Microfilm #15, Library of Virginia, abstracted by William R. Kidd, November 2003. Available upon request.

[32] Amelia County, VA Deed Book 39, pages 176-177, retrieved via familysearch.org from FHL #30448, images 105-106.

[33] Amelia County, VA Deed Book 39, pages 157-158, retrieved via familysearch.org from FHL #30448, images 96-97.

[34] "Old Homes and Buildings of Amelia County, VA, vol. 1, Amelia Historical Committee, 1964. p. 129.

[35] Amelia County Personal Property Tax Lists, 1853-1858, retrieved from FHL #31116 (unrestricted access) via familysearch.org), images 219 (1855), 316 (1856), 413 (1857) and 516 (1858).

containing 210½ acres.
This deed was recorded in Amelia Court on 26 March 1857.[36]

1857 – **Asa Kidd** appears for the first time on the Dinwiddie Land Tax Lists in 1857, on the list of Thomas A. Farley (whose district seems to be largely in the eastern half of Dinwiddie County. In this year, he's taxed on two parcels of land: a parcel of 171 acres "on Rohowick Swamp," 11 miles NE of the Courthouse; and a second parcel of 20 acres (designated as "Lot 3, near Petersburg." A marginal note by both entries reads, "Deeds from J. Dupuy." See Appendix 5 for more details about his land.
This is the last year for which we have checked the Dinwiddie LTLs.

1860 – On the federal census in **Dinwiddie** County, p. 120 of Revenue District 2, along with James Kidd (p. 86) and Dolly Kidd (p. 104).
Asa Kidd 59MW farmer $10,000/$9820 VA
Jane C. "   42FW VA
(no others)
On the slave schedule for this census, he owned 15 slaves.[37]

1864 – **Asa Kidd** signed his last will and testament on 4 September 1864 in Dinwiddie County, VA. In it, he left to his wife and widow Jane C. Kidd, "so long as she lives or remains my widow, the farm on which I now reside, together with all my household and kitchen furniture, plantation utensils, my two horses, wagon, ox cart, one yoke of oxen, and either my buggy or carriage as she may choose, together with one-third of all my cattle, sheep, hogs, and crops of corn, oats, wheat and fodder." He stipulated that his daughter Virginia A. Traylor and all her children "shall have a home with her mother on my said farm during the present War, or until she can return with safety to her home in the City of Petersburg."
He stipulated that after the death of his wife, or her remarriage, the above bequest of property should all be sold, and the proceeds given to his daughter Virginia. His will also directed that the other two-thirds of his livestock and crops, and all other of his property not devised otherwise by this will to be sold, and the proceeds to be held in trust by his friend, J. T. Sutherland, for the equal benefit and support of his two children, Virginia A. Traylor and George F. Kidd.
He further stipulated that "my good and old faithful slave Will shall be supported, clothed and taken care of as long as he shall live by my estate and that he shall be hired out to homes of his own selection by my executor, and that the proceeds of his hire be given to him…as he may need it. Under no circumstances I do not wish him to be sold."
He appointed "my friend, J. T. Southerland" as his executor.[38]
His will was proved in Dinwiddie County Court by the oaths of two of the subscribing witnesses and admitted to record on November 24, 1864.[39]

From the record above we know that he died sometime between 4 September 1864 and 24

---

[36] Amelia County, VA Deed Book 39, pages 410-411, retrieved via familysearch.org from FHL #30448, images 242-243.
[37] image 36/46.
[38] John T. Southerland was Jane Southerland Kidd's brother.
[39] Dinwiddie County, VA. WB 9, pages 88-89., retrieved from FHL#1929696 via familysearch.org (restricted access, affiliated library), image 210 of 555 on this reel. Digital image available upon request. For some reason, this will was not copied into the Dinwiddie Court record until December 27, 1877.

November 1864 in Dinwiddie County.
He is buried in the Sutherland family cemetery in Dinwiddie County, VA.[40]

1869 – 21 June 1869. In Dinwiddie County Court in its June Term, John T. Southerland, the executor of the estate of **Asa Kidd, deceased**, returned to Court with an "Account Current" report of his handling of the estate. The Court had previously in its October 1867 term appointed John Mann, a Commissioner of the Circuit Court of the City of Petersburg, to audit, state and settle the account of said Southerland as executor, and to return his report to the Dinwiddie Court Clerk.

In this record, Commissioner Mann's report dated 10 April 1869 was entered into the Court record. It stated that John T. Southerland on 28 December 1867 had "produced and laid before him a statement of all the money which he had received or become chargeable with or had disbursed as executor of the last will and testament of **Asa Kidd, deceased** since the date of his qualification, together with the vouchers for such disbursement." Southerland's account for the estate was closed on13 February 1868, showing a balance due the estate of $51.65. "The executor qualified on the estate on the 21st day of November 1864, and the assets of the estate except for two notes of George W. Southerland were received by him in Confederate currency. When the Confederate currency became worthless, which was within six months of his qualification, the executor had on hand $257.21 of that currency. Your Commissioner is of the opinion that the Executor is not chargeable therewith, and that the estate must bear the loss. The debits in the account were sustained by satisfactory vouchers. It appears from these records that while Asa's Confederate currency became worthless after his death, his heirs were able to hold on to at least some of his land, transferred to his wife and at her death to her children.[41]

March 25, 1870, Dinwiddie County Court. The heirs of **Asa Kidd** returned to Court and presented a statement acknowledging the receipt of the distribution of Asa's estate by John T. Southerland. It reads:
We, Jane C. Kidd (widow of Asa Kidd, deceased), George F. Kidd, his son, and A. A. Traylor in right of his wife, Virginia A. Traylor, who is a daughter of said Asa Kidd, have received of John T. Southerland, Executor of Asa Kidd the balance ($45.00) in full, we having agreed to share it equally between us. All four parties signed this receipt, and it was filed with the Dinwiddie County Court Clerk on 16 May 1870.[42]

1887 – Asa's widow, Jane C. (Sutherland) Kidd, died 23 June 1887, and is buried in the Sutherland family cemetery in Dinwiddie County, along with Asa and their son George F. Kidd. Her cemetery record states that she was the daughter of F.C. and E.T. Sutherland (We suspect that the T. in her mother's name was for TRAYLOR), and that she died in her 79th year.

---

[40] Graveyards, Dinwiddie County, Virginia. Frances Bland Randolph Chapter, Daughters of the American Revolution, 1945. From Library of Virginia (1-11-03 by WRK). His headstone is evidently unreadable, other than his name, according to this book.

[41] Dinwiddie County Will Book 8, 1863-1875, pages384-386, retrieved from FHL #31103 via familysearch.org (restricted access – affiliated libraries), images 217-218. Scanned images available from authors on request.

[42] Dinwiddie County Will Book 8, 1863-1875, page 428, retrieved from FHL #31103 via familysearch.org (restricted access – affiliated libraries), image 239. Digital image available upon request.

**<u>BARTHOLOMEW KIDD</u>, the son of George4 (Benjamin3, William2, Thomas1) Kidd and
his wife Elizabeth.**[43]
Born about 1786 in Amelia County, VA
Married Polly Moore 24 May 1806, Amelia County, VA [44]
<u>No known children</u>
Died abt. 1836 in Amelia County (see below)

1793 – Along with his brother Jasper, **Bartholomew Kidd** is named in his father George4 Kidd's
will, which was signed in 1793, and proved in Amelia County Court in 1797. After John
Neal declined to be the executor of George Kidd's estate, the court granted letters of
administration to **Bartholomew Kidd** on 22 June 1797.[45]

1802 – **Bartholomew** first appears on the Amelia County, VA Personal Property Tax Lists in 1802
(We believe that previously he's been listed as an unnamed tithable in his deceased father's
estate) with 2 free males over 16 and no slaves.

1803 – **Bartholomew Kidd** again appears on the Amelia PPTL as a single free male over 16; his
younger brother Jasper was evidently previously in Bartholomew's HH in 1802, and then
appears on his own in 1803.

1804, 1805 – **Bartholomew Kidd** is again on the Amelia PPTLs in these years; he then disappears
from them until 1818 (see below).

1806 – **Bartholomew Kidd** appears on the **Nottoway County** PPTLs in 1806, joining his brother
Benjamin Kidd, who appeared first on these lists in 1800 and also in the years 1802-1807.
Bartholomew may be in Chesterfield County after 1806, when he drops from sight for a few
years. We've not checked there yet.

1810 – Not found on the federal census, to date.

1813 – Private "**Bartholomew Kidds**" is listed on the muster roll of Captain Daniel Flournoy's
Company of Virginia Militia from the 23rd Regiment, **Chesterfield** County, commanded by
Col. William Brown from the 18th to the 30th of March, from the 26th to the 28th of June
and from the 30th of June to the 2nd of July 1813. Time of service was 18 days.[46]

1815 – A deed from Jasper Kidd to **Bartholomew Kidd** was recorded on 27 July 1815 in Amelia
County, VA.[47] In it, Jasper Kidd "of **Chesterfield** County" for $250 good and lawful money
of Virginia sold "my right and title in the tract of land that was willed to us by our father
George Kidd, deceased...in Amelia county...together with houses, outhouses, ways, waters,
woods, profits, commodities, etc." to Bartholomew Kidd. Jasper signed with an X, and
could not write.[48]

1815 – **Bartholomew Kidd** is found this one year on the **Chesterfield** County PPTLs (along with
his brother, Jasper). Bartholomew was taxed in one WM over sixteen (himself)and one slave

---

[43] Amelia County, VA Will Book 5, pp. 359-360, and 390 - Will of Geo Kidd, Sr. AND Amelia County Deed Book 24,
p 126
[44] DAR 67:154-159, Marriage Bonds of Amelia County, VA.
[45] Amelia County, VA Order Book 21, p. 490; image of this record on Dropbox in the Amelia Shared Folder.
[46] "Virginia Militia in the War of 1812, vol. 2, from the rolls of the Auditor's Office", page 328, located at LVA, viewed
7-17-2009, WRK.
[47] Amelia County, VA Order book 29, 1814-1817, page 371, Amelia County CH.
[48] Amelia County, VA Deed Book 24, pp. 126-127, scanned image in the Amelia Shared Folder on Dropbox.

over 16, but no livestock.[49] Neither of them are found on subsequent Chesterfield County PPTLs through 1851.

1816 – **Bartholomew Kidd** appears on the **Amelia** County VA PPTL.[50] After this, his name does not appear again on the Amelia County PPTLs (he could be back in his father's household some of this time) until 1830, and is there annually through 1835, the last year I checked.

1817 – **Bartholomew Kidd** appears on the **Dinwiddie** County VA PPTL, with no slaves or property.

1818 – He appears for the first time on the **Amelia** County, VA Land Tax List, taxed on 100 acres on Long Branch, adjoining William Coleman and others. This land was previously Elizabeth Kidd's land, per the will of his father George Kidd Sr.[51] Evidently Elizabeth Kidd has died, and the land became Bartholomew's.

1819 – Bartholomew is NOT found on the Dinwiddie or Amelia Land tax lists in 1819. Nor is there a deed whereby Bartholomew disposes of the 100 acres he was taxed for in 1818. We're unsure what became of that land. It's possible that the land was taken to repay a debt, or otherwise taken from him, but the Amelia County Deed Books contain no reference to him in this period.

1820 – **Bartholomew Kidd** is not found on the federal census in Dinwiddie, Nottoway, or elsewhere, despite the records below.

1820, 1821 – **Bartholomew Kidd** is found on the **Nottoway** County PPTLs, with 1WM>16 and 1 horse each year.
He drops from the Nottoway PPTLs after 1821.

1823 – **Bartholomew Kidd** reappears on the **Amelia** County Land Tax records, taxed on 84 acres adjacent to Thomas Barrett and Laurence Wills, purchased from Laurence Wills. The deed for this transaction evidently states that Bartholomew is a resident of Amelia County at the time.[52]

1828 – **Bartholomew Kidd** testified in an Amelia County Chancery Court suit concerning the estate of Andrew Waugh of Amelia County In this testimony he states that he went to live with Daniel W. Clay (one of the defendants) as overseer about 1824.[53]

1830 – I have NOT found him in either Amelia or Dinwiddie County, VA, but he SHOULD be in Amelia, given the tax lists below.
A *different* Bartholomew, the son of Henry Kidd and Nancy Hill of Fluvanna County, VA, is listed in the Fluvanna County, VA census, p. 356, where he lived out his life.

---

[49] Chesterfield County Personal Property Tax Lists, 1812-1826, retrieved from FHL #2024512 via familysearch.org (unrestricted access), image 197.

[50] 1WM>16 (himself); no property.

[51] From WRK, who writes: "I do not now know how it was stated, but my note is land was previously Elisabeth Kidd's land, per will of his father. Source on that was reel 115 at the LVA, 1 Nov 2003. Additional note is that the microfilm was poor so I verified it by looking at the tax book from the archive at LVA." Bill believes that this land went from George to his widow Elizabeth, and upon Elizabeth's death to Bartholomew.

[52] Personal correspondence from William R. Kidd of Newport News, VA.

[53] Amelia County Chancery Court cases, #1830-001, images 36 and 95 of 228, available online at https://www.lva.virginia.gov/chancery/case_detail.asp?CFN=007-1830-001 .

1830-1835 – **Bartholomew Kidd** is found on the **Amelia** County, VA PPTLs for these years, but not thereafter.

1836 – This **Bartholomew Kidd** probably died in 1836 in Amelia County, VA.[54] The date here is perplexing, because even though recorded in 1836, the documents listed the date as 1826, according to the transcribed notes of Troy Kidd. I believe that this is a mis-transcription, and that he intended 1836, since Bartholomew appears on the Amelia County VA PPTLs through 1835.

BENJAMIN KIDDS

There were at least two Benjamin Kidds in Amelia County, VA. The first was **Benjamin4 Kidd**, born 1739 in Middlesex County, VA, the son of Benjamin3 Kidd. This Benjamin was in Amelia County briefly before returning to Middlesex County by 1771.

The second Benjamin, **Benjamin5 Kidd**, was born about 1761 in Amelia County, VA, the son of George4 Kidd, and grandson of Benjamin3 Kidd.

<u>**BENJAMIN4 KIDD**</u> **(Benjamin3, William2, Thomas1 Kidd), the brother of George4 Kidd**
>**Born 1739, MSX County, VA**
>**Migrated to Amelia County by 1762; left just one record (below) in Amelia and Dinwiddie counties, and we believe that he returned to MSX County. See below.**

1762 – a **Benjamin Kidd** appears on the Amelia County Colonial Tithes List below Deep Creek in Raleigh Parish (David Greenhill's List), among the tithables of William Cassells; Benjamin is listed as the overseer of Cassell's slaves.
>This is his only listing in Amelia County during the period 1736-1764, and is the EARLIEST MENTION OF ANY KIDD IN AMELIA COUNTY. This has to be Benjamin4, son of Benjamin3, because Benjamin3 died in 1761, and Benjamin5 was born in 1761, in Amelia County.

>The authors believe that Benjamin4 (Ben3, William2, Thomas1) Kidd returned to MSX County by 1771, when the birth of his son James is recorded in MSX County. This is consistent with Benjamin4 Kidd returning to Middlesex County by that year (if not earlier), and remaining there the rest of his life.
><u>See the MSX compilation for more information about Benjamin4 Kidd.</u>

<u>**BENJAMIN5 KIDD**</u>**, the son of George4 (Benjamin3, William2, Thomas1) Kidd**
>**Born abt. 1761, probably in MSX County, VA**
>**Married (date and place unknown) Mary _____, who lived until at least 1844**
>**Died abt. 1821 in Dinwiddie County, VA**
>**Had as many as 3 sons who survived him (see his entry on the 1820 census, and his widow, Mary's entry on the 1830 federal census).**

---

[54] The Index to Wills of Amelia County, VA lists an inventory of his estate (Will Book 13 [1833-1837], p. 456) and other estate papers (Book 14 [1837-1841], p 83 and p. 195; also Amelia County Order Book 1834-1837, p. 169 - B's brother George Jr. was administrator of B's estate). In addition, Amelia County Order Book _, 1834-1837, p. 169 records the motion of George Kidd, "who with Frances Coleman his security, entered into bond of $100 for letters of administration on the estate of Bartholomew Kidd, deceased." This entry is dated MARCH 1826, even though it's recorded a decade later.

We believe that these three sons were James6a Kidd, Thomas J. Kidd and John Kidd. See their entries in this compilation.

1778 – The Colonial Tithe Lists of Amelia County for the years 1772-1777 are not extant. A **George Kidd** again appears on these lists in 1778, paying his tithe and that for a **Benjamin Kidd**. They appear on the list of Vivion Brooking, the tax collector for lower Raleigh Parish. We believe that this **Benjamin Kidd** is George's eldest son, born abt 1761.[55]

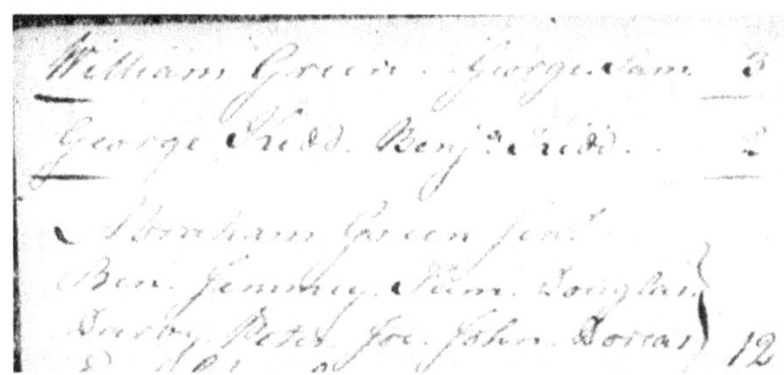

Also in 1778, a George and **Benjamin Kidd** of Amelia County signed the oath of allegiance, refusing allegiance to the Crown, on 25 August 1778.[56] This is most likely Benjamin5 Kidd, since all males over the age of sixteen were expected to sign these oaths of allegiance.[57]

1781 – a **Benjamin Kidd** is found on a 1781 list of Amelia County militia under the command of Edward Munford.[58] This could be either Benjamin4 (Benjamin3, William2, Thomas1) Kidd, or Benjamin5, the son of George4 Kidd. The latter is more likely, since Benjamin5 was back in MSX County by 1771.

1782 – The Virginia Personal Property Tax Lists (PPTLs) began in 1782. The list for Amelia County includes George Kidd with two free males over 21; this list names **Benjamin Kidd** as the second male in the household.[59] We believe that this Benjamin is George's eldest son, and conclude that he's turned 21 years of age in the last year; this would indicate that he was born in or about 1761. No other Kidds are listed in 1782.

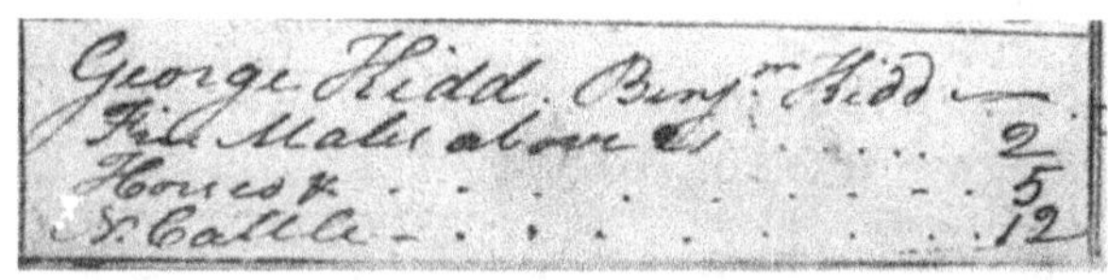

Benjamin Kidd does not appear on Amelia County PPTLs again until 1787 (see below).

1784 – On August 9, 1784, **Ben (X) Kidd** witnessed a deed from Isaac Coleman of Amelia County, VA to Solomon Coleman.[60] This is most likely Benjamin5, son of George; born in 1761; he'd have been 23 years old.

1787 – On the 1787 Amelia County, VA PPTL, a **Ben Kidd** is listed as one of the tithables (white males over 16) in the household of Vivion Brooking, a wealthy landowner, and that he was

---

[55] *Tithe Lists of Amelia County, Virginia, 1765-1778*, by Reiley Kidd MD, Colonial Roots, Millsboro, DE, 2016, citing FHL #190267. This particular entry is viewable online via Familysearch.org (unrestricted access) on image 20 of this reel.

[56] Original in County Court Clerk's office, Amelia County, VA; published in DAR Magazine 93:119, February 1959.

[57] Per one of the Archivists at the Library of Virginia.

[58] *Magazine of Virginia Genealogy*, volume 49, inside back cover, issue 1. We have not seen the original record.

[59] Amelia County, VA PPTLs, 1782-1813, retrieved via familysearch.org from FHL #2024454, image 21.

[60] "Amelia County, VA Deed Books 15-17, 1778-1786", p. 121.

between sixteen and twenty-one years old at the time of the list. [61] This should be
Benjamin5, born about 1761, son of George Kidd, Sr.

1790 – **Benjamin Kidd** is mentioned twice in the **Dinwiddie** County Court Order Book for this
year.[62]
In the March entry, Benjamin Kidd was the security for a James Lewis, who entered into a
debt agreement with William Dwire. Dwire did not make good on the debt, and sued Lewis
and his security **Benjamin Kidd** for payment. The court ruled in favor of Dwire, and
ordered Dwire and Kidd to pay the debt, plus the plaintiff's costs.

The second entry, in the minutes of the November Court session, are extremely faint, and I
cannot make much of the entry out. However, a professional researcher abstracted this
document in 1987 from the original record, which was evidently legible. His abstract says
that Jeremiah Ford, plaintiff, was suing **Benjamin Kidd** and John Williams over a debt. He
was awarded an attachment against the said Kidd's estate, and "executed on some corn", but
the defendant Kidd failed to appear and "replevy the attached effects," so the Court ruled
that the plaintiff recover the debt from John Williams and Nathaniel Epes, Kidd's security.
Despite the record mentioning the "estate" of **Benjamin Kidd**, he was very much still alive,
judging from this entry, and the term refers to the property of an individual in this context.

1790 – **Benjamin Kidd** is also listed for the first time in the **Dinwiddie** County, VA Personal
Property Tax List, with no taxable property.[63]

Benjamin is mentioned twice in **Dinwiddie** County, VA Court of Pleas records in 1790, in
March as a security for another defendant,[64] and again in November, as a defendant
regarding a debt.[65]

1791 – **Benjamin Kidd** is again listed in the **Dinwiddie** County, VA Personal Property Tax List,
with no taxable property.[66]

1792 – **Benjamin Kid** is listed in **Dinwiddie** County, VA PPTL in Braddock Goodwin's district,
with one horse (first taxable property). [67]

1793 – **Benjamin Kid** is listed on the **Dinwiddie** PPTL, in Braddock Goodwin's district (one white
male over 16, 2 horses).

1794-1807 – no Benjamin Kidd listed on the **Dinwiddie** County tax lists; simultaneously has
brother, Lodowick Kidd "disappears" from the district list he appeared in, save for 1794 and

---

[61] Volume 1, page 342.

[62] *Dinwiddie County, VA Surveyors Platt Book, 1755-1796, and Court Orders 1789-1791; An Every Name Index*, published 1995
by TLC Genealogy, P.O. Box 403369, Miami Beach, Florida 33140-1369. Copy in the Library of Virginia, reviewed
1-11-03 by WRK. Microfilm 31090 reviewed April 29, 2011 by RK: pages 172-173 (March 1790 Quarterly Sessions
Court) and 283 (November Court, 1790).

[63] Nicholas district. From "Dinwiddie County, VA Personal Property Tax Lists, 1782-1799".

[64] Dinwiddie County Order Book, 1789-1791, p. 117; the defendants were James and Herbert Lewis, against William
Devine.

[65] Dinwiddie County Order Book, 1789-1791, p. 283.

[66] Wood Rucker District. ibid

[67] His presumed brother, "Laddick Kid" (Lodowick) shows up for the first time on the Dinwiddie County Tax Lists in
this same year, also with one horse, but in William Wall's district.

1799. Lodowick shows up on **Dinwiddie** County, VA Land Tax records from 1795-1823. **Benjamin Kidd** is seen there intermittently during this period.

1800 – a **Benjamin Kidd** appears on the **Nottoway** County, VA PPTL, with 1WM>16, and no property. He's not there in 1801, but reappears in 1802 (see below).
No census records for 1800 survive for Virginia. They were destroyed during the War of 1812, when the British invaded Washington, DC.

1801 – a **Benjamin Kidd** is found in **Dinwiddie** County, in the household of John North, probably as a tenant farmer or employee.[68]

1802-1807 – **Benjamin Kidd** appears again on the **Nottoway** County, VA PPTLs.[69]
In 1806, he has another white male over 16 in his household (probably a son), but that person isn't named; and the following year, there's no other WM in the household, implying that this son may have died. Alternatively, this son may be in someone else's household, as a worker, partner, or tenant farmer.

1803 – On Aug. 26, 1803, Britain Moore and his wife Nancy, of Dinwiddie, sold to **Benjamin Kidd of Nottoway** a tract of 78 acres in Nottoway County for £80.[70]

1804 – On 5 Apr, 1804, the above deed from Britain Moore to **Benjamin Kidd** was recorded in Nottoway Court.[71]

1805 – On 2 May, 1805, a suit was heard in **Nottoway** County: **Benjamin Kidd** versus William Thompson. The attorney for Thompson stated that Thompson would pay debt or surrender himself to be put in jail.[72]

1805-1807 – **Benjamin Kidd** appears on the **Nottoway** County LTLs for the first time in 1805,[73] taxed on the above (1803) tract of 78 acres purchased from Brittain Moore. This entry repeats in 1806 and 1807. He evidently disposed of this land in 1808 (no land tax was collected in Virginia in 1808, and he's not on these LTLs in 1809 or later. He doesn't appear on the 1807 land tax alterations list, and the 1809 LTL doesn't include an alterations list, so we're unsure what became of this land. Perhaps this land was part of the two 1807 deeds cited below.

1806 – Nottoway County Court, 5 May 1806. **Benjamin Kidd** vs. William Thompson. Judgment goes against Thompson for £32 for a debt owed to Kidd.[74]

---

[68] Dinwiddie County VA Data, 1752-1865, Hughes, p. 104.
[69] 1802 – 1WM>16, no property
    1803 – 1WM>16, 1 horse
    1804 – 1WM>16, 1 slave>16, no horse
    1805 – 1WM>16, 1 slave>16, 4 horses
    1806 – 2WM>16, 1 slave 12-16, 4 horses. (A SON HAS COME OF AGE IN 1806.)
    1807 – 1WM>16, 1 horse. (What happened to his son? Probably died.)
[70] Nottoway County, VA deed book 2, page 489. Located at Nottoway County Circuit Court, transcribed by WRK. Scanned image available.
[71] Order book 4, Nottoway County, VA. Page 361. Located in Nottoway County, VA Circuit Court.
[72] Order book 5, Nottoway County, VA. Page 67. Located in Nottoway County, VA Circuit Court.
[73] Nottoway County, VA Land Tax Lists, 1789-1813, from Library of Virginia reel 221, reviewed by RK November 2018 via interlibrary loan. Benjamin Kidd is the only Kidd appearing on these annual lists in this period, as shown here.
[74] Order book 3, Nottoway County, VA. Page 454. Located in Nottoway County, VA Circuit Court.

1807 – 12 September 1807. **Benjamin Kidd and his wife Polly** of **Nottoway** County, sold to Davis Paylor of Nottoway County at tract containing 90 acres in Nottoway County for £135. Recorded 3 Dec, 1807.[75]
12 September 1807. **Benjamin Kidd and his wife Polly** of Nottoway County sold 50 acres in Nottoway County for £65 to John Beech of Nottoway County. [76]

Notice that these two deeds are for a total of 140 acres, although the LTLs never show Benjamin with more than the 78 acres cited below.

1808 – No taxes were collected in Virginia this year, and so no PPTL was created for any of the counties.

1809 – **Benjamin Kidd** is not listed on the Nottoway PPTL, but IS on the **Dinwiddie** PPTL (see below). This confirms that this Benjamin that is intermittently in Nottoway is almost certainly the same Benjamin who's found in Dinwiddie County.

1810 – Benjamin isn't found in Amelia or Dinwiddie County census (the Amelia County census microfilm is VERY faint, and he may be listed, but not recognizable on this census),[77] and was either missed, or he's still in his father's household, or is listed in another taxpayer's household in Dinwiddie County, perhaps as a tenant farmer or employee. He is in Dinwiddie County in 1810, because he's on the personal property tax list that year (see below).

1809-1821 – **Benjamin Kidd** appears on **Dinwiddie** County, VA **personal property tax lists** in these years. He first has a second white male over 16 on the 1819 tax list, possibly his son.[78] However, this other white male over 16 is not listed in 1820, suggesting that either the 1819 entry was Benjamin's son, and that son died, or that it was another poor, single man (like Benjamin) who is working land with Benjamin for economic reasons.
In the early years of this span, Benjamin has no slaves, and 1-3 horses or cattle. In the latter half of this period, he had 1-2 slaves over 16 each year, and 4-5 livestock. And in 1820, for the first time he had a 2-wheel carriage or gig, a sign of the middle class for this period. See Appendix Four for more details.

1814-1821 – **Benjamin Kidd** appears annually on the **Dinwiddie** County, VA **Land Tax Lists** for these years.
His 1814 entry states that he obtained 218 acres on White Oak Creek, 13 miles NW of the courthouse, by deed from H.B. Duvall in the prior 12 months.
For the next 4 years, he's taxed annually on those 218 acres.
His 1818 entry is for 211 acres; in the prior year he transferred 7 acres to Armisted Cassel's Estate.

---

[75] Nottoway County, VA deed book 3, page 323. Located at Nottoway County Circuit Court. Scanned images available.
[76] Nottoway County, VA deed book 3, page 331. Located at Nottoway County Circuit Court. . Scanned images available.
[77] Three Benjamins ARE listed in the 1810 VA census, one in King and Queen County, one in Caroline and one in Middlesex County, VA. I prefer to think that he was among the illegible names on the Amelia County census - RK
[78] These lists enumerate "the number of white males living in the household". In each instance, the individual charged with paying the tax is listed in this column. From 1811 to 1818, Benjamin has no other white male in his household. His property gradually increased during this time (from 1 to 5 horses, and one carriage). He first has TWO white males over sixteen in 1819. This would most likely be a son who has reached the age of majority, usually 16.

From 1819 through 1821, he's taxed annually on this same 211 acres. See Appendix Five for more details on his LTLs.

1820 –**Benjamin Kidd** is found on the 1820 federal census in Dinwiddie County, VA with three males 0-9, one 10-15, one 26-44, and one 45 and older; and one female 0-9, 2 10-15, two 16-25, and two 26-44. Other Kidd households in Dinwiddie County on the 1820 census were James Kidd, James Kidd Jr., Thomas J Kidd, and William Kidd.[79]

1820-1821 – **Benjamin Kidd** is found on the Dinwiddie County VA PPTLs these two years. He also appears on the Dinwiddie Land Tax Lists, now taxed on 211 acres (down 7 acres) on White Oak Creek, 13 miles NW of the Dinwiddie courthouse.

1822 – **Benjamin Kidd** is not found on the Dinwiddie County VA Personal Property Tax Lists or the Land Tax Lists, and his wife/widow **Mary Kidd** pays tax for personal property and land identical to Benjamin's in prior years (see her section in this paper). He appears to have died in 1821 or early 1822.
He's not found in any Dinwiddie County records after 1821.
Unfortunately, no wills or other probate records survive for Dinwiddie County prior to 1831, so even if he left a probate record, it has not survived.

DELITHA ANN (WILLIAMS) KIDD HOGWOOD, the daughter of Robert and Mary Williams, and the wife of William W. Kidd – (see his section of this paper for more information about him)
Born abt 1823 in Virginia
Married (1) William W. Kidd before 1841
Married (2) Alexander Hogwood in 1859
No known children by either marriage

1841 – On Sept. 25, 1841, William W. Kidd and **Delitha Ann Kidd** his wife sold 60 acres to Joseph F. Williams for $100.25, the same amount they paid for it.[80]

1850 – I cannot find Delitha or her husband on the 1850 federal census, in Dinwiddie or elsewhere in Virginia. However, during 1850, he is listed as a U.S. Army soldier; see William W. Kidd's section in this paper, which could explain his absence from the census. When Delitha married again in 1859, she was listed as a "widow."

1855 – On March 9, 1855, Prussian E. Fraser and Martha E. his wife, of Dinwiddie County sold to **Delitha A. Kidd**, also of Dinwiddie County, for $50 a tract of land containing 25 acres in Dinwiddie County, being part of a tract now owned by Fraser, including the improvements adjoining the lands of Stephen Reams, Benjamin G. Walker and others; also one cow and yearling, 2 sows and 8 pigs, one sorrel mare named Fly, household and kitchen furniture, and all the corn and fodder on the premises. The deed was recorded in court on March 19, 1855.[81]
Delitha A. Kidd also appears on the 1855 Dinwiddie County PPTLs this one year only, in

---

[79] no TWP listed, p 12A. 310011-12220 (one male 26-44, one 45 or above), 3 in agriculture; one male slave 26-44 yo. This census is alphabetized by the first letter of the last name (i.e., all Ks, then all Ls), so one cannot draw any conclusions about geographic proximity from it.
[80] Dinwiddie County Court House, Deed Book 3, page 154, viewed 1-14-2010 by WRK.
[81] Dinwiddie County DB 8, pp. 253-4, from LDS microfilm #31096, reviewed and abstracted by RK on 2/11/10.

the district of Robert G. Boisseau, with no white males over the age of 16 in her household, no slaves, but 1 horse valued at $30 and 12 cattle, sheep or hogs, also valued at $30.[82] She drops from the PPTLs in 1856, and does not reappear.

1856-1863 – **Delitha A. Kidd** appeared annually on the Dinwiddie County LTLs in this period, taxed on the above 25-acre parcel. See Appendix 5 for details on the land she owned.

1859 – A license for the marriage of **Delitha A. Kidd** and Alexander Hogwood was issued on May 31, 1859 in Dinwiddie County, VA,[83] and on 3 June 1859, **Delitha A. Kidd** married Alexander Hogwood in Dinwiddie County, VA.[84] Alexander was 28 and single; Delitha was 36 and a widow. Both were born in Dinwiddie County. His parents are listed as (Charles? illegible) and Sarah Hogwood, and hers as Robert and Mary Williams. Alexander was a farmer.

1860 – Delitha is on the federal census in the west ward of Petersburg, VA, p. 194, HH 1816/1777:
Hogwood, Alex[r] 26MW laborer $0/25 VA cannot read or write
  " , **Delitha** 36FW seamstress VA   evidently can read and write

1864 – On 12 September 1864, **Alexander Hogwood** and **Delitha** his wife sold to George S. Williams for one cow and calf "twenty-five acres of land with general warrantee, it being one-half of a tract or parcel of land given by a deed of gift to Joseph F. Williams by the late David Williams and admitted to record on the 18th day of March 1844, the said land lying in the county of Dinwiddie …bounded by the lands of Stephen Reams, F. C. Gittman and others. The above Joseph F. Williams sold the said land to Prussian E. Frayser being fifty acres as given him by David Williams, the said Frayser selling one-half that is twenty-five acres to **Delitha A. Kidd** …who has since intermarried with Alexander Hogwood." Alexander Hogwood signed this deed with an X, while Delitha apparently signed her name.[85]

We could find no other mentions of Delitha after 1864. Since there were no Kidd children in her household in 1860, we conclude that She and William W. Kidd most likely had no children that survived.

EDWARD KIDD, son of William and Matilda Wells Kidd
Born about 1832. Died after 1860.

1850 – On federal census in Lower district of Chesterfield County, VA, p. 134, HH 338 (mis-indexed at Ancestry.com as "Ridd"):
Kidd, William 47MW "operator" (Matoaca cotton mill) VA cannot read or write
  " , Matilda 43FW VA cannot read or write
  " , **Edward** 18MW operator VA
  " , James 15MW operator VA
  " , Thomas 12MW VA
  " , Ann E. 10FW VA (is this Sarah? We believe that it is.)

---

[82] Dinwiddie County PPTLs, 1853-1858, on FHL #31116, retrieved via familysearch.org, image 264.
[83] LDS microfilm 31110, DCVA Marriage Register, 1850-1867, reviewed by RK on 3/14/10.
[84] Dinwiddie County, VA Marriage Register, 1853-1861, p 13, from LDS #1929644, item 1, reviewed and transcribed by RK 4/6/2010..
[85] Dinwiddie County Deed Book 11, pages 106-107, retrieved from FHL # 31097, image 488 via familysearch.org.

1853 – On Nov 1853, **Edward Kidd** sold to Robert H. Sydnor for $75 a tract of land (now in the possession of said Kidd's father and mother until their death) in Dinwiddie County containing 60 acres bounded on the south and east by the land of Robert H. Sydnor, west by the land of Upton Crow, and north by the land of Richard P. Pike.[86]
[In this transaction, Edward was selling his interest in a parcel of land deeded to his mother, Matilda by her father, as a life estate rather than in fee simple. Martha's other children completed similar transactions. See Matilda's section of this compilation for more details.]

1854 – **Edward Kidd**, aged 22, married Susan Freeland, aged 20, in Chesterfield 14 Oct 1854.[87]

1860 – On the federal census in S. District (Mattoaca Factory), Chesterfield County, VA, p. 67, HH 486/496:
Kidd, Edward 27WM (no occupation listed) $0/30 VA
  " , Susan 28FW VA
  " , Rebecca J. 4FW VA
  " , William A. 2MW VA
  " , infant 11/12MW VA
(No others, but next door)
487/497
Seay, Armistead 60MW laborer $0/75 VA
  " , Martha 60FW domestic VA cannot read or write
  " , Martha 30FW weaver VA
Kidd, Harriet 25FW ditto VA married w/in year; cannot read or write
  " , Thomas 23MW works in mill married w/in year; cannot read or write
Williams, Peter 17MW farm laborer VA   cannot read or write
Seay, Emily 35FW weaver VA   cannot read or write
  " , Selden 14MW VA
  " , Mary 9FW VA
  " , Harriet 7FW VA
  " , Martha 3FW VA
Stiles, Jane 40FW seamstress VA

1870 – I cannot find Edward on the federal census. His daughter Rebecca appears to be in the HH of Joshua and Mary A. Moore in Manchester, Chesterfield County, VA. Did Edward or go elsewhere looking for work, because his wife had died? (See note below).

1870 – Susan Kidd, white female died 25 May 1870 in Matoaca Village, disease of the womb, at age 38. Parents Archer and Martha ___ Freeland? Born in Prince George County,VA. Occupation weaver, husband **Ed J Kidd**. A.S. Tucker, friend, was the informant for this record, in Matoaca Township, Samuel A. Mann district.[88]

**ELIZABETH (   ) KIDD, the wife of George4 Kidd (see his section in this paper).
Her maiden name and her approximate year of birth are unknown.**

---

[86] Dinwiddie Court House, deed book 8, pages 17-18, viewed by WRK 14 Jan 2010, copies on file. Retrieved from FHL #31096, images 14-15.
[87] Personal correspondence from WRK, 2/14/10, from old notes, source not certain now.
[88] Chesterfield County, VA death records, 1870. Reel 8 on microfilm, viewed at LVA by WRK on 2-22-03.

1798-1817 – **Elizabeth Kidd** was taxed on George Kidd's land in these years after his death (see next entry, below).[89] Her land was on Long Branch, with John Neal and Richard Allen and William Coleman as neighbors.

1807 – **Elisabeth Kidd** appears on the Amelia County, VA Personal Property Tax List (previously this was listed as "George Kidd's Estate") with 2 free males over 16 (her youngest sons Bartholomew and Jasper) and one slave.
She drops from the Amelia County PPTLs in 1809 (no taxes were collected in 1808), and does not reappear on them, despite the fact that she continued to appear on the Amelia County Land Tax Lists through 1817.

1818 – We believe that she died in 1817 or 1818, because she disappears from the Land Tax records in 1818. No further records have been found that mention her.

ELIZABETH (KIDD) HOOD, the daughter of George4 Kidd, named in his will of 1797.

1793 – George4 Kidd wrote and signed his will in Amelia County on 10 March 1793. It names sons Jasper, Bartholomew, and "all the rest of my sons," along with his wife Elizabeth and daughters Usley and **Elizabeth Kidd**. See George4 Kidd's section for full details.

1802 – In March of 1802, an **Elizabeth Kidd** of Amelia County, VA married Richard Hood. [90]
The Surety for this marriage bond was Bart. Kidd. We believe that this is Elizabeth, the daughter of George4 Kidd, and her brother Bartholomew is serving as bondsman.

We have found no other records for Elizabeth or her husband, Richard Hood.

ELIZABETH KIDD, born ca 1735, died 1801 in Petersburg

1801 – An **Elizabeth Kidd** died and was buried in Petersburg, Dinwiddie County, VA on 29 April 1801, at the age of 66.[91]
This cannot be George Sr.'s widow, and is evidently a different person, given the Amelia Tax List info above. We have no idea who she was.

FRANCIS KIDD, the son of Jasper5 (George4, Benjamin3,William2, Thomas1) Kidd and his
wife, Susan/Susannah Powell Kidd
Born abt. 1825 in VA[92]
Married Mary Slaughter in Petersburg, Virginia in 1860
Died sometime after the 1880 federal census
Evidently had no surviving children

---

[89] Amelia County Land Books, George Booker's district; see notes of Forrest Sheets, researcher (RK).

[90] Amelia County, VA Marriages, 1735-1850 (CD) - (screen 21 of 49, Peggy K. Mitchell). Also cited in *Marriages of Amelia County, Virginia, 1735-1815*, by Wright, p. 55.

[91] Inscription as follows, "Died April 29th, 1801 aetas 66 years". Source is a from "Memoranda of Tombstones in the Courtyard of Blandford Church, Petersburg", compiled by Patrick Henry Drewry, made from a copy at Centre Hill Museum, dated 1949, copy viewed and transcribed at Petersburg Public Library, 3-14-03, WRK.

[92] His year of birth is problematic, ranging from 1820 (he's listed as age 50 on the 1870 federal census) to 1835 (his age on his 1860 marriage record is shown as 25 years old). Curiously, his age on the 1860 census (the same year that his marriage record lists him as only 25) was 32 years of age. And his 1850 census entry lists his age as 25.

[For more information on this man, contact Rebecca Starr via one of the contributors to this compilation.]

1847-1858 – a **Francis Kidd** first appears on the Dinwiddie County, VA PPTL in 1847, on the list of Lewis P. Lanier, joining his brother, Archer Kidd, who first appeared two years earlier. No taxable property.
He appears on the annual PPTLs there through 1858, never with taxable property, the last year of these records that we've reviewed.

1850 – On the federal census in the Northern District, Dinwiddie County, VA, p. 456, HH 338:
Kidd, Susan 52WF VA
" , **Francis** 25WM laborer VA cannot read or write
" , Archer 20WM laborer VA cannot read or write

1860 – On 29 February 1860, **Francis Kidd**, aged 25, married Mary Slaughter, aged 30, in Petersburg, VA. Francis was single, age 25, born in Dinwiddie County; his father is listed as Jasper Kidd and his mother as "Sukey" (with no last name listed). Sukey is a nickname for Susan. Mary is listed as single, age 30, born in Dinwiddie, the daughter of Louis and Jane Slaughter. His residence at the time of the marriage is listed as Chesterfield County; hers was Petersburg.[93]

Later this year, he and his new wife are found on the on the 1860 federal census in District 1, San Marino P.O., Dinwiddie County, VA, p. 21,
HH 154/151:
Kidd, Francis 32M day laborer no property VA cannot read or write
" , Mary A. 30FW VA cannot read or write
Slaughter, William J. 12MW VA
Vaden, Mary A. 17FW housekeeper $15 personal property   VA

1862 – **Francis Kidd** initially enlisted in the Confederate army on June 11, 1861 in Petersburg, Virginia for a 12-month term in Capt. A. M. Goodwyn's Company, the Hargrove Blues (Company I, 12th VA Infantry). It appears from their Compiled Service Records, which are incomplete, that his younger brother, Archer enlisted in the same unit a year later, on 30 April 1862. Both survived the war.

1870 – On the federal census in the Darvilles district of Dinwiddie County, VA, page 494, Dinwiddie C.H. post office, HH 1059/1097:
Frank Kidd 50WM laborer VA cannot read or write
Mary A. Kidd 45FW keeping house VA cannot read or write

1880 – On the federal census in the Namozine District of Dinwiddie County, VA, ED 82, sheet 4D, HH 32/34:
Frank Kidd 50WM laborer VA VA VA
Mary " 53FW wife keeping house VA VA VA

This is the last record we've been able to find for Francis. We do not know when or where he died. It appears he had no children.

---

[93] Virginia Marriages, 1785-1940 on familysearch.org, citing FHL #33441, record #419; I retrieved this record via familysearch.org (restricted access – affiliated library), image 399 on this reel.

<u>GEORGE KIDDS</u> – There are at least FOUR George Kidds in the three-county area of SE
Virginia that we're interested in, and are trying to distinguish from each other:
George4 Kidd (George Sr., 1737-1797)
George5a Kidd (George Jr., 1763-1844)
George5b Kidd, identity and connection (if any) to George4 Kidd unknown
George Fendale Kidd, son of Asa Kidd (b. abt. 1833)

<u>GEORGE4 KIDD</u>, the son of Benjamin3 (William2, Thomas1) Kidd
> **Born 3 May 1737, Middlesex County, VA**
> **Married Elizabeth (maiden name unknown), in MSX County[94]**
> **Moved to Amelia County, VA ca 1762/1763 after his father's death in MSX County**
> **Died testate there in 1797.**

**This George Kidd and his wife Elizabeth are the progenitors of the Kidd family of Amelia,
Dinwiddie and Nottoway Counties, with eight of their children (six of them sons) surviving
to adulthood. Nearly every Kidd listed in this compilation is a proven or probable
descendant of this couple.**

**Although George4 Kidd died testate, his will, written in 1793, listed only his four youngest
children by name. This document mentions their older children only as "all the rest of my
sons," but not naming them. Relying on the annual Amelia County PPTLs, we see these
sons appearing first within George4 Kidd's household, and subsequently joining him on
these annual lists.**

THE KNOWN CHILDREN OF GEORGE4 KIDD AND HIS WIFE ELIZABETH
> **(See their sections of this document for more information.)**
1. <u>Benjamin5 Kidd</u> – born abt 1761; died abt 1821 in Amelia County
2. <u>George5a Kidd</u> – born in Amelia County, 1763; died there in 1844
3. <u>Lodowick Kidd</u> – abt 1765, Amelia; died in 1856 in Tippah County, MS
4. <u>James5a Kidd</u> – born abt 1767, Amelia; died in 1842 in Mecklenburg County, VA
5. <u>Usley Kidd</u> – born abt 1774 in Amelia; died sometime after 1812
6. <u>Elizabeth Kidd</u> – born abt 1782 in Amelia; died sometime after 1802
7. <u>Bartholomew Kidd</u> – born about 1786 in Amelia; died there in 1836
8. <u>Jasper Kidd</u> – born abt 1790 in Amelia; died sometime after 1830, place unknown

For further information on his descendants, see his page in our Middlesex County Kidds family tree
on Ancestry.com, at this URL: https://www.ancestry.com/family-
tree/person/tree/37652986/person/19120498914/Gallery?_phtarg=kqz1139

1737 – **George Kidd**, the eldest of the four sons of Benjamin3 Kidd and his wife Judith Chowning,
> was born 3 May and baptized 27 May 1737 in Middlesex County, Virginia.[95]

---

[94] She was his wife by 1762, when George4 served as executor of his father, Benjamin3 Kidd's estate and sold the family
land in MS County.
[95] *Parish Register of Christ Church Parish, Middlesex County, Virginia, 1635-1812*, p. 144.

1762 – On 17 May 1762, **George Kidd** and his wife Elizabeth sold 50 acres of land in Middlesex County, VA to a Henry Thurston of Middlesex County; the quantity and description of this land matches that of his father Benjamin3 Kidd's land, supporting our hypothesis that George was the eldest son of Benjamin3 Kidd.[96] George was serving as administrator of his father Benjamin's estate and selling his father's land, which he inherited as the oldest son when his father, Benjamin, died intestate. This deed was proved in MSX Court on 3 August 1763.

Following this event, George Kidd drops from the Middlesex County records and appears in Amelia County, Virginia

1763 – Troy Kidd, an excellent Kidd researcher and descendant, now deceased, said he had a reference to George Kidd Sr. buying land in Amelia County, VA; however Troy died before he could provide a copy of the deed, and we have been unable to find such a record. We think that Troy may have been in error on this.

Regardless, the Revolutionary War pension application for George Kidd Jr., **George4 Kidd's son**, states that he was born in Amelia County in 1763, placing the arrival of this family in Amelia County in either 1762 or 1763.

In addition, **George Kidd** DOES start appearing on the Amelia County, VA Personal Property Tax Lists in 1763 when he is listed among the tithables (taxable white males and slaves) of William Cassells. The listing is ambiguous, because there appears to be a comma between "George" and "Kid", raising the possibility that Cassells had two slaves by these names. These lists are incomplete, but I'm almost certain this citation is proof of his presence in Amelia by 1763.[97] The PPTL for 1764 is incomplete, and I don't find George Kidd on those lists that survived. But he is present on the 1765 list, and thereafter. [The 1764 Colonial Tithables Lists are not extant.]

1765 – A **George Kid** is found on the 1765 Colonial Tithables Lists of Amelia County, upon the List of William Crawley, one of the tax assessors of Raleigh Parish. His tithe (and that of another white male) was paid by Vivion Brookings, a wealthy plantation owner with over 2000 acres of land and 18 slaves; presumably George and the other white man were serving as overseers for Brookings.[98]

1769-1770 – **George Kidd is** again found on the Tithes Lists of Amelia County in 1769; this time his tax (along with the tax of Allen Freeman and Evan Mitchell) was paid by Col. Robert Bolling, a large slaveholder who was taxed for 54 slaves in 1769. They appear on the tax list of Vivion Brookings (the plantation owner who George worked for in 1765), the assessor for lower Raleigh Parish in that year.

---

[96] Middlesex County, Virginia Deed Book 8A, pp. 295-296. Digital images and transcript of the document available upon request.

[97] He's listed among the tithables (taxable white males and slaves) of William Cassells. The listing is ambiguous, because there appears to be a comma between "George" and "Kid", raising the possibility that Cassells had two slaves by these names. However, Benjamin Kidd was William Cassell's overseer in 1762, and I believe that George took over his brother's job.

[98] *Tithe Lists of Amelia County, Virginia, 1765-1778*, by Reiley Kidd MD, Colonial Roots, Millsboro, DE, 2016, citing FHL #190266.

The following year, George Kidd's tax was again paid for by Col. Robert Bolling, again in lower Raleigh Parish. [99]

1771 – In a deed signed 28 November 1771, **George Kidd** purchased 100 acres of land "on the east side of Tucker's branch" in Amelia County from John Clardy Sr. and Susannah his wife, for "80 pounds current money of Virginia."[100] Neighbors included Clardy, Daniel Allen, Colemans, and Bevils. The deed was recorded the same date.

He continued to pay taxes there until he died in 1797, and his wife Elizabeth took over paying the taxes until 1817; presumably she died that year.

1778 – The Colonial Tithe Lists of Amelia County for the years 1772-1777 are not extant. A **George Kidd** again appears on these lists in 1778, paying his own tithe and that for a **Benjamin Kidd.** As before, they are found on the list of Vivion Brooking, the tax collector for lower Raleigh Parish. We believe that this Benjamin Kidd is George's eldest son, born abt 1761.[101]

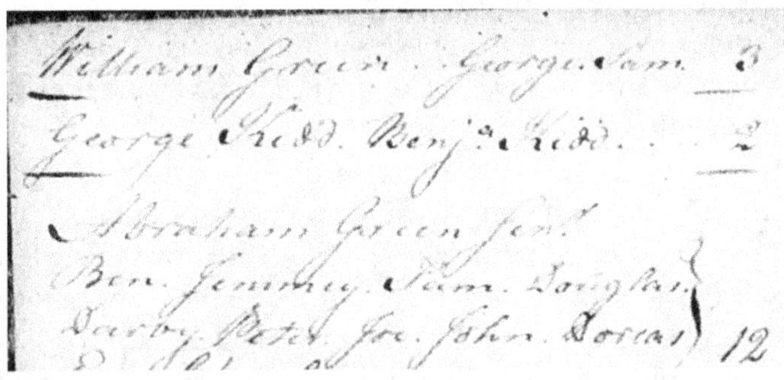

Also in 1778, **George Kidd** and Benjamin Kidd of Amelia County signed the oath of allegiance, refusing allegiance to the Crown, on 25 August 1778.[102]

We believe that this Benjamin Kidd was this George4 Kidd's son, since all males over the age of sixteen were expected to sign these oaths of allegiance.

1779 – in a deed dated 15 March 1779, George Worsham of Amelia County sold to Evans Mitchell of same, for £20, a parcel of 244 acres adjacent to the lines of John Hood, Robert Hood, Tucker Hood, Abraham Coleman, **George Kidd**, Thomas Tucker, and Matthew Tucker.[103]

On 28 October 1779, **George Kid** owned land near Namozine Creek "as it meanders" in Amelia County, adjacent to Abraham & Francis (x) Coleman (Coleman's land sold to John Neal).[104] The other neighbor of this parcel was Daniel Allen.

1782 – The Virginia Personal Property Tax Lists (PPTLs) began in 1782. The PPTL for Amelia County includes **George Kidd** with two free males over 21; this list names Benjamin Kidd as the second male in the household.[105] We believe that this Benjamin is George's eldest son,

---

[99] Ibid.

[100] Amelia County Deed Book 11, page 347.

[101] *Tithe Lists of Amelia County, Virginia, 1765-1778*, by Reiley Kidd MD, Colonial Roots, Millsboro, DE, 2016, citing FHL #190267. This particular entry is viewable online via Familysearch.org (unrestricted access) on image 20 of this reel.

[102] Original in County Court Clerk's office, Amelia County, VA; published in DAR Magazine February 1959.

[103] Amelia County, VA Deed Book 15, p. 67, as abstracted in *Amelia County Virginia (Deed) Books 15, 16, & 17, 1778-1786*, by Gibson Jefferson McConnaughey, Amelia, VA, 1993, p. 12.

[104] Amelia County, VA Deed Book 15, p. 206, as abstracted in *Amelia County Virginia (Deed) Books 15, 16, & 17, 1778-1786*, by Gibson Jefferson McConnaughey, Amelia, VA, 1993, p 29.

[105] Amelia County, VA PPTLs, 1782-1813, retrieved via familysearch.org from FHL #2024454, image 21.

and conclude that he's turned 21 years of age in the last year; this would indicate that he was born in or about 1761. No other Kidds are listed in the 1782 Amelia County PPTL.

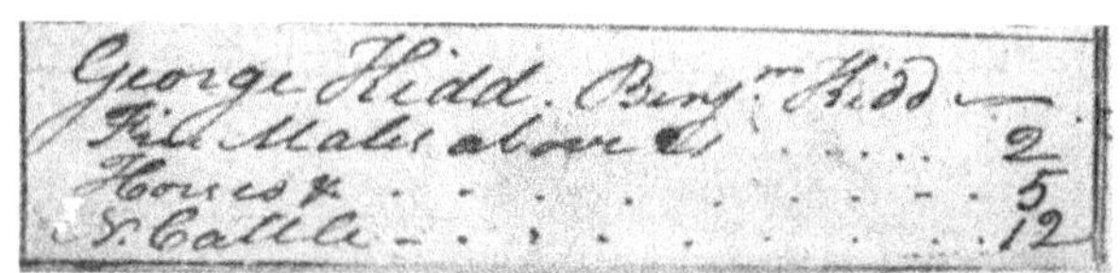

1782-1797 – **George Kidd** appears on the first Amelia County, VA **Land Tax list** in 1782,[106] taxed on 100 acres of land in George Booker's district. This is the tract of land that he purchased in 1771 (see above). He continued to appear annually on these LTLs through 1797. Beginning in 1798 (after George4's death in 1797), his widow Elizabeth is taxed for these 100 acres through 1817. Thereafter, she disappears from the tax lists, and we believe that she died in 1817 or 1818.[107]

1783 – **George Kidd** again appears on the Amelia County PPTL, taxed for two free males over 16 (the age threshold for taxation was changed since 1782), 3 horses and 10 cattle. At this time he owned no slaves.
The 1783 PPTL listed only the name of the person charged with the tax, and did not name the other taxable males in the household. As in 1782, there were no other Kidds named on the 1783 PPTL.[108]

1784 – **George Kidd** again appears on the 1784 Amelia County PPTL, with 4 Tithes (in this one year, this category seems to have included BOTH free white males AND taxable slaves (those over age 16). He had no slaves under 16, and owned 3 horses & 9 cattle.
ALSO on the 1784 Amelia PPTL is a second George Kidd (almost certainly George Sr.'s son), charged with one free white male (himself), no slaves, 3 horses and 9 cattle.[109]

1785 – George Kidd again appears on the Amelia County PPTL in 1785. The column headings changed from the previous year, listing the following for each taxpayer:
Taxpayer/Whites above 21/Whites <21/Black tithes/young Negroes/Horses/Cattle
George Kidd/   1   /   1   /   1   /   0   / 4 / 8
This almost certainly is George4 Kidd, given the other tithes he is charged with; it suggests that some of the tithes he paid in 1784 were for tithable slaves.
No other Kidd taxpayers appear on the 1785 PPTL for Amelia County.

Also in 1785, **George Kidd** is among the signees of a petition dated 9 November 1785 in Amelia County, VA.[110]

1786 – **George Kidd** again appears on the Amelia PPTLs in this year. As before, the column headings changed again (making it nearly impossible to create a coherent, illustrative Table depicting these annual lists); the column headings in 1786 were:
Taxpayer/White tithes > 21/WM 16-21/Slaves >16/Negroes <16/horses/cattle

---

[106] The new state of Virginia began the annual PPTLs and LTLs in 1782, after the Rev. War.

[107] Amelia County, VA Land Tax records, copied by Troy Kidd (copy in RK's Amelia County, VA file).

[108] Ibid, image 85.

[109] Ibid, image 111.

[110] from *Early VA Religious Petitions*, on VSLA website. There are 20 petitions from Amelia County, VA on this website, from 5/12/1780 and later.

George Kidd / 2   / 1   / blank   /   0?   /4   / 11[111]
As before, there were no other Kidd taxpayers on the 1786 Amelia County PPTL.

1787-1791 – Starting in 1787 and continuing through 1791, the Amelia County PPTLs listed not only the name of every person charged with the tax, but also listed <u>the names of ALL white tithables in each household</u>; in addition, each year's list contains a column listing the number (but not the names) of white males in each household between the ages of 16-21. This permits one to identify a taxpayer's sons within the household as they age, then leave the family home and become household heads themselves.

Sadly, this didn't last long. But for those interested in George4 Kidd and "all the rest of my sons" not named in his will, the timing was fortuitous.

The Table below depicts the Amelia PPTLs for these years, illustrating the appearance of several of his sons, first within his household, and then as neighboring households.

[N. B. The column titled "White tithes over 21" **includes** the taxpayer.]

TABLE DEPICTING THE AMELIA COUNTY PPTLS, 1787-1791 [112]

YEAR	Person charged with the tax	White males > 21	White Males 16-21	Negro Tithables (>16)	Negroes <16	Horses, etc.	Microfilm image
1787	George Kidd Sr.	George Kidd Lodwick Kidd	1	0	0	3	157
	George Kidd Jr.	George Kidd	0	0	0	1	
1788	George Kid Sr.	George Kid, Lod. Kidd, Jas. Kidd	this column left blank, 1788-1791	0	0	4	180
	George Kid Jr.	George Kid	-	0	0	1	
1789	George Kid Sr.	George Kid, Lod. Kidd, Jas. Kidd	-	0	0	4	209
	George Kid Jr.	George Kid	-	0	0	2	
1790	George Kid Sr.	George Kid, Lod. Kidd, Jas. Kidd	-	0	0	4	220
	George Kid Jr.	George Kid	-	0	0	2	

---

[111] Ibid, image 142.

[112] Entries in this Table were retrieved from FHL #2024454, Amelia County PPTLs, 1782-1813 via familysearch.org (unrestricted access). The column labeled "Microfilm image" refers to the image number on the reel for each entry.

1791	George Kid Sr.	George Kid Jams Kid Bartholomew Kid	-	0	0	3
	George Kid Jr.	George Kid	-	0	0	2
	Lodwick Kid	Lodwick Kid	-	0	0	1

The image below is a scanned image of their entry in the 1789 Amelia PPTL:

1787-1797 – **George4 Kidd** is also listed annually on the Amelia County, VA <u>Land Tax Lists (LTLs)</u> in George Booker's district, taxed on 100 acres of land. Beginning in 1798 (after his death in 1797), his widow Elizabeth is taxed for these 100 acres, through 1817. Thereafter, she disappears from the tax lists, and we believe that she died in 1817 or 1818.[113]

1791 – On 15 August 1791, **George Kidd** was one of the witnesses, along with Jesse Coleman and Robt. Johns, to Joseph Coleman and his wife selling land in Amelia County to Daniel Coleman.[114]

1792-1804 – The Table below depicts the Amelia County PPTLs for these years.

YEAR	TAXPAYER	WM >16	Blacks >16	Blacks 12-16	Horses, etc.	COMMENTS
1792	**George Kidd** (no others)	2	-	-	3	FHL #2024454, image 249
1793	**George Kid**	2	-	-	2	ibid, image 266
	George Kid Jr.	1	-	-	0	
1794	**George Kid Sr.**	3	-	-	4	ibid, image 284
	George Kid Jr.	1	-	-	-	
1795	**George Kid Sr.**	3	-	-	4	ibid, image 300

---

[113] Amelia County, VA Land Tax Lists, 1782-1857, abstracted from reels 14-16 and 385 at the Library of Virginia by William R. Kidd, one of the authors of this compilation, in November of 2003. Copy available upon request.

[114] *Unrecorded Deeds & Other Documents, Amelia County, Virginia, 1750-1902*, by Gibson Jefferson McConnaughey, Iberian Publishing Co., 1996, p. 12.

	George Kid Jr.	1	-	-	-	
1796	**George Kidd Sr.**	3	-	-	3	ibid, image 316
	George Kidd Jr.	1	-	-	-	
1797	**George Kidd's Est.**	2	-	-	3	ibid, image 332
	George Kidd Jr.	1	-	-	-	
1798	**George Kid's Est.**	2	-	-	3	ibid, image 349
	George Kid	1	1	-	-	
1799	**George Kid's Est.**	2	-	-	3	ibid, image 367
	George Kid	1	1	-	-	
1800	**George Kid's Est.**	2	-	-	3	ibid, image 385
	George Kid	1	1	-	-	
1801	**George Kid's Est.**	2	-	-	4	ibid, image 405
	George Kid	1	1	-	1	
1802	Bartholomew Kidd (no others)	2	-	1	3	ibid, image 425 (George Jr. in Dinwiddie this year)
1803	Bartholomew Kid (no others)	1	-	-	-	ibid, image 447
	Jasper Kid	1	-	-	1	
	George Kid	1	1	1	2	
1804	**George Kidd's Est.**	1	1	-	1	Ibid, imge 465
	Bartholomew Kid	1	-	-	-	
	George Kid	1	1	1	2	

1793 –On 10 March 1793, **George Kidd** wrote and signed his will in Amelia County, Virginia. See below.

1797 – The will of **George Kidd Sr.**, written in 1793, was proven in Amelia County, VA Court on 22 June 1797. It names sons Jasper, Bartholomew, and "all the rest of my sons;" we believe that this refers to Benjamin, George (Jr.), Lodowick and James, who, being older and already out on their own, likely already had received their inheritance when they left their father's household. This would account for their not being named individually, but just referred to as "my other sons").
An inventory appraisal of his estate was made in 1797 as well.[115]

---

[115] Amelia County Will Book 5, page 390 (digital images available upon request).

Below is a word-for-word transcription of the original will, which was discovered in his Probate packet in the Amelia County Court Clerk's office.[116] <u>The original spelling has been preserved, as was punctuation</u> (or rather, the lack thereof).

In the Name of God, Amen I **George Kidd** of Amelia County in the Colloney of Virginia being sick and weak but of sound and perfect Memory do Make this my Last Will and Testament in Manner and form as Followeth Item first I give to my Beloved wife Elizabeth Kidd My land and all the Rest of my Estate During her Life or Widderhood and at her Death or Marriage my Land to be Eakley Devidded between Bartholomew Kidd and Jasper Kidd and their hars for Ever <u>and all the Rest of my sons</u> (added emphasis mine – RK) I give them Two shillings and six pence apeace to them and their hars forever. I give to Isack Coleman Two shillings and to his heirs for Ever all the rest of my Estate I Give to be Eakly Devided between Bartholomew Kidd Jasper Kidd Usley Kidd and Elizabeth Kidd At the Death or Marriage of My Wife Elizabeth Kidd to Them and there hars forever Lastly I do Appoint George Bevell and John Neal to be Executors of this My Last Will and testament in witness where of I have hereunto Set My hand and seal this Tenth Day of March in the Year of our Lord one Thousand seven hundred and Ninty three published and Delivered in presents of
Teste
Abraham X Coleman (his mark)   George Kidd {seal}
William Coleman

At a Court held for Amelia County the 22nd day of June 1797, The Last Will and Testament of George Kidd dec'd was Exhibited into Court and proved by the oath of William Coleman a witness thereto who also made oath that he also saw Abraham Coleman the other witness subscribing the same attest the said will at the request of the said Testator and in his presence who is since dead John Neal the Executor therein named came into Court and Refused to take upon himself the burthen of the Execution thereof and adm(inistration) with the Will annexed is granted to Bartholomew Kidd who took the oath by Law prescribed and entered into and acknowledged Bond who together with John Neal his security in the penalty of 2000 Dollars certificate is granted him to obtain Letters of Administration in due form and the same is ordered to be recorded.

[In 1814, Jasper Kidd sold his share of the tract of land in Amelia County "willed to us by our father **George Kidd**," for $250, to his brother Bartholomew Kidd.[117]]

1798-1817 – Amelia County LTLs reveal that **Elizabeth Kidd** was taxed on George Kidd's land in these years after his death (see next entry, below).[118] Her land was on Long Branch, with John Neal and Richard Allen and William Coleman as neighbors.

1807 – **Elisabeth Kidd** appears on the 1807 Amelia County, VA Personal Property Tax List this one year (previously this was listed as "George Kidd's Estate") with 2 free males over 16 (her youngest sons Bartholomew and Jasper) and one slave.

------

[116] A <u>transcription</u> of this will was entered into Amelia County Will Book 5, pages 359-360; this copy is viewable online via familysearch.org (unrestricted access) on FHL #30451, images 391-392.

[117] Amelia County Deed Book 24, page 126. Both were residing in Chesterfield County VA at the time. (I have a copy of this.)

[118] Amelia County Land Books, George Booker's district; see notes of Forrest Sheets, researcher (RK).

She drops from the Amelia County PPTLs in 1809 (no taxes were collected in 1808), and does not reappear on them, despite the fact that she continued to appear on the Amelia County Land Tax Lists through 1817.

<u>GEORGE5a KIDD</u> – the son of George4 (Benjamin3, William2, Thomas1) Kidd
Often referred to in Amelia County records as George Kidd Jr.
Born 1763, Amelia County, VA
Married Mary Southall in Amelia County in 1786
Died testate 24 Nov 1844, Amelia County, VA
Four children named in his will: James6b Kidd, Asa Kidd, Nancy L. Coleman,[119] and Martha (Kidd) Young.[120]

1763 – **George5a Kidd** was born in Amelia County, VA in the year 1763, and lived there and in Dinwiddie County, VA all his life, according to his Revolutionary War pension application, dated 23 August 1836.[121] His application said he was "Known particularly to Henry H. Southall, William Coleman, and Parson William Hubbard." This application was pursued unsuccessfully by his son Asa Kidd after George's death in 1844.
George was literate, and signed his own name to many documents.

1784 – George5 Kidd first appears on the Amelia County, VA PPTL:[122]
George Kidd – 1 free white male over 21
(also on the list was his father. George Kidd, with 4 FWM>21. No others)

1785, 1786 – there is only ONE George Kidd on the Amelia County, VA PPTLs for these years, and they appear to be George Sr. Not sure where George Jr. is, given the marriage record below. Perhaps he's back in his father's household (See George Kidd Sr.'s listings for these years).

In 1786, **George Kidd** married Mary[123] Southall, daughter of James Southall.[124]
This couple had two sons Asa and James Kidd (this James is the ancestor of Albert Ray Kidd[125] and Troy Kidd) and at least two daughters, Nancy Kidd Coleman and Martha Kidd Young.
[There are numerous mentions of the Southall family in connection with George Kidd. In

---

[119] Nancy L. was the wife of Braxton Coleman.
[120] Martha was the wife of Elliott Young. She and her family migrated west, along with her brother, James Kidd.
[121] Revolutionary War Pension File R5907. Digital images of this record available upon request.
[122] Amelia County, VA PPTLs, 1782-1834, personally transcribed by Reiley Kidd, 2008.
[123] Amelia County DB 21, p. 67, George Kidd and his wife Mary sold to Henry H. Southall a parcel of land...;Amelia County DB 25, p. 58 records the sale of land by George Kidd and Mary his wife to Elliott Young (who married their daughter Martha on Jan. 1816 (Amelia County Marriage Bonds - 17W(1)49).
[124] Amelia County Marriage Bonds, page 1. June 12, 1786. Witnesses Jno. and Daniel Southall. Sur. Jesse Coleman. (16W(1)211).
[125] Troy Kidd was a marvelous researcher, and collected a great deal of information on this family. Troy died suddenly and unexpectedly in 1999, just as Y-DNA studies were beginning to be used for genealogical purposes. With the help of others, we tracked down Troy's older brother, Albert Ray, and although he didn't share Troy's passion for family history, he agreed to participate in the Kidd Y-DNA Project. Doing so enabled us to confirm Troy's research, and to get a better picture of George4 Kidd's Y-DNA structure, as well as serving as a gold standard with which to measure other potential descendants, whose paper trail back to George4 was not as strong as Troy's was.

addition, George5 Kidd's nephew (the son of his brother, Lodowick), William Kidd married Elizabeth A. Southall in June of 1818 in Amelia County.[126]]

1787-1791 – Starting in 1787 and continuing through 1791, the Amelia County PPTLs listed not only the name of every person charged with the tax, but also listed the names of ALL white tithables in each household; in addition, each year's list contains a column listing the number (but not the names) of white males in each household between the ages of 16-21. This permits one to identify a taxpayer's sons within the household as they age, then leave the family home and become household heads themselves.

Sadly, this didn't last long. But for those interested in George4 Kidd and "all the rest of my sons" not named in his will, the timing was fortuitous.

The Table below depicts the Amelia PPTLs for these years, illustrating the appearance of several of his sons, first within his household, and then as neighboring households.

[N. B. The column titled "White tithes over 21" includes the taxpayer.]

TABLE DEPICTING THE AMELIA COUNTY PPTLS, 1787-1791 [127]

YEAR	Person charged with the tax	White males > 21	White Males 16-21	Negro Tithables (>16)	Negroes <16	Horses, etc.	Microfilm image
1787	George Kidd Sr.	George Kidd Ladwick Kidd	1	0	0	3	157
	George Kidd Jr.	George Kidd	0	0	0	1	
1788	George Kid Sr.	George Kid, Lod. Kidd, Jas. Kidd	this column left blank, 1788-1791	0	0	4	180
	George Kid Jr.	George Kid	-	0	0	1	
1789	George Kid Sr.	George Kid, Lod. Kidd, Jas. Kidd	-	0	0	4	209
	George Kid Jr.	George Kid	-	0	0	2	
1790	George Kid Sr.	George Kid, Lod. Kidd, Jas. Kidd	-	0	0	4	220
	George Kid Jr.	George Kid	-	0	0	2	

---

[126] Virginia, Marriages, 1740-1850 on Ancestry.com, citing "Marriage Bonds in Amelia County Marriage Bonds, image 62 of 804 in this database. Barnett Southall listed as witness or security.

[127] Entries in this Table were retrieved from FHL #2024454, Amelia County PPTLs, 1782-1813 via familysearch.org (unrestricted access). The column labeled "Microfilm image" refers to the image number on the reel for each entry.

1791	George Kid Sr.	George Kid Jams Kid Bartholomew Kid	-	0	0	3	233
	George Kid Jr.	George Kid	-	0	0	2	
	Lodwick Kid	Lodwick Kid	-	0	0	1	

The image below is a scanned image of their entry in the 1789 Amelia PPTL:

1792 – On 1 September 1792, Daniel Coleman and Francis his wife of Amelia County sold to **George Kidd** of the same place for the sum of £96.10 a tract of land in Amelia County containing 96½ acres and adjoining Robert Tanner, William Hale, Thomas V. Brookings, and Andrew Waugh.[128] <u>Lodowick Kidd</u> is listed as a witness, along with Jesse Coleman and Ebenezer Coleman.

This is **George5a Kidd**, because he first appears on the Amelia Land Tax Lists in 1793 as George Kidd <u>Jr.</u>, taxed on 96.5 acres, and distinguished from the older George Kidd, who was listed as George Kidd <u>Sr.</u>

1792-1804 – The Table below depicts the Amelia County PPTLs for these years.

YEAR	TAXPAYER	WM >16	Blacks >16	Blacks 12-16	Horses, etc.	COMMENTS
1792	George Kidd (no others)	2	-	-	3	FHL #2024454, image 249
1793	George Kid	2	-	-	2	ibid, image 266
	George Kid Jr.	1	-	-	0	
1794	George Kid Sr.	3	-	-	4	ibid, image 284
	George Kid Jr.	1	-	-	-	
1795	George Kid Sr.	3	-	-	4	ibid, image 300
	George Kid Jr.	1	-	-	-	

---

[128] Amelia County Deed Book 19, pp. 217-218, retrieved from FHL #30438, image 312 via Familysearch.org.

Year	Name					Source
1796	George Kidd Sr.	3	-	-	3	ibid, image 316
	George Kidd Jr.	1	-	-	-	
1797	George Kidd's Est.	2	-	-	3	ibid, image 332
	George Kidd Jr.	1	-	-	-	
1798	George Kid's Est.	2	-	-	3	ibid, image 349
	George Kid	1	1	-	-	
1799	George Kid's Est.	2	-	-	3	ibid, image 367
	George Kid	1	1	-	-	
1800	George Kid's Est.	2	-	-	3	ibid, image 385
	George Kid	1	1	-	-	
1801	George Kid's Est.	2	-	-	4	ibid, image 405
	George Kid	1	1	-	1	
1802	Bartholomew Kidd (no others)	2	-	1	3	ibid, image 425 (George Jr. in Dinwiddie this year)
1803	Bartholomew Kid (no others)	1	-	-	-	ibid, image 447
	Jasper Kid	1	-	-	1	
	George Kid	1	1	1	2	
1804	George Kidd's Est.	1	1	-	1	Ibid, imge 465
	Bartholomew Kid	1	-	-	-	
	George Kid	1	1	1	2	

1793-1800 – Beginning in 1793 and continuing through 1800, **George Kidd Jr.** also appears on Amelia County **LTLs**, taxed for 96.5 acres.

1794 – A **George Kidd Jr.** was plaintiff in a suit dated 27 Feb 1794 against William Willson and Robert Colquhouser, executors of William Walthall dec'd in Amelia County, VA Court. In this suit, the defendants failed to appear, and the court ruled that the plaintiff recover the sum of £3.15.0 and costs, on 6 Apr 1794.[129]

1795 – The Amelia County Chancery Court records for this year contain a suit brought by Lucy Walthall, the widow of Robert Walthall, deceased, against **George Kidd, Jr.** regarding a half-acre tract of land lying in Amelia County, part of the land "purchased of Joseph Coleman by said Kidd," and deeded by George Kidd Jr. to Robert Walthall during his lifetime. The deed was never recorded in court, and following Walthall's death, George Kidd Jr. repeatedly refused to provide details regarding the deed.[130]

---

[129] Amelia County, VA Order Book 20, p. 218, abstracted by Forrest Sheets, a researcher hired by RK in 1987.
[130] Copies available from WRK. The 10-page document he provided doesn't include the final outcome of this suit.

1797 – On 27 July 1797, **George Kidd** was granted letters of administration on the estate of Isaac Coleman deceased.[131] Since George Kidd Sr.'s will was proved on 22 June 1797, this entry must be for **George Kidd Jr**.

1799 – In an Amelia County deed signed 1 November 1799, Anderson Tucker of Amelia County for £138 sold to **George Kidd** of Amelia County a parcel of land in Amelia containing 138 acres, bounded by the lands of Allen, Adams, Jones, Neals, Parkinson and Bevills. This deed was admitted to record on 22 January 1801.[132]

1800 – On September 25, 1800, **George Kidd** and Mary his wife of Amelia County sold to Henry H. Southall for £110 current money of Virginia a parcel of land containing 96 acres, adjacent to lands of Walthalls, William Jones, Robert Tanner, Field Tanner, and Stephen Southall.[133] Witnesses were John Southall and Claiborn Perkinson.

1801 – In Amelia County January Court 1801, a deed from Anderson Tucker to **George Kidd** was acknowledged by the said Tucker, and ordered to be recorded.[134]

In Amelia County, October Court 1801, a deed from William Adams and wife to **Geo. Kidd** was presented into court and proved by the oath of one of the witnesses thereto and ordered to be continued for further proof.[135]

1799-1848 – Between 1799 and 1840, numerous land purchases and sales are recorded for a **George Kidd** of Amelia County.[136] Henry H. Southall (brother of Mary Southall Kidd, George Kidd's wife) served as witness for many of these transactions.

The Amelia County, VA Land Tax Records reflect these acquisitions. From 1793-1800, **George Kidd** is taxed on 96.5 acres. From 1801-1802, he is taxed on 138 acres; in 1803 he adds 68 more acres. From 1808-1812 he has 221 acres. Beginning in 1814, he has 333 acres.[137]

The acreage varies from year to year, through 1848 (even though he died in 1844); evidently his son Asa left things in George's name for this period.

His land is described as being on Beaverpond Branch, with John and Archer Neal and Herod Crowder as neighbors.

---

[131] Amelia County Order Book 21, p. 506, abstracted in Amelia County Will Book 5, 1793-1799, with additional deaths and heirs from Order Books 21, 22 and 23, abstracted by Bel Hubbard Wise, Mountain Press, Signal Mountain, TN, p. 57.
The next entry in this Order Book binds out Nancy, Usley and Mary Coleman, orphans of Isaac Coleman, deceased.

[132] Amelia County DB 21, pp. 107.

[133] Amelia County DB 21, pp. 67-68. Scanned images available.

[134] FHL #30466, Amelia County, VA OBs 23-26, 1800-1812, OB 23, page 119 (image 77 on this reel).

[135] FHL #30466: Amelia County, VA OBs 23-26, 1800-1812, OB 23, 1800-1801, image 6 on this reel (via FamilySearch.org's digital images, August 2018).

[136] Deed Book 21, p. 67 (1800) and p. 107 (1799); DB 22, p. 201 (1806); DB 23, p. 159 (1810) and p. 413 (1811); DB 24, p. 126 (1815); DB 25, p. 58 (1818); DB 28, p. 460 (1828); DB 30, p. 76 (1828); DB 32, p. 83 (1834), and DB 34, p. 378 (1840). RK has digital images of all of these; they add little specific information, except to show the continued contact of this George Kidd with the Coleman, Southall, Allen, Adams, Neal and Bevill families.

[137] Amelia County, Virginia Land Tax Records, transcribed by Troy Kidd (copy in RK's Amelia County, VA file).

1802 – In 1802, a **George Kidd** appears for the first time on the **Dinwiddie** County Personal
Property Tax List.[138] (Lodowick has appeared intermittently since 1792, and a Benjamin
Kidd was listed intermittently from 1790 through 1793.)[139]

1806 – On 8 February 1806, Richard Cardwill Jr. and Lucy his wife of Dinwiddie County for £18.6
current money of Virginia sold to **George Kidd** a parcel of land in Amelia County of 15 ¼
acres "beginning at the said Kidd's corner… and running to Mrs. Rebecca Adams tract…to
Mr. David Adams, dec'd." Witnessed by William Coleman and others.[140]

1806-1809 – A **George Kidd** is found on the **Dinwiddie** PPTLs from 1806-1809, without personal
property. (No lists were recorded statewide in 1808.)

1810 – The 1810 VA census lists one George Kidd in **Amelia** County:[141]
George Kidd 12001-1100-8 (1M 0-9, 2M 10-15 & 1 45 & up; 1F 0-9 & 1 10-15; 8 total
(therefore two slaves).
Jasper Kidd 0001-0011-7 (7 total, therefore 4 slaves)
The 29 names next to George and Jasper Kidd are illegible, but appear to be surnames
starting with L. Meanwhile, Lodowick Kidd is listed in Dinwiddie County.

1810 – In an Amelia County deed signed 22 February 1810, Burrel Featherston and Rebecca his wife
of Nottoway for £18.6 sold to **George Kidd** a parcel of land in Amelia containing 15 ½
acres adjoining the lands of **George Kidd** and the widow Adams.[142]

1810-1811 – No Kidds listed on Amelia County, VA PPTLs.

1811 – In an Amelia County Deed of Gift dated 24 May 1811, Francis (X) Clay of Nottoway County
to her son, Thomas Clay of Amelia County. In consideration of the natural love and
affection, and $1, 110 acres in Amelia County adj. the lines of **George Kidd**, Daniel Allen
Sr., Polly Coleman and Rebecah Adams.[143]

In an Amelia County deed signed 24 October 1811, Archer Coleman of Amelia County for
£138.19 sold to **George Kidd** a parcel of land in Amelia containing 97 acres, adjoining the
lands of John Neal, Thomas Woodward and Archer Neal. Witnesses were Henry H.
Southall, Geo. Pollard and L. Wills.[144]

1812 – On the Amelia County, VA PPTL:
George Kidd – 2 free WM >16 (George & son James, b. 1794), 5 slaves, 2 gigs

1813-1815 – On the Amelia County, VA PPTL:
George Kidd – 2 free WM >16 (George & son James, b. 1794), 7 slaves, 2 gigs

1816 – On 26 Jan 1816, Martha Kidd married Elliott Young in Amelia County, VA. **George Kidd**
(this is George5a Kidd, son of George Sr.) was listed as father of the bride.[145]

---

138 Dinwiddie County Personal Property Tax Lists, 1800-1819.

139 Dinwiddie County Personal Property Tax Lists, 1782-1799.

140 Amelia County DB 22, pp. 201-202 (scanned images available).

141 1810 VA census, Amelia County, page 237.

142 Amelia County DB 23, p. 159 (scanned image available).

143 *Unrecorded Deeds & Other Documents, Amelia County, Virginia, 1750-1902*, by Gibson Jefferson McConnaughey, Iberian
Publishing Co., 1996, p. 44, citing "Packet #1, Labeled "Deeds not Proven, A-H".

144 Amelia County DB 23, p. 413 (scanned image available).

145 *Amelia County, Virginia Marriage Boonds, Consents, and Ministers' Returns, 1816-1852*, by T.P. Hughes.

And a James Kidd served as security. This James may have been George Jr.'s son, who just turned 21; the alternative is that this is James5, George5a's brother, but this is improbable, as James5 Kidd was in Mecklenburg County, VA in 1816.

1816 – On the Amelia County, VA PPTL:
George Kidd – 2 free males over 16, 6 slaves
James Kidd – 1 free male over 16, one slave (this is George5a's eldest son, b. 1794)

1817 – On the Amelia County, VA PPTL:
George Kidd – 2 free males over 16 (George and son Asa[146], or a previously unknown son[147]; 7 slaves
James Kidd – 1 free males over 16

1818 – On the Amelia County, VA PPTL:
George Kidd – 2 free males over 16 (looks like James6b moved back home)
Bartholomew Kidd – 1 free male over 16 (George5a's younger brother)

In a deed signed 18 February 1818, **George Kidd Senr.** and Mary his wife sold for $800 to Elliott Young (their son-in-law who married their daughter Martha) a parcel of land containing 130 acres adjoining David Adams, Burwell Coleman, George Kidd, Herod T. Crowder, Jack Bevill and David Allen.[148]

1819 – On the Amelia County, VA PPTL:
George Kidd – 3 free males over 16 (probably James6b and Asa [right age for his known son, Asa, now age 16]); 6 slaves; no others.

1820 – On the Amelia County, VA PPTL:
George Kidd – 3 free males over 16 (again, probably James6a and Asa)

The 1820 VA census finds a **George Kidd** "over 45 years old" in Amelia County, along with Barnett, Field, and Henry H. Southall.[149] Again, Lodowick and William are in Dinwiddie County along with other Kidds.[150]

1825 – In a deed signed 3 November 1825, Asa Kidd of Amelia County for $393 sold to John H. Brown of Petersburg, Virginia a parcel of land containing 65 ½ acres, adjoining **George Kidd**, the estate of Archer Neal, Bolling's old mill pond, and John H. Brown. This land had been purchased by said Kidd from Jack Neal. Asa signed this deed, and could write.[151]

1827 – In a deed signed 8 October 1827, Elliott Young and Martha his wife, and **George Kidd** and Robert Bevill & Frances his wife, all of Amelia County, for $800 sold to Elizabeth C. Tarborne 150 acres adjoining the lands of Wm. Scott, Bevill, **George Kidd**, Herod T. Crowder, Joel Bevill, the estate of Allen, Daniel Allen and Wm. B. Scott.

---

[146] From his census entries, we believe that Asa was born about 1805; he'd be only 12 in 1817, so this may not be him.

[147] George Kidd Jr. had only two known sons, James and Asa. James is named in this list, and Asa would appear to have been too young. Thus this listing MAY be a third son, one who died in the next few years.

[148] Amelia County DB 25, pp. 58-59 (scanned images available).

[149]. 1820 VA census, Amelia County, (failed to record page!);(000201-00001; 8 slaves).

[150] Kidds listed on the 1820 Dinwiddie County census include Lodawick (210001-11231, 6 slaves); Lodawick's son William (100100-00100, no slaves); James (100011-12220); Benjamin (310011-12220); Thomas I [J?] (110110-10100); and James Jr. (000010-10100).

[151] Amelia County, VA DB 27, pp. 420-422 (scanned images available).

On Dec. 17, **George Kidd** served as security for the marriage of Benjamin Caudle & Susannah A. Coleman in Amelia County, VA.[152]

1828 – Amelia County Chancery Court records contain an affidavit given by **George Kidd** on 23 April 1828 at "Braxton Coleman's tavern," in a dispute between Peter Woodward and Eppes Allen over a horse Woodard had earlier purchased from Allen. George Kidd's affidavit states that he thought the horse was suffering from a condition called "yellow water," and thought the horse was unsound and should be returned.
Others providing affidavits in the case included the surnames Cousins, Southall, Coleman and Bevill.
THIS DOCUMENT CONTAINS GEORGE KIDD'S SIGNATURE.[153]

In a deed signed 21 October 1828, **George Kidd**, William Puryear and John P. Bolling, acting as commissioners of the Court, sold to James H. Southall for $371.50 a parcel of land on which the late George Pollard resided, containing 218 acres. This deed was recorded in Court in August 1830.[154]

1830 – The 1830 VA census lists a **George Kidd** in Amelia County, page 143:[155]
George Kidd 000010001-10001 (one male 20-29 and one 60-69; one female 0-4 and one 60-69) plus 5 male and 3 female slaves (one male and one female between 55-100 years old). The younger male in this household should be his remaining son Asa. (The older son James left VA for KY in 1828.)

1834 – On 19 April 1834, Alexander Allen and Martha his wife of Amelia County conveyed a parcel of land in Amelia County "on which Adams meeting house now stands, containing and laid out for one acre of land" to a group of Trustees of the Methodist Episcopal Church. The Trustees, listed by name, were Henry H. Southall, James Allen, **George Kidd**, William T. Green, William Coleman, William D. Southall, **Asa Kidd** and John Clay. The deed stipulates that the land is conveyed in Trust, with the understanding that the trustees "will erect or build, or cause to be built…a place of worship for the use of the members of the Methodist Episcopal Church" and that it remain in use for this purpose, in coordination with and ministers provided by this denomination.
The deed was proved in court and admitted to record in Amelia County Court on 26 June 1834.[156]

In a Deed of Release signed 1 November 1834, **George Kidd** and Peter Woodward acknowledged that a Deed of Trust entered into with them by John B. T. Brown in 1830 had been satisfied.[157]

---

[152] *Amelia County, Virginia Marriage Boonds, Consents, and Ministers' Returns, 1816-1852*, by T.P. Hughes.
[153] Amelia County, VA Chancery Court Book for 1828, pp. 40, ff.
[154] Amelia County DB 30, pp. 76-77 (scanned images available).
[155] 1830 VA census, Amelia County, Eastern District, list of Fabius Lawson, page 143, (misindexed as "George Hdd" at Ancestry.com).
[156] Amelia County Deed book 31, pp. 400-402, photostatic copy obtained from the County Court Clerk's office, because the online images via familysearch.org were too faint to be interpreted, January 31, 2021.
[157] Amelia County DB 32, pp. 83-85 (scanned images available).

1835 – On 19 August 1835, **George Kidd** of Amelia County, VA was among the deponents in a suit by Levi B. Crowder and Nancy D. Crowder his wife (formerly Nancy D. Davis) against the executors of George Pollard.[158] Other deponents included Joel Bevill, Barnett Southall, and Henry H. Southall.

1836 – In 1836, a **George Kidd** of Amelia County filed a Revolutionary War pension application, claiming intermittent service in the Virginia Militia during the war. His affidavit states that he was born in Amelia County in 1763, that he lived there and in Dinwiddie County ever since, that he was always drafted a militia man and served with Generals Layfayette and Mecklenburg, but never served during a battle, and that he was regularly discharged, but lost his papers; he stated that he was "particularly known to Henry H. Southall, William Coleman, and Parson William Hubbard."[159]
Also in 1836, **George Kidd** of Nottoway County gave an affidavit on 3 Aug 1836, stating that he served in the Revolutionary War as a private in a company commanded by James H. Munford's father, in which James H. Munford was an ensign.[160]

1840 – on 16 May 1840, **George Kidd** received $100 from William Nance "for the use of the Presbyterian Church built near Phaup's"[161] Kidd's right, title and interest in this land had been transferred to him by Braxton Coleman in April 182? (illegible). The land was on Cousins Road, "commencing at Nance Corner."
Asa Kidd, **George Kidd**'s son, was one of the Justices of the Peace admitting this deed to record on 13 May 1840.[162]

1844 – **George Kidd** wrote and signed his will on 19 November 1844:[163]

I, George Kidd of the county of Amelia and state of Virginia being of sound mind but feeble in body do make this to be my last will and testament in manner and form following.

Item 1 I give unto my son Asa Kidd this land on which I reside to him and his heirs for forever the wagon and plantation utensils.

Item 2 My son Asa Kidd is to pay unto my two daughters Nancy S. Coleman and Marth Young one hundred dollars each.

Item 3rd After my just debts are paid I wish my personal estate to be equally divided between my four children, Asa Kidd James Kidd Nancy L. Coleman & Martha Young also the proceeds of my crops and stock and all my perishable property to be divided equally among the same.

Item 4th I give unto my daughter Nancy L. Coleman one hundred and fifty dollars to be raised out of my estate. Signed sealed and delivered Nov. 19th, 1844.

(witnesses)
Benj. C. James   Geo Kidd {seal}
Wm. H. Perkinson

---

[158] Amelia County, VA Chancery Court record 1846-006, image 25, online.
[159] Revolutionary War Pension File R5907. Digital images of this record available upon request.
[160] Rev. War pension applications on Fold3.com, the application of James H. Munford.
[161] Amelia County, VA DB 34, p 378.
[162] Amelia County DB 34, pp. 378-379 (scanned images available).
[163] Amelia County, Virginia Will Book 15, pages 369-370, retrieved from FHL #30456 via familysearch.org (unrestricted access), images 471-472.

Robert Coleman
   his X mark

According to family records, **George Kidd** died in Amelia County on 24 November 1844.

On 26 December 1844, his will was proved in Court and ordered to be recorded:
> In Amelia County Court 26th December 1844 this the last Will and testament of George Kidd was this day presented in Court and proven by the oaths of two subscribing witnesses thereto and ordered to be recorded.
> And on motion of Asa Kidd(,) leave is given him to qualify as admr. with this will annexed of said George Kidd and thereupon he took the oath prescribed and together with Robert Cousins his security entered into and acknowledged a bond in the penalty of $2000 conditioned as the law directs certificate is granted him for obtaining letters of administration with the Will annexed in due form.[164]

His son Asa Kidd pursued George Kidd's pension application as his heir. However, this pension request was rejected.[165]

GEORGE5b KIDD – <u>We do not know who this George Kidd belongs to</u>.

1798 – a **George Kidd** appears for the first and only time on the Nottoway County, VA Personal Property Tax Lists (1 WM >16, no property).

1802 – In 1802, a **George Kidd** appears for the first time on the <u>Dinwiddie</u> County Personal Property Tax List.[166] (Lodowick has appeared intermittently since 1792, and a Benjamin Kidd was listed intermittently from 1790 through 1793.)[167] A **George Kidd** is found on the same tax lists from 1806-1809, without personal property.
THIS GEORGE MAY BE THE SON OF BENJAMIN5 KIDD; he was born abt. 1771; or he may be George5a, born 1763, the son of George Kidd Sr. (George4).

1803 – Yet ANOTHER **George Kidd** first appears in Land Records at Amelia Courthouse [1787 ?]-1807, <u>along</u> with Elizabeth Kidd, George Kidd Sr., and George Kidd Jr. This George Kidd is taxed on 68 acres in 1803; by 1807 his holdings were 83.5 acres.
This George could be the son of George5a Kidd, but he is not named in George Jr.'s will of 1844, and this seems unlikely.
At present, we have no plausible explanation.

1806 – A **George Kidd** bought 15.5 acres in Amelia from Dinwiddie neighbors Richard Cardwell and wife.[168] This reference could be to either George5a or George5b.

No other records that might pertain to George5b Kidd have been found to date in this three-county area. Either he died, or he moved elsewhere, and remains to be discovered.

---

[164] Ibid. Other estate records include p. 390 (inventory and appraisal), p. 392 (acct. sales), and p. 641 (executor's account).
[165] Rev. War pension application R-5907 (RK have a copy).
[166] Dinwiddie County Personal Property Tax Lists, 1800-1819.
[167] Dinwiddie County Personal Property Tax Lists, 1782-1799.
[168] Sheets research report for RK, 7/30/88).

GEORGE FENDALE KIDD, the son of Asa (Asa6, George5a, George4, Benjamin3, William2, Thomas1) Kidd and his wife, Jane C (Sutherland) Kidd
Born abt 1833, VA; died in 1885 in Petersburg, VA.
Evidently never married or had children

His year of birth is uncertain. He's said to have served in the Civil War, but no documentation has been provided.

1850 – I believe that he's the man below, living in the household of one of his mother's relatives, in Petersburg, VA, HH 552/648, p. 425A:
Southerland, George W. 26MW grocer $1000 VA
  " , William 21MW clerk VA
  " , Prudance 21FW
Kidd, George 17MW clerk VA

1853-1857 – he appears annually on the PPTLs of Petersburg, VA.[169]

1860 – I can't find him on the federal census, and don't know where he is.

1864 – He is named in his father's 1864 Amelia County, VA will.

1870 – We can't find him on this census, either.

1876-1877 – residence in Petersburg, VA: **Kidd, George F** gen agt 21 Bank bds 158 High.[170]

1880 – I cannot find him on the federal census in 1880, in Petersburg, or elsewhere. His obituary (see below) said that he'd left Petersburg for business several years before his death.

1885 – **Geo F Kidd**, white male, died 9 Jan 1885 in Petersburg, at age 52 of alcoholism. Parents Asa and Jane C. Kidd. Born in Dinwiddie, single. D. Steel, physician reporting. [171]
His obituary was published in The Petersburg Index-Daily Appeal on Saturday, 10 January 1885.[172]

1885 – George F. Kidd is buried in the Sutherland Graveyard in Dinwiddie County. The inscription on his headstone reads: "**George Kidd** son of Asa and Jane S. Kidd." [173]

GEORGE T. KIDD, named in Dinwiddie County deeds in 1856 [likely refers to George Fendale Kidd, son of Asa, above]

1856 – **Kidd, George T**. to D Milie ?Force), book 22, p. 688.[174]
Kidd, George T. account sales. Book 23, p. 64.[175]

---

[169] See William R. Kidd's transcriptions of these PPTLs, 1787-1871.

[170] Petersburg City directory 1876-77, page 96, located at LVA, reviewed 2-22-03

[171] Petersburg death records, 1853-1892, reel 34, from microfilm at the Library of Virginia.

[172] Available at NewspaperArchives.com. It states he was "a well-known and respected citizen," and that his remains were returned to the home of John T. Sutherland of Dinwiddie County, to be interred in the family burial ground.

[173] Graveyards, Dinwiddie County, Virginia. Frances Bland Randolph Chapter, Daughters of the American Revolution, 1945. From Library of Virginia (1-11-03 by William R. Kidd)

[174] *Virginia, Dinwiddie County, Petersburg Court Records, Part I, Index to Deeds, 1784-1869*, p. 425.

[175] *Virginia, Dinwiddie County, Petersburg Court Records, Part I, Index to Deeds, 1784-1869*, p. 425.

GEORGE W. KIDD, the son of **William R. Kidd (William R7, James6a, Benjamin5, George4, Benjamin3, William2, Thomas1 Kidd) and his first wife Martha F. Young Born December 1845 in Chesterfield County, VA, died 4 August 1909 in Chesterfield County, VA.**

1860 – On the federal census in Amelia County, VA, living with his father, page 77, HH 606/581:
W.R. Kidd 40 MW lumberman $2000/5914 VA
George W Kidd 13MW VA

1864 – **George W. Kidd** served in the Civil War, and was wounded in the right temple at the battle of Cold Harbor in 1864, at which time he was only 16 or 17 years old.[176]

1867-1869 – **George W. Kidd** appears annually these three years on the Amelia County, VA PPTLs, according to William R. Kidd.[177]

1870 – On the federal census in Sussex County, Va, Stony Creek Township, p. 193, HH 80/80:
Kids (sic), **George** 25MW farmer b. VA
" , Robert 7MW VA
" , John 3MW VA
" , William 53MW farmer b. VA
Harvel, Manerva 16FB domestic servant b. VA cannot read or write
We're confident that this is George W. Kidd, with his two half-brothers, John and William (by his father's second wife, Martha Phillips, who died in 1869), and his widowed father living in his household.[178]

1879 – **George W. Kidd** applied from Chesterfield County, VA for a disability pension related to his war wounds at the battle of Cold Harbor in 1864.[179]

1880 – On the federal census in Chesterfield County, VA, Clover Hill district, Enumeration District 66, page 36D, household 323/328:
Kidd, G. W. WM 34M sawyer VA VA VA
" , Susan WF 25M keeping house VA VA VA
" , Martha S. WF 2S VA VA VA
" , Wm. W. WM 2/12S VA VA VA (born March 1880)
Robertson, Mary BF 15S servant VA VA VA

1900 – On the federal census in Chesterfield County, VA, Clover Hill district, ED 003, page 6B, household 109/109:
Kidd, George W. WM b. Dec. 1845 54M marr. 23 yr VA VA VA farmer
" , Samantha S. WF wife b. Oct. 1855 44M marr. 23 yr; 5 children/4 living VA VA VA
" , Waverly M. WM son b. May 1886 14S at school VA VA VA
" , Mary E. WF dau. B. July 1892 7S at school VA VA VA

---

[176] WRK, personal correspondence, February 2010. This George W. Kidd was living in Chesterfield County, VA in 1879, when he applied for a pension.

[177] No details provided.

[178] At the time of the 1880 federal census, John and William are living in the household of John Philips, their grandfather, in Amelia County, VA.

[179] Personal correspondence, WRK, an author of this paper. He writes: There was an act that provided for artificial limbs for men wounded in combat. It appears he received $30.00 compensation.

1909 – He is buried in the cemetery of Second Branch Baptist Church in Chesterfield County, VA, next to Samantha P. Kidd.[180]

JAMES KIDDs – There were at least <u>six</u> James Kidds in this three-county area (as well as in Warren County, NC, and Mecklenburg County, VA), and three of them were born around 1794. Teasing the records below apart, and deciding which of these men they belong to, was a challenge; we have tried diligently to segregate the various citations of a James Kidd by age, amount of property and land, the names of their wives, and associations with other residents, listing each citation where we think it most likely belongs. But the way we have sorted them here may not be entirely accurate.

They are listed here chronologically by the year of their birth.

1) **James5a Kidd** (aka **James Kidd Sr.**; b abt. 1767-d. 1842), son of George4 Kidd. Y-DNA evidence and records analysis supports that James5a, son of George4, is the same man as the James Kidd who lived in Warren County, NC, and Mecklenburg County, VA, and was the father of John B. Kidd.

2) **James6a Kidd** (abt. 1794 - 10 April 1874), probable son of Benjamin5 Kidd

3) **James6b Kidd** (abt. 1794 - abt. 1882, Grayson County, TX), son of George5 Kidd – left VA in 1828 for Kentucky

4) **James Kidd** (abt. 1794 - 9 August 1874), identity currently unknown.

5) **James7 Kidd** (abt. 1820, VA - ??) - His ancestry is unproven, but we believe that he was the eldest son of Thomas J. Kidd, based upon their shared occupation, his age matching that of Thomas J.'s eldest son, and the fact that James7 named his only son Thomas J. Kidd.

6) **James Kidd** (abt 1834 - 1855) , son of William and Matilda (Wells?) Kidd

JAMES5a KIDD, the son of George4 Kidd (Benjamin3, William2, Thomas1) Kidd
    & his wife (name unknown) [181]
    Born before 1767, most likely in Amelia County
    Married Elizabeth Beasley before 1792
    Moved to Warren County, NC, then to Mecklenburg County, VA
    Died 31 March 1842, most likely in Mecklenburg County, VA

SOME OF THE DATA BELOW MAY NOT PERTAIN TO THIS JAMES KIDD. While we have made every effort to assign each historical record to the proper James Kidd, we acknowledge that some of these decisions may not be accurate.

If we are correct in allocating the citations below, James5a remained in Amelia County until 1798 or 1799, when he moved to Warren County, NC, evidently following his future wife,

---

[180] From Findagrave.com.

[181] We base this upon the fact that a James Kidd appears on the Dinwiddie Personal Property Tax Lists in the household of George4 Kidd from 1788-1791, and George pays his tax, as he has done for his other known sons. While James COULD be a nephew or other distant relative, it's highly likely that this James is indeed George4's son.

Elizabeth Beasley[182] and her parents and family. He remained there until at least 1814, then moved just north, across the NC-VA border into Mecklenburg County, VA. He remained in Mecklenburg County until at least 1827, when he sold his land there to his son John B. Kidd. He then disappears from VA records.

However, we are confident that he is the **James L. Kidd** whose death on March 31, 1842 was recorded in John B. Kidd's almanac, since this James Kidd was referred to by this name in the 1825 marriage record of his daughter Elizabeth Ann Kidd (see below).

1788-1791 – a "**Jas. Kidd**" is listed by name in the household of George4 Kidd on the 1788 Amelia County PPTL. Unlike earlier lists, this list named all the free white males in a household above the age of 21 years.[183]

1788:

Person paying tax	WM>21 (including taxpayer)
George Kid Sr.	George Kid, Lod. Kidd, **Jas. Kidd**
George Kid Jr.	George Kid

His calculated age, based upon his attaining the age of 21 in this year, matches perfectly with the dates in his son John B. Kidd's Copy Book.

This listing repeated annually through 1791, but not after this. [A different James does begin appearing in 1812, but this James is James6b, the son of George5a Kidd.]

James Kidd is not found on the Amelia County PPTLs after 1791.

Abt. 1793?[184] – **James Kidd** married Elizabeth Beasley (location unknown, but probably in Warren County, NC). We have been unable to find a record of this marriage.

Some researchers have stated that James and Elizabeth married in 1796. We are not sure where this date came from, but have found no record to substantiate that.

Elizabeth Beasley's father, John Pitts Beasley, died about 1792 in Warren County, NC, and his will was entered into record in May 1792. That will does not name his children.[185] The first record we've found that names James and Elizabeth Kidd among the heirs of John Pitts Beasley was not until September 1805, when the division of John Pitts Beasley's land was presented in Warren County Court; his land was divided into nine lots, with "James Kid" receiving Lot No. 7.[186] Later records (March 1815) of the heirs of John Pitts Beasley selling their right, title and interest in his lands list "James Kid and Elizabeth his wife" among his

---

[182] Elizabeth was the daughter of John Pitts Beasley. The 1792 Warren County, NC will of John Pitts Beasley names among his heirs "James Kidd and wife Elizabeth," confirming that Elizabeth Beasley was James' wife, and providing us with Elizabeth's maiden name. According to land records, John P. Beasley bought land in Amelia County, 1761, in Bute County, NC in 1777, and in Warren County, NC in 1778. (Bute County was discontinued in 1779, becoming Warren County.) JPB had moved to NC by 1778, when he served as overseer of one of the roads there. He was in Warren County, NC at least until 1781, when he was reimbursed for losses during the Revolutionary War. In 1789, he was in Mecklenburg County, VA, where he witnessed a will. But he also appears to have continued to live just over the state line in Warren County, NC, appearing in several records there. And his will was written there in 1783, and probated there in 1792. Given that his will was probated in 1792, it's evident that Elizabeth Beasley married James Kidd prior to that date.

[183] Amelia County. VA PPTLs, FHL US/CAN microfilm #2024454. Digital images available upon request.

[184] The Copy Book kept by their son, John B. Kidd, lists his date of birth as 26 February 1794. This would indicate that they were married by 1793, assuming that they were married when John B. was conceived.

[185] Warren County, NC Will Book 6, pages 97-98. A transcription of his will was provided to me by Sandra K. Kidd

[186] Warren County, NC Deed Book 17, pages 251-252, found on FHL #20071, images 627-628, viewable online via familysearch.org (unrestricted access).

heirs.[187] All we can conclude from these records is that they were married by September 1805 (and perhaps years earlier).

1798 – a **James Kidd** witnessed the will of John Brewer (wife USLE Brewer, probably James' sister) in Dinwiddie County, VA on 4 October 1798.[188] This must be James5a, brother of Usley Kidd Brewer, and son of George4, because James6b (son of George5a) was born about 1794.

1800 – there is a **James Kidd** on the federal census in Warren County, NC, the right age to be James5a Kidd:
Halifax, Warren County, NC, p. 814:
Kidd, James 10001-00010; no slaves.
No other Kidd household heads there. This James Kidd is 45 or over in age, with a son 0-9, and a wife 26-44. (The young son in this household is the right age to be John B. Kidd – see his section in this paper.)

Also in 1800, in the marriage records for Warren County, an Allen Burton married Elizabeth Brooks on March 12, 1800. The bondsman was **James Kidd**.[189]

1805 – **James Kidd** served as bondsman to the remarriage of his widowed mother-in-law Elizabeth Beasley to Abraham Puckett on 27 May 1805, in Warren County, NC.[190]

James Kidd is named in the 1805 Warren County, NC land division, along with his wife Elizabeth, as heirs to John Pitts Beasley (see records below for John Pitts Beasley). This division was prompted by the remarriage of John Pitts Beasley's widow Elizabeth to Abraham Puckett.[191]
On 16 Dec 1805, in Warren County, NC, **James Kidd** was named in an account of sale of the estate of John Pitts Beasley, deceased, [as buyer? Not noted.] [192]

1807 – **James Kidd** was bondsman for his brother-in-law Pitts Beasley's marriage to Martha Acree in 1807 in Warren County, NC.

1810 – On 13 Mar 1810, William Kimball of Warren County, NC sold to **James Kidd** of the same place for $150 a tract of 50 acres of land in Warren County, lying on Six Pound (Creek) and adjoining Thomas Beasley's line. This deed was proved in Warren County Court February Term 1811.[193]
We do not find him on the 1810 federal census in Warren County, NC, despite the deed record above, and the subsequent tax lists below.

---

[187] Warren County, NC Deed Book 20, pages 217-218, found on FHL #20073, images 232-233, viewable online via familysearch.org (unrestricted access).
[188] VGS Quarterly, vol. 10, p. 3, Acc.27293-15 and Acc. 28657-2, reprinted in "Some Wills from the Burned Counties – Dinwiddie County," p. 26. Also available at the VAGenWeb pages for Dinwiddie County, VA: http://www.vagenweb.net/dinwiddie/wills/wills-unrecorded.htm.
[189] Personal correspondence from John Paul Kidd, contained in his document which I retitled, "James, father of John B," and placed in my Genealogy/Kidd folder. (RK)
[190] Marriages of Bute and Warren Cos, NC, 1764-1868 (at ancestry.com).
[191] Warren County, NC Deed Book 20, pages 217-218, found on FHL #20073, images 232-233, viewable online via familysearch.org (unrestricted access).
[192] Warren County, NC WB 14, p 221.
[193] Warren County, NC DB 19, p 28

1811-1814 – **James Kidd** appears on the **Warren County, NC** tax lists in these four years, as follows:[194]

YEAR	DISTRICT	TAXPAYER	Land	W. polls	B. polls
1811	Six Pound	James Kidd	109	1	1
1812	Six Pound	James Kidd	119	1	1
1813	Hawtree	James Kidd	119	1	1
1814	Six Pound	James Kidd	119	1	1

We have not been able to locate subsequent tax lists for Warren County, to see if he appears on the tax lists for 1815 or 1816.

1816 – Sometime in 1816, **James Kidd** relocated to Mecklenburg County, VA, just over the state line from Warren County, NC. He was still "of Warren County, NC" in January of 1816, when he entered into two deeds in Mecklenburg County (see below).
The family may not have moved far. In fact, several of John B. Kidd's children later married in Warren County, NC, suggesting that they lived very near the state line. Another possible explanation, offered by Wayne Rainey, is that "the Kidds like many other families of the southeastern part of Mecklenburg County, VA, married in neighboring Warren County mostly because the Warren County courthouse was closer than the one in Boydton, VA (Mecklenburg's county seat), plus after the railroad came in, it was very much closer, as the railroad went into Warrenton, NC," the county seat of Warren County.

On 24 January 1816 in Mecklenburg County, VA, **James Kidd** of **Warren County, NC** entered into a Deed of Trust with James Critchlow of Brunswick County, VA, to obtain the purchase price for a 500-acre tract in Mecklenburg County, purchased from Winnifred Winn for $500.[195]

On the same date, Winnifred Winn of Mecklenburg County, VA sold to **James Kidd of Warren County, NC** for $500 the above-described tract in Mecklenburg County.
Both deeds were recorded in the Mecklenburg County Clerk's office on 17 October 1821.[196]
This **James Kidd** also first appears on the Mecklenburg County, VA Personal Property Tax Lists in 1816, as shown in the Table below.[197] He continued to be listed on these PPTLs through 1822.

---

[194] The Warren County, North Carolina Tax Lists for these four years were recorded in the county's Will Books 16-18 for unknown reasons. Digital images of the listings for James Kidd were retrieved via familysearch.org from FHL #531533, Warren County. NC will books, v. 14-18, as follows:
1811: WB 16, p. 146 (image 465 of 932); 1812: WB 17, p. 109 (image 659 of 932)l 1813: WB 17, p; 309 (image 767 of 932); and 1814: WB 18, p. 206 (image 904 of 932). Images available upon request.
[195] Mecklenburg County Deed Book 19, page 262-293, retrieved via familysearch.org from FHL #32541, image 156.
[196] Ibid, pages 263-264, images 156-157 on that reel. Digital images available from the authors.
[197] Mecklenburg County, VA Personal Property Tax Lists, 1806-1828, US/CAN Film 20007, researched by professional genealogist Nancy Heuser for Paula Kidd (transcription of Kidd and Beasley entries in RK's file on John B. Kidd).

Year	Taxpayer	WMT tithes	Slaves	Cattle	Horses
1816	James Kidd	2	3	-	2
1817	James Kidd	1	3	-	3
1818	James Kidd	2	3	-	3
1819	James Kidd	2	2	-	2
1820	James Kidd	2	2	-	3
1821	James Kidd	X[198]	2	-	3
1822	James Kidd		3	-	6

(The other male tithe would be for his son, John B. Kidd, born abt. 1794, not yet out on his own.)
This James has land, slaves and other property; he's more prosperous than most of the
Kidds in this paper. This is important circumstantial evidence distinguishing him from the
others as he moves about.

1816-1827 – This **James Kidd** also appears on the Mecklenburg County Land tax lists in 1816,
when he is taxed on 500 acres, valued at $250. In this entry, he's listed as "James Kidd Sr."
In 1817, this parcel of land is described as "west side, Great Creek, 14.8 miles from
Courthouse. These entries repeat annually through 1827, when he sold this land to John B.
Kidd (his son), then end.
In 1820, he's taxed on 510 acres, "east and west sides of Great Creek," and a $240 evaluation
was added for buildings. In 1822, his entry describes revenue returned to **James Kidd**,
"debit for too much charged," and his acreage drops back to 500 acres.
[Great Creek is in the southeastern part of Mecklenburg County, flowing south to the
Roanoke River and lying just east of the community of Maringo and less than two miles west
of the Mecklenburg-Brunswick county line, which it parallels. It is visible on sections 12 and
16 of the 1870 map of Mecklenburg County, coursing past the lands of William
Reany/Rainey and "Mrs. Kidd's." [199]

1817-1822 – **James Kidd** is found on the Mecklenburg County, VA Personal Property Tax Lists in
these years, as follows:[200]
1817 - one white male tithe, 3 slaves over 16, and 3 horses. No other Kidds.
1818 - two white male tithes, 3 slaves over 16, and 3 horses. No other Kidds.
1819 - two white male tithes, 2 slaves over 16, and 2 horses. No other Kidds.
1820 - two white male tithes, 2 slaves over 16, and 3 horses. No other Kidds.
1821 - (lists stopped recording white tithes in this year); 2 slaves over 12, 3 horses.
1822 - 3 slaves over 12, 6 horses. No other Kidds.

---

[198] In this year, the PPTLs changed, and no WMTs were listed; only slaves and horses.
[199] Mecklenburg County, VA Land Tax Lists, 1815-1830, researched by professional genealogist Nancy Heuser for Paula
Kidd; transcript in RK's John B. Kidd file. No other Kidds on these lists.
[200] Mecklenburg County, VA Personal Property Tax Lists, 1806-1828, US/CAN Film 20007. See above.

1823 - James Kidd drops off these PPTLs, and his son John B. appears for the first time, with 2 slaves over 12, and 4 horses. No other Kidds.
1826 - **James Kidd** reappears on the Mecklenburg County, VA PPTL this year (and John B. doesn't appear this year), and then isn't listed again through 1828.

1820 – In 1820, **James Kidd** appears on the federal census in Mecklenburg County, VA:
James Kidd – 1WM 16-25 & 1 >44; 2F<10, 1 10-15, 1 16-25, and 1 >44. Three slaves (1 male <14, 1F 16-25 and 1F >45).[201]

1823 – **James Kidd** drops from the Mecklenburg County PPTLs, and his son, John B., to whom he recently sold land, appears for the first time on these tax lists. See his section, below.

1825 – On 20 July 1825, James Kidd's daughter Elizabeth Ann Kidd and Riddick Temple obtained a marriage bond in Mecklenburg County, VA. John B. Kidd was the surety for this bond, and consent was given by **James L. Kidd**.[202]

1827 – On 3 March 1827, **James Kidd** sold 500 acres to his son John B. Kidd of Mecklenburg County for $500.[203]
No further mention of James Kidd is found in Mecklenburg County, Virginia, to my knowledge (though not all records for 1810-1830 may have been searched.)

1830 – No record of him is found on the 1830 federal census, or on indexes for this census. Most likely he was living with John B. Kidd or some other relative; see 1840, below.

1840 – John B. Kidd (**James5a Kidd's son**) was the only Kidd household head on the federal census in Mecklenburg County, VA, , East District, p. 411:[204]
John B. Kidd: 2M <4, 1M 5-9, 1M 10-14, 2M 15-19, 1M 40-49, & **1 60-69;** 3F 5-9, 2F 15-19, and 1 30-39; eleven slaves; 25 total, with 11 in agriculture.
We believe that the oldest male in this household is **James5a Kidd**, who died less than two years later, most likely while living with John B. and his family. See below.

1842 – According to the Copy Book of his son John B. Kidd, **James L. Kidd** died in 1842.[205]
Because the only other death recorded in the Copy Book is that for Elizabeth Kidd[206] (James' wife was Elizabeth Beasley), we feel sure that this is the date of death for his father

---

[201] p. 157A.

[202] The Copy Book of John B. Kidd. I believe but am not certain that this occurred in Mecklenburg County, VA, primarily because the notation mentions the specific time of his death on "March 31, 1842, at 10 o'clock in the evening." It does not provide the location of his death.

[203] Mecklenburg County Deed Book 22, Page 342, also from John Paul Kidd: Deed dated 3 Mar 1827 - James Kidd of Mecklenburg County sells John B. Kidd same county 500 acres for $500 land bounded by lands of Presly Hinton, James Carrol, Charles Jones, and estates of John Martain and William Jones.
We are not sure whether this is the same parcel that James Kidd had bought a few years earlier, but it most likely is.

[204] 1840 federal census, Mecklenburg County, VA, East District, p. 411A:
John B. Kidd 211200101-030201 (oldest males 40-49 and 60-69; oldest female 30-39)

[205] The dates of James L. Kidd's birth and death are recorded in a Copy Book, apparently copied from the John B. Kidd family Bible. A typed transcript from this Copy Book , entitled "Kidd family Bible record, 1794-1842" is available online at the Library of Virginia, Archives and Manuscripts Room, Manuscript call #25295a, 1 leaf.
The citation reads: "March 31 – 1842 was the Day that James L. Kidd died 10 o'clock in the night."

[206] "June they 17th – 1821 was they Day that Elisabeth Kidd died in the Evening."

James L. Kidd. (John B. Kidd also had a son named James L. Kidd, but this son was alive at the time of the 1850 federal census.) See Appendix Three for a transcription of this Copy Book.

No will or other probate record has been found for this James Kidd, in Mecklenburg or other counties.

<u>JAMES6a KIDD</u>, most likely the son of Benjamin5 (George4, Benjamin3, William2, Thomas1) Kidd
> **Born abt. 1794[207] in Amelia or Dinwiddie County, VA**
> **Married twice – to Ann Eliza ___ (1839 deed below), then circa 1847 to Ann/Nancy M. Sutherland Thweatt, the wife and widow of Allen Thweatt**
> **Died 10 April 1874**
> **Only one known child, William R. Kidd,[208] born by James' first wife, Ann Eliza**

We know that one of the James Kidds in Dinwiddie in this era was the son of Benjamin, because of the 1821 Dinwiddie PPTL, which reads, "James (son Ben)".
We believe that this James Kidd and Thomas J. Kidd (see his entries in this book) were brothers.[209]

1813 – a **James Kidd** appears for the first time on the **Dinwiddie** County, VA PPTLs, List B.[210] He is the only Kidd on List B, and is taxed only on himself, with no horse or slaves, or other property. The other Kidds are on List A, a different district.

1817 – TWO **James Kidds** appear on the Dinwiddie County PPTL (and a third appears on the Amelia County, VA PPTL this year). Neither of the Dinwiddie James Kidds has any property, slaves or horses, likely indicating that they are young and just getting started on their own. One is likely James6a, the son of Benjamin5a; the other is probably James6b, the son of George5a.
[The reader may find Appendix Two : The MALE descendants of George4 Kidd, useful in visualizing the relationships of these two James Kidds, and the other (male) descendants of George4 Kidd.]

---

[207] Age 26-44 in 1820; 57 in 1850; 65 in 1860; 75 in 1870; enlisted in War of 1812 in 1813.

[208] This is the ancestor of William R. "Bill" Kidd, one of the authors of this work.

[209] Bill writes (Nov. 2009): Here is part of what I think links Thomas and James as brothers:

1. War of 1812-A James Kidd and a Thomas Kidd both served in the 83rd Regiment of WM in the War of 1812 from Jul 1 to Jul 6 1813, different companies but same Regiment and dates. My James Kidd and a Thomas Kidd served in the 1st Regiment of the VM in the War of 1812, service dates both started at 28 Aug 1814, end dates were 5 Dec 1814 for James and 30 Nov 1814 for Thomas. I think the James listed first may be my James, even though this is not in his service record. Same counties, same basic dates of enlistment.

2. Mary C Kidd, daughter of Thomas J Kidd. Samuel H Clarke married Mary C Kidd 8 Jun 1838, then Mary C Clark married Trent E Harrison 16 Nov 1842. 24 Dec 1854 William R Kidd wins a suit against Samuel Clarke, a business partner in a saw mill. This always made me think William and Mary may have been close cousins if he went into business with her husband. Can't be sure it was the same Samuel Clark but pretty good coincidence.

3. Trent E Harrison. Both Thomas and James left their property to Trent E Harrison in their wills. Also, Trent E Harrison was listed as a witness in the pension record of James Kidd. There was a Benjamin Harrison (relations unknown) living at South Pine near Smiths Lane in the 1870's, which looks like the same address for James Kidd in the mid to late 1860's.

[210] Binns Genealogy (online paid subscription), Dinwiddie County, Virginia PPTLs, 1782-1819, 1813, list B, image 6.

1818 – Only ONE **James Kidd** is found on the Dinwiddie PPTL this year. He has one slave, and no horse, but has a gig (a two-wheeled carriage) valued at $30.

1819 – TWO James Kidds again appear on the Dinwiddie PPTL in 1819. Both have one slave and one gig, but no horse. Again, these are probably **James6a** and his cousin, James6b.

1820 – There are TWO James Kidds in Dinwiddie County on the 1820 federal census; they are close in age, and the "Jr." most likely indicates the younger of the two, and not a father-son relationship:[211]
Kidd, James – 1M 0-9 & 1 26-44; 1F 0-9 & 1 16-25, 1 in Ag, 2 F slaves <14.
   (either of these could be James6a, but we think he's this one)
Kidd, James Jr. – 1M 26-44, 1F 0-9 & 1F 16-25. 1 in Ag, no slaves. This is presumably James6b, the son of George5a Kidd.

1821-1823 – In each of these years, two James Kidds appear on the Dinwiddie PPTLs.
   In 1821, one of them is specifically listed as "**Kidd, James (son Ben)**,"[212] meaning James, the son of Benjamin Kidd (who died in 1821, perhaps prompting this specific entry).
   In 1822 and 1823, one James has no slaves or horses, but a gig, just as James, son of Ben did in 1821. This James is referenced as "**James Sr.**" these two years.
   The other James (whom we suspect is James6b) is listed annually as "James Jr.", apparently to distinguish him from the only slightly older James6a; each of these years he has one slave and one horse, but no gig.

1824-1830 – The Dinwiddie PPTLs go back to showing only ONE James Kidd, which must be **James6a**, because James6b is back in Amelia County, on that county's PPTL from 1824-1828, then disappearing, and we know that James6b migrated west to Kentucky in 1828 (see James6b's entries that follow).

1828 – a **James Kidd** appears for the first time since 1823 on the **Dinwiddie** County, VA **Land Tax List** of Lewis P. Lanier. He is taxed on 60 acres on the waters of Georges branch, 17 miles NW of the Courthouse. A note in the margin by his entry reads "by deed from Wm. E and Hannah Hardaway.[213]
   [All Dinwiddie Deed Books prior to 1832 are no longer extant; the same is true for chancery records.]

1829-1839 – This **James Kidd** appears annually on the Dinwiddie County, VA Land Tax Lists, taxed on the same 60-acre parcel of land on George's Branch, 17 miles NW of the courthouse. George's Branch is a short creek that runs north, draining into Namozine Creek, the boundary between Amelia and Dinwiddie Counties.
   For more specifics about the Dinwiddie land he owned, see his section in Appendix Five.
   He drops from this list in 1840, having sold the land in 1839. See below.

1830 – **James Kidd** is on the VA federal census in Dinwiddie County, along with Jasper, Mary,

---

[211] 1820 federal census, Dinwiddie County, VA, p. 12A; this census was recorded by first letter of last name, rather than by geographic location, so no conclusions can be drawn by proximity on the census.

[212] A scan of this record is available from Reiley Kidd, one of the authors of this paper; it was retrieved from FHL #31114, Dinwiddie County, VA PPTLs, 1820-1841, image 31.

[213] Dinwiddie County, VA Land Tax Lists, 1824-1835, FHL microfilm 0029922, retrieved via familysearch.org (unrestricted access), image 315 of 786.

Thomas J. and William Kidd.[214]
[This should be James6a Kidd, judging from his age; the James below is too young for
James5a, and James6b has moved to KY.]
Kidd, Jasper – 0200001-0020001 (oldest M & F both 40-49)
Kidd, Mary – 00111- 0020101 (males 10-14, 15-19 & 20-29; oldest F 40-49)
   This is evidently Mary Kidd, widow of Benjamin.
Kidd, James – 001001-0001, 1F slave>55 (James 30-39; female 15-19)
Kidd, William – 310001-00001, 1M & 1F slave 10-24 (oldest M 30-39; female 20-29)
Kidd, Thomas J. – 0010001- 000102, no slaves (oldest M 40-49; 2F 30-39).

1831-1833 – We don't find any records of him in any of the three counties.

1834 – a **James Kidd** sued Thomas Jordan & Thomas B. Grigg in Dinwiddie Superior Court over a
debt from June 1833, and was awarded the debt ($70) with interest until paid, plus his court
costs.[215]

1835 – 2 Apr 1835. A **Nottoway** County, VA deed dated 2 Dec 1834 from Archer J. Bevill and his
wife Susan to **James Kidd,** conveying real estate, was received on 22 March 1835. F.
Fitzgerald. Present were Nathan Ward, Thomas Howson, Peterson W. Harper and George
N. Seay, gentlemen justices.[216] Because the Deed Books of Nottoway County were destroyed
during the Civil War, this deed is not available to us. However, the description of the land in
the annual Nottoway Land Tax Lists (LTLs) record this as 259 (1836) or 257 (1837) acres in
Nottoway on Butterwood Creek, 12 miles East of the courthouse.

1835-1847 – a **James Kidd** appears annually on the **Nottoway** County, VA PPTLs.
   1835 – 2WM>16, 2 slaves >16, 2 horses.
   1836 – 2WM>16, 1B>16, 1B 12-16, 3 horses.
   1837 – 2WM>16, 2B>16, 2 horses.
   1838 – 1WM>16, 3B>16, 2 horses.
   1839 – 1WM>16, 3B>16, 1 horse.
   1840 – 1WM>16, 3B>16, 3 horses.
   1841 - 1WM>16, 2B>16, 3 horses, a two-wheel coach valued at less than $50.
   1842 – 1WM>16, 2B>16, 2 horses, one 4-wheel carriage valued at $150.
   1843 – 1WM>16, 3B>16, 2 horses, one 4-wheel carriage valued at $100, 1 wooden clock.
   1844 – 1WM>16, 3B>16, 3 horses, one 4-wheel carriage valued at $75, 1 clock @ $.25.
   1845 – 1WM>16, 2B>16, 1B 12-16, 3 horses, one 4-wheel carriage valued at $40.
   1846 – 1WM>16, 3B>16, 1B 12-16, 3 horses, one 4-wheel carriage valued at $40.
   1847 – 1WM>16, 4B>16, 1B 12-16, 2 horses, one 4-wheel carriage valued at $40

His presumed son William R. Kidd first appears on these lists in 1838; in this year, the
number of White Males over 16 in James Kidd's household drops from 2 to 1, consistent
with the second male being James' son, William R. Kidd. See William R.'s Notes (below).
This James doesn't appear in Nottoway after 1847. See 1848 for him in Dinwiddie County.

1836-1847 – **James Kidd** appears for the first time on the 1836 Land Tax List of **Nottoway**

---

[214] 1830 federal census, Dinwiddie County, VA. All but Thomas J. and William are on p. 390. William is on p. 392 and
   Thomas J. is on p. 410.
[215] Dinwiddie Order Book 1A, p. 205, sent by Bill Kidd, August 2011.
[216] Order book 11, Nottoway County, VA. Page 237. Located in Nottoway County, VA Circuit Court.

County, taxed upon 259 acres on Butterwood Creek,[217] 12 miles E of the Courthouse, transferred from A J Bevill. He continues to be listed through 1847, and in 1848 drops from the Nottoway LTLs. No Kidd appeared on these lists otherwise from 1814 through 1861, according to William R. Kidd, who reviewed these lists.

1839 – On 4 September 1839, **James Kidd** and Ann Eliza his wife of **Dinwiddie** sold 60 acres for $80 to Merideth C. Clardy.[218] Both James and Ann Eliza Kidd signed this deed, indicating that they could read and write. The deed was presented in court, proved and admitted to record on 21 October 1839.

1840 – **James Kidd** is on the federal census in **Nottoway** County, VA, p. 279: 000001-000101, and 1 free colored male 10-24, and 6 slaves.[219] [James and wife both 30-39; one younger white female 15-19.]

1847 – On 7 October 1847, a Nottoway County, VA deed of real estate was recorded from **James Kidd** to W. W. Jones, proven by the oaths of E. G Booth and Archer Jones on 2 Sept 1847, and further proven on 10 Sept 1847 by Thomas D. Sammons. A deed of trust conveying real estate from WW Jones to Edwin G Booth, trustee for the benefit of **James Kidd**, dated 8 May 1847, was acknowledged 2 Sept 1847 by Jones and Booth.[220] Again, because the deed book containing this record was destroyed, we only have this Order Book citation.

1848 – a **James Kidd** appears for the first time in 9 years on the **Dinwiddie** County Land Tax Lists (as "James Kidd & wife", taxed on 425.5 acres "on the Great Branch," 5 miles NW of the courthouse.[221] This description is problematic, because I find no waterway called Great Branch on the 1820 Hargrave map of Dinwiddie County. There is a Great Creek, but it's almost due south of the Dinwiddie Courthouse, lying just above the Nottoway River, into which it drains. However, this may be a mis-transcription of George's Branch, the location of another parcel of land owned at one time by James Kidd. This seems unlikely, because the term Great Branch is repeated on subsequent LTLs. And a table of waterways in Dinwiddie County[222] shows "Great Branch as an alternate name for the "Great Licking Place Branch" of Buckskin Creek. This is also due south of the Dinwiddie Courthouse, and drains into the Nottoway River.
The notation for this entry says, "deed from Ann M. Thweat." This James is considerably more wealthy (judging from the value of his land and buildings, valued at $1382) than he was earlier. Most likely his second marriage, to Ann M. Thweatt, brought more wealth.
He and his wife are also taxed on another parcel of 4.75 acres in the same location.
This is the land that he evidently swaps with James Boisseau (see below).

1848 – As stated above, this **James Kidd** was in Nottoway County through 1847. In 1848, he bought the above land, and for the next 5 years, appears annually on the **Dinwiddie PPTLs**

---

[217] Judging from the 1820 Hargrave map of Dinwiddie County, this land was just across the county line separating Dinwiddie from Nottoway; Butterwood Creek originates in Nottoway County and runs almost directly east, crossing into Dinwiddie County.

[218] Dinwiddie County, VA DB 2, page 372, retrieved from FHL #31093, image 195. Digital image available upon request.

[219] Slaves: 1M <10, 2M 24-35; 1F<10, 1 10-23 and 1 24-35.

[220] Order book 14, Nottoway County, VA. Page 57. Located in Nottoway County, VA Circuit Court.

[221] FHL #29924, Dinwiddie LTLs, 1841-1850, image 390 (image available upon request).

[222] *Dinwiddie County. Carrefour of the Commonwealth*, by Richard L. Jones, published by the Dinwiddie Board of Supervisors under the direction of the Dinwiddie County Historical Book Commission, 1976, page 317, ff.

again:

Year	Slaves	Horses	Gig(value)
1848	5	4	0
1849	8	4	1($70)
1850	8	4	0 (but one carryall, a 4-wheel wagon, worth $50)
1851	8	3	1 ($50)
1852	5	2	1 ($120) and 49 livestock (counted only this year)

Another James Kidd appears on the Dinwiddie PPTLs for these 5 years (and in the preceding 12 years). He's far less prosperous, with 0-1 slaves and usually no or one horse and no gig. I'm not sure who he is. These later references may be to James7 Kidd, who we believe was the son of Thomas J. Kidd.

1848 – On 27 July 1848, **James Kidd** and his wife Ann M. Kidd of Dinwiddie Country sold to James Boisseau of the same place for $1.00 and a satisfactory consideration, a tract of land containing 430 acres bounded east by A. K. Boisseau and other, north and west by John W. Gilliam, and on the south by Dr. William B. Scott. Signed **James Kidd**, and Ann M. Kidd, who consents. James H. Boisseau and William B. Scott, justices. Recorded 19 Aug, 1848.[223]

On 19 August 1848, Boisseau and Scott sold 430 acres in Dinwiddie County to **James Kidd** for $1.00.[224]
He and James Boisseau have made some sort of land swap, trading the land previously by James' second wife, Ann M. Thweat.

1849-1854 – **James Kidd** continues to be taxed for 430 acres total in Dinwiddie County on the Great Branch, 5 miles NW of the courthouse.[225] See Appendix Five of this compilation for more information on his entries on the Dinwiddie LTLs.
He and his wife sold this land in 1854 (see below), and drop from the Dinwiddie LTL in 1855.

1850 – On the federal census in the northern district of Dinwiddie County, VA, p. 454, HH 302:
Kidd, James 57MW farmer $3250 VA [too young for James5a]
" , Nancy M. 49FW VA
Ellison, Betty 16FW   VA (apparently a domestic servant)
Pritchet, Washington 18 mulatto male laborer VA (apparently a free black male)
" , David 30BM laborer VA cannot read or write (apparently a free black male)

1850 – On the 1850 Slave Schedule of the Dinwiddie County census (Northern District), James Kidd is listed with 7 slaves:[226]
James Kidd:
1. 60 year old female black
2. 48 year old male black
3. 40 year old male black

---

[223] Dinwiddie County, VA. DB5, page 599. Deed book located at Dinwiddie County Courthouse.
[224] Dinwiddie County, VA. DB 5, page 600. Boisseau and Scott sold back the same land they purchased from Kidd and wife on 27 Jul, 1848. The first sale was from James Kidd and wife to Boisseau and Scott. The sale back was only to James Kidd. Deed book located at Dinwiddie County Courthouse.
[225] The 1849 entry is found on FHL #29924, Dinwiddie LTLs, 1841-1850, image 437 (image available upon request).
[226] Dinwiddie County, VA, Northern District. Slave Schedule, reel 986,page 379. 28 Aug, 1850; viewed by WRK 14 Jan 2010, copies on file.

    4.   24 year old female mulatto
    5.   4 year old male mulatto
    6.   2 year old male mulatto
    7.   3 month old male mulatto

1853 – On 3 September 1853, **James Kidd** and Ann M his wife of the County of Dinwiddie sold to George Hawkes of the County of Amelia of the second part a tract of 100 acres of land in Amelia County, bounded by the Hudgins estate on the north and west, by the lands of ___ on the south and by the lands of Joseph Mann on the east for $100. This deed was recorded 23 December 1853.[227]

1853-1858 – **James Kidd** continued to be listed annually on the Dinwiddie County, VA PPTLs through 1858, the last year that we have checked these records.[228]

1854 – On 24 February 1854, **James Kidd Jr.**, trustee for Jane C. Vaughan, entered into a Deed of Trust, as follows between Peter E. Vaughan of the first part, James Kidd Jr. of the second part and Jane C. Vaughan of the third part, all of the County of Dinwiddie. Peter granted unto Kidd the land on which Jane was currently residing and any other land that Peter had in Dinwiddie as well as Peter's interest to a negro man Ric?o now in the possession of his mother, the said Jane C. Vaughan, and all of his property. In trust to secure a debt due to Jane by bond for $350.[229]
Given the designation of this James Kidd as "Jr.", this record may belong to a different James Kidd.

1854 – On 30 November 1854, **James Kidd** and wife Ann M. of Dinwiddie sold 430 acres where they lived to Thomas W. Scott for $2,600. The land was bounded on the north by Mrs. M. Gilliam, on the east by the lands of Manassah Audas and Charles Moody, on the south by the lands of Mrs. Kizzie Boisseau and E. P. Scott, and on the west by Mrs. Gilliam's land. Both James and Ann M. Kidd signed this deed. The deed was proved in Court and admitted to record on 1 December 1854.[230]

1855 – On 16 April 1855, John W. Tucker and Nancy his wife sold to **James Kidd** a plot of land in Petersburg for $1,500, bounded on the east by and extending on a street called Pine Street (in a plat made by Jonathon Smith for Leslie & Birden & C. D. McIndoe?), 130 feet; on the west by a parallel line of equal extent, on the north by the land of John Fords; and on the south by A Fords lot, the whole depth of the lot being westwardly and at right angles to Pine Street aforesaid, 134 feet and is a part of lot number 10 of which D. Lumsden by deed of 15 Dec, 1851 conveyed his interest therein to the aforesaid James Smith and the said James Smith by deed of 1 Jan, 1852 and wife conveyed their interest therein to the aforesaid J. W. Tucker.[231]
This deed was acknowledged in Court by Tucker on 16 April 1855. For some reason it was not entered into record until 10 December 1857.

---

[227] Deed book Amelia County, VA. Page 39. Copy in deed file (WRK)
[228] See WRK's Excel file, "Amelia & Dinwiddie PPTLs, 1814-1853-WRK" in RK's Kidd folder.
[229] Dinwiddie County, VA. DB 7, page 511. Deed book located at Dinwiddie County Courthouse.
[230] Dinwiddie County, VA. DB 8, pages 170-171. This is the same land traded from Kidd to Boisseau and Scott, and then traded back to Kidd in 1848. Image retrieved from FHL #31096, image 95. Copy available from authors.
[231] City of Petersburg, DB 24, pages 196-197, from microfilm reel 13 at the Library of Virginia. Images available from the authors.

1856 – On 18 June 1856, John W. Gill and Mary E. Gill his wife sold to **James Kidd** two certain lots or parcels of land in Petersburg called Pridesfield, each of said lots fronting on Dunlop Street… for $165. This is the same land that conveyed to Gill by Robert H Mann. The deed was recorded 11 December 1857.[232]

1857 – On 26 Feb 1857, William R Kidd (the son of James6a Kidd) entered into a Deed of Trust with Charles Lumsden and **James Kidd**. Whereas the said Kidd and William C. Lumsden have formed a partnership under the name of Lumsden and Kidd for the purpose of cutting and sawing timber and grinding corn &c …on a piece of land in Amelia County called the Brown tract, which they recently bought from A.H. Burke. Kidd and Lumsden agreed to share equally in all expenses. William Kidd provides a note of trust to secure Lumsden against any payment Lumsden may make to behalf on Kidd's part, held by W. L. Watkins, trustee of Samuel Clarke, and which will be due 1 Jan 1859. Charles Lumsden and **James Kidd** paid William Kidd $5.00 for five Negroes currently residing in Petersburg. All three signed this instrument, and could write.

This deed of trust was acknowledged by William R. Kidd, **James Kidd**, and Charles Lumsden before a notary public in Petersburg on 2 March 1857. It was admitted to record in the Clerk's Office of the Hustings Court in Petersburg on 23 January 1858.[233]

1858-1861 – **James Kidd** also appears for the first time on the Petersburg, Virginia PPTLs in 1858:
Kidd, James 1 WM >21, 3 slaves >12, 2 horses $235, 2 cattle $35, 1 clock $8, furniture $200, aggregate value $478, tax $6.31.[234]
He continues to be listed annually through 1861,[235] then drops from these PPTLs until 1868 (see below).

1859 – On 20 May 1859, **James Kidd** and Ann M. Kidd his wife sold to Abel Head for the sum of $400, two lots in Petersburg, called Pridesfield (the land that they had purchased in 1856 for $165). James and Ann M. Kidd acknowledged this deed before a notary public on 24 May 1859, and it was admitted to record on 27 May 1859.[236]

1860 – On the federal census in the South Ward of Petersburg district, p 301, HH 418:
Kidd, James 65MW no occupation $1000/8000 VA
 " , Ann M. 60FW VA
(no others)

There are TWO James Kidds on the 1860 Slave Schedule in the South Ward of the city of Petersburg.[237] One has eleven slaves and two slave houses; nearby, the other James Kidd has two slaves (a 35-year-old female and a 12 year old male) and no slave house.

---

[232] City of Petersburg, DB 24, pages 194-195, from microfilm reel 13 at the Library of Virginia. . Scanned images available from the authors.

[233] City of Petersburg DB 24, pages 242-243, from microfilm reel 13 at the Library of Virginia. Scanned images available from the authors.

[234] PPTL Petersburg, VA 18857-1859, reel 814, page 554, line 26

[235] For the details of each of his listings, see the Petersburg PPTLs document by WR Kidd in the Dinwiddie Sources folder on Dropbox.

[236] City of Petersburg DB 25, pages 30-31, from microfilm reel 14 at the Library of Virginia. Scanned images available from the authors.

[237] 1860 federal census, Slave Schedule for Petersburg, Dinwiddie County, VA on Ancestry.com, page 9.

I suspect, but cannot be certain, that both entries are for the same James Kidd, because he's the only one who lived in Petersburg in 1860.

1860 – On 10 October 1860, David May and W. L. Watkins, commissioners appointed by the Circuit Court of Petersburg in the May term 1860 in Chancery to make the sale of certain lands and lots belonging to S. G. Wells' estate sold to **James Kidd** in consideration of (blank) paid by said Kidd to the said Commissioners …lot number 72 in the plat of lots made at the instance of the said Commissioners and filed by them for record in the Hustings Court of Petersburg…this lot having been purchased by said Kidd at public auction. It was admitted to record on 1 February 1862.[238]

1863 – On 6 February 1863, Joseph B. Willson and Mary Ann his wife sold to **James Kidd** (residence not specified for either the sellers or the buyer) for $1000 a certain tract of land in the county of Amelia containing 100 acres and bounded by the following lines, viz., beginning at William Kidd's corner (we believe that this is William R. Kidd, this James Kidd's son, and that this is the site of his lumber and grist mill venture) on the Petersburg Road, thence with his line …to the Appomattox River, thence up the river 159 poles to a small stream near a large red oak, thence a new line to the Petersburg Road, thence along the road to the beginning. Joseph B. Williams and Mary Ann Williams both signed this deed. The deed was acknowledged by the sellers before a notary public on 11 August 1866 in Amelia County, but wasn't entered into record in Amelia County until 16 March 1868.[239]

1867 –In a deed made 5 March 1867 between **James Kidd** and Ann M. Kidd his wife of the one part and Bolling G. Heath of the other part.
Witnesseth that whereas the said James Kidd sold to the said Bolling G. Heath in the year 1863 a certain lot with improvements in the City of Petersburg lying on the south side of Shepherd Street, being the same (lot) purchased by the said Kidd of the Commissioners appointed for the division and sale of Stephen G. Wells' estate… and whereas the said James Kidd received of the said Bolling G. Heath the sum of $2350 the purchase money for the said lot, and whereas the said James Kidd and Ann M his wife executed a duly authenticated deed…but which said deed was lost or mislaid prior to being recorded and cannot now be produced, now the said James Kidd and Ann M. his wife do grant and convey said land to Bolling G. Heath. Ann M. Kidd and James Kidd both signed this deed, and it was admitted to record the following day.[240]

Also in 1867, this **James Kidd** was the informant for the birth record of his grandson:
A son, Jno. Kidd, was born 10 Mar 1867 in the City of Petersburg, VA to William R Kidd, occupation – Lumber Dealer, and Martha Kidd. The person giving the information was "Jas. Kidd, grandfather."[241]
[This record substantiates that this particular James Kidd was the father of William R. Kidd;

---

238 City of Petersburg DB 26, pages 519-520, from microfilm reel 15 at the Library of Virginia. Scanned images available from the authors.
239 Amelia County Deed Book 40, p. 608, retrieved by WRK at LoV, reel 18, in January 2003. Image available upon request.
240 City of Petersburg DB 29, pages 693-694, from microfilm reel 74 at the Library of Virginia. Scanned images available from the authors.
241 Petersburg, Virginia Register of Births, 1853-1871, page 111, retrieved from FHL #33443, image 92 of 450, via familysearch.org (unrestricted access).

there were no other James Kidds living in Petersburg at this time.

1868 – In a deed dated 7 Feb 1868, **James Kidd** and Nancy M. Kidd his wife of the City of
Petersburg sold to Daniel Robertson of Amelia County a tract of 100 acres of land in Amelia
County for $500, this being the same land James Kidd had purchased from Joseph P.
Wilson. The deed was apparently witnessed and signed in Court on 18 November 1870 by
James Kidd, and contains a note that Nancy M. Kidd was deceased at this time. The deed
was admitted to record 28 September 1871.[242]
James Kidd signed this deed with an X on 18 November 1870.
On this transaction, he received only half of what he paid for this land 5 years earlier.

The Petersburg Daily Index (newspaper of Petersburg, Virginia) on 6 Aug, 1868 contained a
notice from **James Kidd** about a missing Bible, lost at the registration desk of the West
Ward with the name Ann Thweatt inscribed, containing the family record of the Thweatt
and Kidd family. Since James is taxed on land in 1848 that is noted as received from Ann M.
Thweatt, this appears to be the family Bible. She is buried in Blandford in James Kidd's plot
but apparently there is no marker.[243]

1868-1870 – **James Kidd** appeared annually on the Personal Property Tax List for Petersburg, VA
in these years, with little property.[244] Following the Civil War, his fortunes declined
considerably.

1870 – On the federal census in Petersburg, VA, 4th Ward, p. 326, HH 836, apparently a duplex:
Kidd, James 75MW no occupation VA
  " , Nancy M. 68FW keeps house VA cannot read or write

1870 – a Nancy Kidd, age 75, died in Petersburg, Virginia on 13 June 1870.[245] This must be James
Kidd's wife. She was buried in Blandford Cemetery in Petersburg on 17 June 1870.[246]

1871 – On 25 March 1871, **James Kidd** of Dinwiddie revoked all earlier wills to compensate his
friend Trent E Harrison for his kindness in the past, and what he anticipates will come in the
future. Kidd gives his entire estate to Harrison to do with as he sees fit. After Harrison's
death, the remainder of the estate is to go to Harrison's wife Mary. **James Kidd** signed the
deed with an X on 12 Apr 1871. Witnesses included E. P. Wells, J.F. Wells, and J. R. Smith.
He acknowledged the deed before a justice of the peace in Darville twp. of Dinwiddie
County on 12 April 1871. The deed was recorded 17 April 1871.[247]
The fact that James Kidd signed this deed with an X is perplexing, since in all previous
records, he was able to sign his name. Nevertheless, we believe that this is indeed our
James6a Kidd, based on the subsequent records (below). James6a Kidd's second wife, Ann
M. Kidd has died, James is elderly and has no one else to care for him at this point. And
indeed, the 1874 records below show that Trent E Harrison did care for him in his last

---

[242] Amelia County DB 42:34, reviewed by William R. Kidd at the Amelia Courthouse.
[243] Personal correspondence from William R. Kidd.
[244] For the details of each of his listings, see the Petersburg PPTLs document by WR Kidd in the Dinnwiddie Sources
folder on Dropbox.
[245] Virginia, Deaths and Burials, 1853-1917, on Ancestry.com, citing FHL #33443, Peterburg, Virginia Deaths.
Scanned image of this record is in the Dinwiddie Shared Folder on Dropbox.
[246] *Index of Interments at Blandford Cemetery*, reviewed by William R. Kidd at Library of Virginia.
[247] Dinwiddie County, VA. DB 12, page 593, retrieved from FHL #31098, image 322. Scanned copy available from the
authors.

sickness, and paid his expenses. We don't know why James6a Kidd signed this deed with an X. Perhaps he'd had a stroke or was otherwise incapacitated.

Trent Harrison married Mary Kidd, daughter of Thomas J. Kidd, who was James6a Kidd's brother. So Mary was his niece. Trent E. Harrison was an important figure to the Kidd family. His wife's brother, Stanfield Kidd, died abt. 1855, and the Harrisons took in Stanfield's daughter, Martha F Kidd; she was living with them at the time of the 1860 census.

In 1871, this **James Kidd** lived in Wilson's, a small town in Dinwiddie County, VA, according to his War of 1812 pension application filed in 1871.

1874 – Both his War of 1812 pension application and the Dinwiddie County, VA Register of Births and Deaths state that this **James Kidd** died on 10 April 1874.[248]
This date of death is confirmed in other Dinwiddie County Court records, of which we have photocopies.[249]

At a Court held for Dinwiddie County on Monday, 21 Sept 1874, T. E. Harrison this day presented to the Court satisfactory evidence to the (illegible) that **Jas. Kidd** is entitled to (illegible) of pension, and that he died in the County of Dinwiddie on 10 April 1874. leaving no widow or minor child and without sufficient assets to defray the expense of his last sickness and burial, and that the same was paid by said Harrison.[250]

JAMES6b KIDD, the son of George Kidd, Jr. (George5a, George4, Benjamin3, William2, Thomas1 Kidd), named in his father's 1844 Amelia County will
Born abt. 1794, Amelia County, VA
Married Rebecca Young in 1816 in Amelia County, VA
Moved to Kentucky in 1828 with his sister Martha,[251] who married Elliott Young in

---

[248] War of 1812 pension record for James Kidd (Copy from the National Archives in Washington, DC (NAB), 7 Aug 2009, by William R. Kidd)
SO 24157, SC 19852, BLW 34187-40-50, BLW 38588-120-55
Service in Captain William Dancy's unit, 1st Regiment of the Virginia Militia, drafted at Dinwiddie CH on 10 Aug 1814 for a term of 6 months, enlisted 28 Aug 1814, honorably discharged 30 Nov 1814, Camp Powell's Creek
Residence in 1851, Dinwiddie County, VA
Residence in 1855, Petersburg, Dinwiddie County, VA
Residence in 1871, Dinwiddie County (P.O. Wilson's Depot), VA
James had 2 wives, but no detail is listed other than the notations of "first wife" followed by a blank and "?", and then the next line below that is simply "wife", again followed by a blank but no question mark. Finally the note "death of wives prior to 1871" appears later.
Death date of soldier 10 Apr 1874
Power of attorney dated 7 Nov 1872 witnessed by Peter King and Trent E Harrison.
This date of death is also found in Dinwiddie County Register of Births and Deaths, 1865-1896 (Item 1 on microfilm FHL US/CAN film 1929708, reviewed by RK, Oct. 2009).
[249] Dinwiddie County Order Book 1A, 1874, pp. 81-82, containing the report of T.E. Harrison to the Court that James Kidd died on 10 April 1874 leaving neither a widow nor a minor child, and without assets to pay his final expenses, so those were paid by Harrison.
[250] Dinwiddie County, Virginia Order Book, 1873-1881, pp. 81-82. Scanned images in Dinwiddie Source Documents folder on Dropbox.
[251] letter from Patrick J. Young, brother of Elliott Young, and from Lutannus Young, nephew of Elliott Young. See Young-Kidd Bible records (Margaret Winders).

VA, 29 Jan 1816.[252]
Later moved to Grayson County, Texas, where he died abt 1882.
This James Kidd was the ancestor of Troy Kidd[253] **and his brother, Albert Ray Kidd,
the latter a participant in the Kidd Y-DNA Project.**
**[The Descendants Chart for George4 Kidd in Appendix Two may aid some readers
in visualizing these two James Kidds and their relationships.]**

1811 – a **James Kidd** is found in the household of Daniel Tucker Sr. on the Dinwiddie County VA
PPTL.[254]

1812 – This **James Kidd** of Dinwiddie County VA served in the War of 1812,[255] and received
bounty land in Green County, Kentucky for his service.

1812 – This **James Kidd** is probably the second WM in George Kidd's household on the 1812
Amelia County PPTL:
George Kidd – 2 free WM >16, 5 slaves, 2 gigs.

1813-1815 – We believe that he is again the second WM in George5a's household on the Amelia
County PPTLs in each of these years (his holdings didn't change in this 3-year period):
George Kidd – 2 free WM >16, 7 slaves, 2 gigs.

1816 – **James Kidd** is listed as surety on the 22 Jan 1816 marriage bond of Elliot Young and Martha
Kidd. George Kidd (this is George5a Kidd, son of George4 Kidd) is listed as father of the
bride. The wedding was apparently 4 days later, on 26 Jan 1816.[256]
James6b, George5a's son, was Martha's brother; he would have been about 21 years of age.

On 29 Jan 1816, this **James Kidd** married Rebecca Young in Amelia County, VA.

Also in 1816, James Kidd appears on the Amelia County PPTL in his own household for the
first time (appearing on this PPTL along with his father):
George Kidd – 2 free males over 16, 6 slaves
James Kidd – 1 free male over 16, one slave (this is George Jr.'s eldest son, b. 1794)

1817 – A **James Kidd** is listed as surety on 29 Mar 1817 in the **Amelia** County, VA marriage of
Henry T. Garrett and Martha Thompson. Ann Thompson is listed as the mother of the
bride.[257] I'm unsure whether this is the same James, but he's the best fit.

1817 – He again appears on the **Amelia** County PPTL for this year, one free white male over 16, no
property:

---

[252] Dinwiddie County, VA Data, 1752-1865, Hughes, p. 432.

[253] Troy Kidd did a great deal of research on this branch of the family, and shared it freely with the authors prior to his
sudden and untimely death on 22 April 1998 in Dennison, TX. Sadly all his work has been lost, as far as I can tell.

[254] Dinwiddie County, VA Data, 1752-1865, Hughes, p. 128.

[255] "Dinwiddie County: The Countrey of the Apamatica", compiled by the Workers of the Writers' Program of the Work
Projects Administration in the State of Virginia, 1942, Whittet and Shepperson Printers, Richmond, Virginia, page
255.

[256] *Amelia County, Virginia Marriage Bonds, Consents, and Ministers' Returns, 1816*-1852, compiled and indexed by T.P. Hughes
Jr., Page 51. Book located at the Library of Virginia.

[257] Amelia County Marriage Bonds, consents and Marriage Returns, 1816-1852. Compiled and indexed by Thomas P.
Hughes Jr. Page 17. Book located at the Library of Virginia.

George Kidd – 2 free males over 16 (Geo. + son Asa[258], or a previously unknown son[259]; 7 slaves

James Kidd – 1 free male over 16

1818-1823 – In these years, **James Kidd** was taxed in **Dinwiddie** County on 110 acres on branches of Bear Swamp, 9 miles NW of Courthouse, conveyed by Elliott Young[260], (his brother-in-law, see above). See <u>Appendix Five</u> for more details about his entries on the Dinwiddie LTLs.

1820 – There are TWO James Kidds in **Dinwiddie** County on the federal census; they are close in age, and the "Jr." most likely indicates the younger of the two, and not a father-son relationship:[261]

Kidd, James – 1M 0-9 & 1 26-44; 1F 0-9 & 1 16-25, 1 in Ag, 2 F slaves <14.

Kidd, James Jr. – 1M 26-44, 1F 0-9 & 1F 16-25. 1 in Ag, no slaves. This is presumably James6b, the son of George5a Kidd (see next).

1820-1823 – a James Kidd appears annually on the **Dinwiddie** County, VA PPTLs. This is most likely James6b, since the above information indicates that he moved across the county line from Amelia into Dinwiddie County by 1818, and later moved back to Amelia County (see below), before leaving Virginia for Kentucky in 1828.

1823 – **James Kidd** sold his 110 acre parcel of land in Dinwiddie County in 1823 or early 1824[262] to Henry Young, and drops from the Dinwiddie County <u>Land Tax Lists</u> in 1824. He evidently moved back to Amelia County. (see below).

1823 – On 9 October 1823, Jesse Coleman II of Amelia County sold **James Kidd** of <u>**Dinwiddie**</u> County for $730 for 65 acres[263] of land in **Amelia** County.[264]

For the next 4 years, **James Kidd** appears on the **Amelia** County, VA Land Tax Lists, taxed on 65 acres. This land was adjacent to Barnett Southall.[265]

He disappears from the land tax lists in 1828.

1824-1828 – **James Kidd** also appears annually on the **Amelia** County PPTLs through 1828.

1824 – one slave, one horse

1825 – one slave, no horses

1826 – 2 slaves, one horse

---

[258] From his census entries, we believe that Asa was born about 1805; he'd be only 12 in 1817, so this may not be him.

[259] George Kidd Jr. had only two known sons, James and Asa. James is named in this list, and Asa would appear to have been too young. Thus this listing MAY be a third son, one who died in the next few years.

[260] *Land Records of Dinwiddie County, VA, 1752-1820*, p 106. ALSO, RK (one of the authors of this paper) personally reviewed the microfilm records of these tax lists for Dinwiddie County and transcribed them, confirming the above.

[261] 1820 federal census, Dinwiddie County, VA, p. 12A; this census was recorded by first letter of last name, rather than by geographic location, so no conclusions can be drawn by proximity on the census.

[262] Dinwiddie County VA Land Tax Lists for 1824 show that in the past 12 months, James Kidd deeded 110 acres on the branches of Bear Swamp to Henry Young. FHC film 0029921, personally reviewed by RK, Dec 2009.

[263] Why did Kidd pay so much for this land?

[264] Deed book 26, Amelia County, VA. Page 385. Copy in deed file (WRK). Boundaries listed in the deed on file.

[265] Amelia County, Land Tax Lists, transcribed by Troy Kidd, copy in RK's Amelia file.

1827 – 2 slaves, two horses
1828 – 2 slaves, two horses

1828 – On 1 January 1828, **James Kidd** (Jr.) and Rebecca Kidd his wife, of **Amelia** County, VA sold to Francis Waddill a parcel of land containing 65 acres in Amelia adjoining the lands of Allen, Crowder, and Southall. [266] Following this, he and his family moved West via Tennessee to his bounty land grant in Green County, KY.

1829, ff. – No James Kidd appears on the Amelia County, VA Personal Property Tax Lists or the Land Tax Lists from 1828 through 1835.

Subsequent records for him are found in Barren County, Kentucky, then Grayson County, Texas, where he died in 1882. Much more information can be found on his page of our Kidds of MSX County, Virginia family tree on Ancestry.com: https://www.ancestry.com/family-tree/person/tree/37652986/person/19120498932/facts

UNKNOWN JAMES KIDD
Born abt 1794 in Dinwiddie County
Died 9 August 1874 in Dinwiddie County, VA

1874 – On 9 August 1874, a **James Kidd's** death is recorded in Darvilles Twp of Dinwiddie County.[267] The informant for this record was William Rogers, listed as "friend" to the deceased. He appears to have been born about 1794, given his age (80) at the time of his death. The informant stated that he was born in Dinwiddie County. The record did not name his parents.[268] Cause of death listed as "old age"; occupation is listed as "farmer," and marital status as "unmarried."[269]

At this time, we do not know who this James Kidd is. He cannot be James6b Kidd, because that James Kidd left Dinwiddie decades earlier for Kentucky and died in Texas. And we have a different date of death (10 April 1874 in Dinwiddie County) for James6a Kidd. It seems possible, but very unlikely that this (or the other 1874 death record) is a clerical error or mistaken claim.
Perhaps he was the father of the William Kidd that died in Darvilles Twp of Dinwiddie County in 1873 at the age of 46, whose identity is also unknown to us.

__JAMES7 KIDD__, **the probable son of Thomas J. Kidd (Thomas J6, Benjamin5, George4, Benjamin3, William2, Thomas1 Kidd) and his wife, Jane Gent,[270] based upon similar occupation, the fact that his age matches that of Thomas J.'s oldest son on census records, and the fact that James named his only son "Thomas J. Kidd."**

---

[266] Amelia County, VA Deed Book 28, page 328 ; RK has photocopy.

[267] Dinwiddie County, Death Registers, 1853-1896, FHL #2056979, image 460; scanned image available.

[268] In fact, the names Alex and Ann Johnson" appear in the Parents column for him, but the same two are listed as the parents of the next person in the roster as well and those names in James' column are smudged, as if being crossed out.

[269] The column heading reads, "Consort or Unmarried," so he could have been widowed, single or divorced.

[270] See his 1855 marriage record, which left the name of his father blank, but named his mother as Jane Gent.

Born about 1816[271] in Dinwiddie County, VA[272]
Married Jane G Haddon, the daughter of Edmund and Sarah H. Haddon, in
Dinwiddie County on 11 December 1855
Died abt. 1892. Occupation: wheelwright/carriage maker

1843-1852 – a new **James Kidd** appears on the annual Dinwiddie County PPTLs, beginning in
1843. He would be the right age to be this James Kidd, newly out on his own:

Year Slaves Horses Gigs(value)
1843   0   0   0
1844   0   0   0
1845   0   1   0
1846 (not listed this year)
1847   1   1   0
1848   1   1   0
1849   0   1   0
1850   0   1   0
1851   0   1   0
1852   0   1   0   (but one 4-wheel wagon valued at $50)
This is the last year checked so far.

1850 – On 26 January 1850, John P. Crump and Susan his wife sold to **James Kidd**, all of
Dinwiddie for $369, a tract of land in Dinwiddie containing 123 acres and adjoining Norman
Crawford's line, Hardaway, John P. Crump, and Oliver Chappell. Recorded 26 Jan, 1850. [273]

1850-1867 – In 1850, a **James Kidd** is taxed for the first time on 123 acres on Vaughan's Rd, 2
miles east of the courthouse, valued at $369. A notation in the margin by this entry reads,
"By deed from Jno. P. Crump & wife."[274] He's on the tax list of William Bishop, the only
Kidd on this list. The other Dinwiddie County Kidd households (James6a, Thomas J. and
William & Matilda Kidd) are in the district of James Boisseau.
He continues to be taxed annually on this land through 1867, the last year of these records
that we have examined. (We know that he owned this land until his death; see 1894, below.)

1850 – On the federal census in southern district of Dinwiddie County, VA, p. 986, HH 385:
Kidd, James 30MW carriage maker $369 VA
Wells, Sarah 70FW VA cannot read or write
Gent, Jane 65FW VA cannot read or write
Cook, Elizabeth 20FW VA
Malone, Payton 32MW blacksmith VA cannot read or write
Butcher, Albert 21MB no occupation VA cannot read or write
" , Thomas 20MB no occupation VA cannot read or write

1855 – **James Kidd** of Dinwiddie County, VA married Jane G. Haddon on 11 December 1855.[275]
James was 39 and single; Jane was 20, and also single. Both stated that they were born in

---

[271] Age 30 on 1850 census, 39 on 11 December 1855, when he married Jane G Haddon; 45 in 1860, 54 in 1870 and 64 in
1880.

[272] His 1855 marriage record states that he was born in Dinwiddie County, Virginia.

[273] Dinwiddie County, VA. DB 6, page 309. Deed book located at Dinwiddie County Courthouse.

[274] Dinwiddie County Land Tax Lists, 1841-1850, retrieved from FHL #29924, image 487.

[275] Dinwiddie County Marriage Register, 1853-1861, p 5, LDS #1929644, item 1, image 11, reviewed and transcribed by
RK on 4/6/2010. Scanned image available upon request.

Dinwiddie County.   James' occupation is listed as "coachmaker." His father's name isn't given; his mother's name is listed as "Jane Gent." This matches the census records in 1850 (above) and later (below). Wife Jane's parents were Edmund and Annie Haddon.

1857 – On 22 April 1857, Sarah Jane Kidd was born in Dinwiddie County to **James Kidd Jr**. and Jane A. Kidd. Father's occupation wheelwright, residing in Dinwiddie.[276] (see below)

1860 – On the VA census in Dinwiddie County, p 86, Revenue District 2, p. 18, HH 149/138:
Kidd, James 45MW farmer $1230/0 VA
" , Jane G. 24FW VA
" , Sarah J. 3FW VA
" , Mary E. 1FW VA
Jones, Scott 16MW VA

This James Kidd is also found on the 1860 Slave Schedule, in Revenue District No. 2 of Dinwiddie County, with three slaves (a 45-year-old mulatto female, and two mulatto males, ages 2 and 12).[277] This entry includes the notation, "employed of Sarah Alford, owner, Dinwiddie County;" it also indicates that this James Kidd owns one slave house. The slave-owning neighbors listed on this schedule match his neighbors on the 1860 federal census itself.

1870 – On the VA census in Dinwiddie County, VA, p. 144, HH145.:
Kidd, James 54MW wheelwright $615/200 VA
" , Jane G. 35FW keeping house VA
" , Sarah J. 12FW at school VA
" , Thomas J. 9MW at school VA
" , Lorena 4FW VA
" , Ann Estelle 2FW VA[278]
" , Mollie B. 11/12FW VA[279]
Ampy, William, 25 mulatto male, laborer VA
" , Becky, 21 mulatto female, domestic servant VA

1880 – On the federal census in Rowanty magisterial district, Dinwiddie County, VA, ED 85, sheet 31C, page 217, HH 292/293:
Kidd, James WM 64M farming VA VA VA
" , Jane FW wife 44M keeps house VA VA VA
" , Sarah FW dau 22S milliner VA VA VA
" , Thomas MW son 19S assists on farm VA VA VA
" , Lorina FW dau 15S at home VA VA VA attended school within the year
" , Ann E. FW dau 13S at home VA VA VA attended school within the year

---

[276] Dinwiddie County, VA. births, 1853-1868, reel 19. Microfilm located in the Library of Virginia.
[277] 1860 federal census, Slave Schedule For Dinwiddie County, Rev. District No. 2, on Ancestry.com, page 16.
[278] According to the Virginia Birth Index (page 91, reviewed and transcribed by WRK), her Dinwiddie County birth record lists her birth name as Nannie Estelle Kidd, born 2 March 1867.
[279] According to the Virginia Birth Index (page 20, reviewed and transcribed by WRK), her Dinwiddie County birth record lists her birth name as Mollie Betty Kidd, born 28 June 1869.

" , Mary E. fw dau 10S at school VA VA VA attended school within the year
" , Patti A.[280] FW dau 7S at home VA VA VA attended school within the year

1883 – On 3 April 1883, W. R. McKenney, a commissioner of the Dinwiddie County Court, sold to
James Kidd and BC Wells a tract of land in Dinwiddie. In the October 1880 circuit court in
the suit of Mortimer Mitchell and wife vs. Ledbetter's administrator and others, McKenney
was appointed commissioner to sell 60 ½ acres in Dinwiddie County, on the north by Cattail
Creek, on the east by the lands of the same **James Kidd**, on the south by what is known as
the old John P (Phillips written, but scratched out) Crump tract, on the west by the land of
<u>Peter Gent</u>, Berryman Scott, and the tract of 7 acres assigned to the widow of the late Henry
Ledbetter. That land was sold to the highest bidder (Kidd and Wells) for $60.50 on 17 Jan
1881. This deed was executed to provide B. C. Wells and James Kidd a "good and sufficient
deed with special warranty" for the said real estate. W. R. McKinney acknowledged this deed
before a notary public in the City of Petersburg on 3 April 1883. It was recorded in the
Clerk's office of Dinwiddie County 21 April 1884.[281]
(The mention of Peter Gent is a clue to James and Jane C; later deeds will confirm this.)

1887 – On 7 March 1887, **James Kidd** of Dinwiddie County entered into a deed of trust with W. R.
McKenney of Petersburg, for the sum of $5.00 paid by McKenney, in order to secure the
payment of a certain negotiable note of ? date for the sum of $92.75 payable 12 months after
the date at the National Bank of Petersburg in Petersburg. In doing so, he used two tracts of
land that he owned as collateral: a tract of 123½ acres lying on both sides <u>of Vaughan's Road
in Dinwiddie, part of which land contains a residence occupied by James Kidd</u>, bounded as
follows, on the north by Chappell's estate. On the east by James Keiser, on the south by
Conally's estate and on the west by Crump's estate; and an undivided one half interest in a
tract of land 60 ½ acres purchased by party of the first part and Bertha Wells of WR
McKenney, commissioner and adjoining the tract above mentioned.
James Kidd acknowledged this deed before a notary public in Petersburg on 7 March 1887,
and it was admitted to record in the Dinwiddie Court Clerk's office the following day.[282]

1889 – On 19 April 1889. **James Kidd** and Jane G. his wife entered into another deed of trust, this
time with Frank Orgain of Dinwiddie County, in order to secure payment of another debt.
In doing so he put up as collateral a tract of land lying in Rowanty Magisterial District,
Dinwiddie County (same land mentioned in 1887 deed above) "which is where James and
Jane currently reside."[283]

On 20 April 1889 W. R. McKenney signed a deed of release, acknowledging that the debt of
$92.75 had been fully paid by **James Kidd** to WR McKenney, and Kidd has requested the
execution of a Deed of Release, therefore this deed of release was granted; it was recorded
29 April 1889.[284]

1894 – On 28 Nov 1894, **Jane G. Kidd**, <u>widow</u> of **James Kidd** deceased, AD Harding and Sarah J
his wife, LM McGee and M? his wife, AB Ellington and Lonie? (this would be Lorina) his

---

[280] According to the Virginia Birth Index (page 155, reviewed and transcribed by WRK), her Dinwiddie County birth
record lists her birth name as Pattie Alma, born 22 Feb 1874.
[281] Dinwiddie Court House, deed book 16 pages 604-605, viewed by WRK 14 Jan 2010, images on file.
[282] Dinwiddie Court House, deed book 17, pages 684-685, viewed by WRK 14 Jan 2010, images on file.
[283] Dinwiddie Court House, deed book 18, pages 651-652, viewed by WRK 14 Jan 2010, images on file.
[284] Dinwiddie County Release Deed Book 1, p. 77, retrieved by WRK June 2009. Scanned image available.

wife, Mollie Kidd and Pattie Kidd, **heirs at law of the said James Kidd dec'd,** sold to V. Arabella Sterne and Edna Frances Ettenborough for $400 the same 2 pieces of land mentioned above in the 1887 deed.[285]

In this Deed of Bargain and Sale, the heirs of James7 Kidd are selling the land he owned prior to his death; this deed gives us the names (and married names) of the surviving children of James Kidd and Jane G. Haddon. Note that their son, Thomas (who was age 19 on the 1880 federal census) is not among them; presumably he died in the interval.

See this James Kidd's section of our MSX County Kidds tree on Ancestry.com at https://www.ancestry.com/family-tree/person/tree/37652986/person/19120499473/facts for more information on this line.

JAMES KIDD, the son of William and Matilda (Wells) Kidd
      born abt. 1834, died in September 1855 at the age of 20 (see below).

1850 – On the federal census in Lower district of Chesterfield County, VA, p. 134, HH 338 (mis-indexed at Ancestry.com as "Ridd"):
   Kidd, William 47MW "operator" VA cannot read or write
    " , Matilda 43FW VA cannot read or write
    " , Edward 18MW operator VA
    " , **James** 15MW operator VA
    " , Thomas 12MW VA
    " , Ann E. 10FW VA

1855 – On 18 January 1855, this **James Kidd** sold all his interest in a parcel of land in Dinwiddie County containing 60 acres "in the possession of Mrs. Matilda Kidd her life" (estate?) to Robert H. Sydnor for $75. The land was bounded on the north by R. H. Sydnor, on the west by Upton Crow, on the south by Cox Road and on the east by R. H. Sydnor. He appeared before a justice in Petersburg to acknowledge the deed, and it was admitted to record in Dinwiddie County Court on 19 November 1855.[286]
[In this transaction, James was selling his interest in a parcel of land deeded to his mother, Matilda by her father, as a life estate rather than in fee simple. Martha's other children completed similar transactions. See Matilda's section of this compilation for more details.]

1858 – **James Kidd** died on 23 Sept 1858 in Chesterfield County at the age of 20. This record lists his parents as William and Matilda Kidd, and his birthplace as Dinwiddie County. The cause of his death was not known.[287]

1866 – On 20 March 1866, William Kidd and his wife Matilda, both of Chesterfield deeded 60 acres in Dinwiddie County to Robert H. Sydnor for $30.00. Recorded 20 Aug 1866.[288]

---

[285] Dinwiddie Court House, deed book 20 (#2), pages 116-117, viewed by WRK 14 Jan 2010, images on file.
[286] Dinwiddie County, VA. DB 8, pages 395-396, retrieved from FHL #31096, images 224 & 225. Copies available upon request.
[287] Chesterfield County Death Registers, 1853-1896. Retrieved via familysearch.org (unrestricted access) from FHL #2056977, image 42.
[288] Dinwiddie County, VA. DB 11, page 269. Deed book located at Dinwiddie County Courthouse.

OTHER James Kidd citations, as yet unassigned

1859 – a James Kidd is found in Amelia County, VA in 1859:

> Eliza Kidd, white female, died Mar, 1859 in Amelia County. Died of New Ralgia? (neuralgia? A stroke, perhaps). Age 34 years, 11 months 3 days. Parents unknown, husband **James Kidd**, who reported.[289]

This James Kidd is not in Amelia County for either the 1850 or the 1860 federal census, and we cannot place him at this time. He cannot be James 6a, the son of Ben, whose wife (one of them) was Eliza Kidd, because James6a Kidd's first wife Eliza predeceased this woman; she died between 1839 (when she's named as his wife in a deed) and 1847, when a subsequent deed and other records show that he was then married to Nancy/Ann M. Thweatt.

JANE G. (HADDON) KIDD, the wife of James7 Kidd

> **Born 24 November 1835 to Edmund and Sally H. Haddon in Dinwiddie County, VA**
> **Married James7 Kidd in Dinwiddie or Amelia County circa 1856[290]**
> **Lived with her daughter, Patti Kidd Bristow in Petersburg in her later years.**
> **Died 19 January 1915 in Petersburg, Virginia.**
> **See James7 Kidd's section of this paper and the MSX Kidds Tree on Ancestry.com for more information about her.[291]**

1894 – On 28 November 1894, **Jane G. Kidd**, <u>widow</u> of **James Kidd** deceased, AD Harding and Sarah J his wife, LM McGee and M? his wife, AB Ellington and Lonie? (this would be Lorina) his wife, Mollie Kidd and Pattie Kidd, **heirs at law of the said James Kidd dec'd,** sold to V. Arabella Sterne and Edna Frances Ettenborough for $400 the same 2 pieces of land mentioned above in the 1887 deed.[292]

> In this Deed of Bargain and Sale, the heirs of James7 Kidd are selling the land he owned prior to his death; this deed gives us the names (and married names) of the surviving children of James Kidd and Jane G. Haddon. Note that their son, Thomas (who was age 19 on the 1880 federal census) is not among them; presumably he died in the interval.

> See the MSX County Kidds tree on Ancestry for more information on this line:
> https://www.ancestry.com/family-tree/person/tree/37652986/person/19120499473/facts

JASPER KIDD, the son of George4 (Benjamin3, William2, Thomas1) Kidd,[293] and brother of Bartholomew Kidd[294]

> **Born abt. 1787 Amelia County VA. From this reference, he was living in Chesterfield**

---

[289] Amelia County, VA death records, 1853-1896, reel 2, p. 43, line 13, reviewed by WRK at LVA 2/17/10; scanned image from FHL #30474, item 4, Amelia County, VA Deaths, (image 435 on this reel) is stored in the Amelia County Shared Folder on Dropbox.

[290] She and James are on the 1860 federal census in Dinwiddie County, with a daughter, age 3 and a son, age 1.

[291] See https://www.ancestry.com/family-tree/person/tree/37652986/person/19120499474/facts

[292] Dinwiddie Court House, deed book 20 (#2), pages 116-117, viewed by WRK 14 Jan 2010, images on file.

[293] Amelia County, VA Will Book 5, pp. 359-360, and 390 - Will of Geo Kidd, Sr. AND Amelia County Deed Book 24, p 126.

[294] Amelia County, VA DB 24, p 126 (copy in Geo II file, RK) - On Oct. 26, 1814 Jasper Kidd of Chesterfield County, VA for $250 sold "my right and title in the tract of land in Amelia County, VA that was willed to us by our father George Kidd, deceased.....to Bartholomew Kidd of Chesterfield County, VA" Recorded in Amelia County, VA 7 June 1815.

County, VA, just NE of Amelia County and N of Dinwiddie County, in 1814, and married his second wife Susannah Powell there on 25 Oct 1814.
This couple had two known, documented sons:
1. Francis Kidd, born abt 1825,[295] and
2. Archer/Archibald Kidd, born abt 1830[296]
He was not able to write; he signed documents with an "X".
He drops from sight after the 1830 census. We believe that he died before 1850.
See below.

1793 – Along with his brother, Bartholomew, **Jasper Kidd** was named as a son of George4 Kidd in George Kidd's will, signed in 1793 and proven in Court in 1797.

1803-1807 – **Jasper Kidd** appears for the first time on the Amelia County. VA Personal Property Tax Lists in 1803; he appears on the Amelia County PPTLs annually 1805-1807 (in 1807, in the HH of his widowed mother Elizabeth Kidd).
1803 – Jasper Kidd – 1 free male over 16; no slaves; 1 horse.
1804 – **George Kidd's Est.** – 1 free male over 16 (Jasper) ; no slaves; 1 horse.
1805 – Jasper Kid – 2 free males over 16 (who is the second one here?); no slaves; 1 horse.
1806 – **Kid, Jasper** – 1 WM>16, no slaves; 1 horse.
1807 –Elisabeth Kidd – 2 free males over 16(most likely Jasper); one slave; and one horse. no others

1808 – No taxes were collected statewide this year.

1809-1811 – No Kidds appear on the Amelia County, VA PPTLs in these years.

1810 – **Jasper Kidd** married Fanny Thompson, daughter of Thomas Thompson on 13 November 1810 in Amelia County, VA. Her father gave his consent in court, suggesting that Fanny was not yet old enough to consent. Thomas Thompson also was the surety for this marriage. [297]

1810 – **Jasper Kidd** appears on the 1810 federal census as a head of household in Amelia County, VA, living next to his older brother, George Kidd:[298]
George Kidd 12001-1100-8 (1M 0-9, 2M 10-15 & 1 45 & up; 1F 0-9 & 1 10-15; 8 total (therefore two slaves).
Jasper Kidd 0001-0011-7 (1WM 26-44; 1F 16-25 & 1 26-44; 7 total, therefore 4 slaves) (no other Kidd household heads on this census in Amelia County).

1812-1814 – He appears on the Amelia County, VA PPTLs in each of these years, with the same personal property:
Kidd, Jasper – 1 WM>16, no slaves.

---

[295] Francis Kidd's 1860 marriage record lists his parents as **Jasper and Susan Kidd**, and his place of birth as Dinwiddie County, VA. Moreover, he and his brother, Archer are in the household of Susan Kidd, evidently their widowed mother. Jasper is nowhere to be seen or found.

[296] Archer's 1859 marriage record listed his parents' names as "Joseph" Kidd and Susan Powell. We think the father's name is a clerk's error, since the record otherwise perfectly matches our Archibald, son of JASPER Kidd and Susan Powell. And his 1868 marriage record marriage record lists his parents as **Jasper and Susan Kidd**, and his place of birth as Dinwiddie County, VA. See his section of this compilation for full details.

[297] DAR 67:154-159, Marriage Bonds of Amelia County, VA.

[298] 1810 VA census, Amelia County, page 237.

1814 – On 25 October 1814, a marriage bond was issued in **Chesterfield** County, Virginia for the marriage of **Jasper Kidd** and Susanna Powell. The surety for this bond was Alexander Powell.[299]

1815, ff. – An Amelia County deed from **Jasper Kidd** "of **Chesterfield** County " to Bartholomew Kidd "of the aforesaid County," was recorded 27 July, 1815. [300] In this deed, he was selling to his brother Bartholomew his share of the land in Amelia County that was given to them by their father, George Kidd in his 1793 will, proven in 1797.
Jasper is not found in Amelia County after this point.

1815 – **Jasper Kidd** is found this one year on the **Chesterfield** County PPTLs (along with his brother, Bartholomew). Jasper was taxed in one WM over sixteen (himself), one slave over 16, 1 horse and one cow.[301] Neither of them are found on subsequent Chesterfield County PPTLs through 1851.

1816-1819 – **Jasper Kidd** appears on the **Dinwiddie** County Personal Property Tax List each year, with no slaves and one horse.

1817-1820 – In these years, **Jasper Kidd** was taxed on 70 acres on Cox Rd., 14 miles NW of the Dinwiddie courthouse, conveyed by Joel Walker of Dinwiddie County in the preceding year (prior to the 1817 Land Tax List).[302]
Jasper Kidd sold this land (70 acres on Cox Rd., 14 miles NW of the Courthouse) in 1820 to Alexander Wells,[303] and drops from the Dinwiddie Land Tax Lists in 1821.

1820 – We do not find him on a federal census this year, BUT he was definitely in Dinwiddie County, VA in the early part of 1820, judging from the land tax record, above.

1820-1826 – **Jasper Kidd** is <u>not</u> found on the Dinwiddie PPTLs or LTLs in 1820 through 1826.

1827 – **Jasper Kidd** again appears for just this year on the Dinwiddie County PPTL, with no slaves, property or horse. We know that he was there in 1830, because he appeared on the federal census that year.

1830 – On the VA census in Dinwiddie County, along with James, Mary, Thomas J and William Kidd.[304]
Kidd, Jasper – 0200001-0020001 (oldest M & F both 40-49) NOTE the two young sons, ages 5-9; this is a reasonable 'fit' for his two documented sons, Francis and Archer. See their sections in this compilation.
Kidd, Mary – 00111- 0020101 (males 10-14, 15-19 & 20-29; oldest F 40-49)
     This is evidently Mary Kidd, widow of Benjamin Kidd.

---

[299] *Marriage Bonds & Ministers' Returns of Chesterfield County, Virginia 1771-1815,* by Catherine Lindsay Knorr, 1958.

[300] Amelia County, VA Order book 29, 1814-1817, page 371, Amelia County CH; also Amelia County Deed Book 24, pp. 126-127 (scanned images of this deed in the Amelia Shared folder on Dropbox.

[301] Chesterfield County Personal Property Tax Lists, 1812-1826, retrieved from FHL #2024512 via familysearch.org (unrestricted access), image 197.

[302] *Land Records of Dinwiddie County, VA, 1752-1820,* p 106. This reference lists the grantor's name as Joel Wells, but I personally reviewed the microfilmed tax list, and believe it clearly says Joel WALKER. (RK, Aug. 2009)

[303] "Land Records, Dinwiddie County, Virginia, 1752-1820" , compiled and indexed by Thomas P. Hughes and Jewel B. Sandifer, indicates that a DANIEL Wells starts paying the taxes for this land in 1820, conveyed from Archer Bevill and Benj. Kidd. Not sure about the discrepancy in the given name of the buyer of this land.

[304] 1830 federal census, Dinwiddie County, VA. All but Thomas J. and William are on p. 390. William is on p. 392 and Thomas J. is on p. 410.

Kidd, James – 001001-0001, 1F slave>55 (James 30-39; the only is female 15-19)
Kidd, William – 310001-00001, 1M & 1F slave 10-24 (oldest M 30-39; female 20-29)
Kidd, Thomas J. – 0010001- 000102, no slaves (oldest M 40-49; 2F 30-39).

We have found no further records of Jasper Kidd. He is not found on the 1840 VA census, the indices of this census, or thereafter. We do not know what became of him, but suspect that he died before the 1850 federal census.

We are confident that he did NOT migrate to Tippah County, Mississippi, a claim made by at least one tree on Ancestry.com, without documentation. The Kidds of Tippah County, Mississippi are the direct line of Reiley Kidd, one of the authors of this publication. He has done extensive research there, without finding any reference to Jasper Kidd.

JEMIMA (KIDD) WHITMORE, very likely the daughter of Benjamin5 Kidd[305]
> **Born abt 1791 in Dinwiddie County**
> **Died in March 1867 in Dinwiddie County**

1839 – On 27 April 1839, **Jemima & Sally Whitmore** of Dinwiddie County, VA sold to Thomas J. Kidd of Dinwiddie County for $100 a tract of 80 acres in the upper part of Dinwiddie County, adjoining P.W. Harper, Perry S. Derby and William B. Thompson. This deed was recorded 11 May 1839.[306]

1850 – On the federal census in Dinwiddie County (southern District), VA, p. 471, HH 23:
Kidd, Thomas J. 64WM Wheelright $100 VA
Whitmore, Jemima 54WF VA cannot read or write
Kidd, Stanfield 19WM wheelright $0 VA married within the year
 “ , Missouri E. 17FW VA married within the year (Stanfield's wife)
[Jemima is living with her presumed brother, Thomas J. Kidd and his son, Stanfield.]

1852 – On 17 September 1852, Stanfield Kidd and his wife Missouri sold to **Jemima Whitmore** and Thomas J. Kidd, all of Dinwiddie County, for the sum of one dollar a tract of 5 acres of land in Dinwiddie adjoining the lands of George Whitmore on the road at the southeast corner of the said Stanfield Kidd, to have and to hold the said Jemima Whitmore and Thomas J. Kidd <u>and at the death of Jemima and Thomas J, the said land reverts back to the former owners and their heirs</u>. Recorded 18 October 1852. [307]

1853-1857 – Thomas J. Kidd and **Jemima Whitmore** paid land taxes on the above 5 acres of land in Dinwiddie County, on Beaver Pond Creek in each of these years.

1857 – **Jemima Whitmore** died in Dinwiddie County, Virginia in March of 1857 at the age of 68. The cause of death was "consumption." Her death record lists her marital status as

---

[305] Although there is no direct evidence for this relationship, her date of birth makes this plausible. And the existing records imply some sort of close relationship with Thomas J. and James 6a Kidd. The most likely scenario, in our opinion, is that they were siblings.
[306] Dinwiddie County, VA. DB 2, page 269. Deed book located at Dinwiddie County Courthouse.
[307] Dinwiddie County, VA. DB 7, page 259, retrieved from FHL #31095, image 416. Copy available upon request.

"unmarried."[308] The space on the form for the names of her parents was left blank. The informant was Trent E. Harrison, "Friend."[309], [310]

<u>JOHN KIDD</u>, most likely the son of Benjamin5 (George4, Benjamin3, William2, Thomas1) Kidd and his wife Polly.
Born abt 1808[311] in Dinwiddie County, Virginia.
Lived in Lynchburg, VA 1858-1862.
Date and place of death unknown.

1820 – On the 1820 federal census in Dinwiddie County, Benjamin Kidd is listed as having 3 males age 0-9 and 1 10-15. Until recently, we knew of only 2 sons of Benjamin and Mary/Polly Kid: Thomas J. Kidd and James Kidd. We now believe that this John Kidd was another of their sons, based upon his 1858 and 1862 marriage records (see below) that name his parents.

1827 – a **John Kidd** appeared on the Dinwiddie County, VA PPTL this year, paying a tax on 1 horse, and no other property (no slaves). Not listed again until 1833 (see below).

1830 –In this year, Benjamin5 Kidd's widow, Mary Kidd appears on the federal census, with 1M 10-14, 1 15-19, and 1 20-29. We believe that this **John Kidd** is the "missing" third and youngest son, based on the 1834 and 1843 records below.

1833 – There is a September 1833 Dinwiddie County Chancery Court record of a complex suit with **John Kidd** and Sally his wife among the defendants in a suit brought by Chastain Ellington and his wife Martha, formerly Martha Featherstone. Other defendants include several Hardaways, Price Pollan, John Featherstone and other Featherstones. Defendant William E. Hardaway, administrator of Peter M. Hardaway, deceased was ordered to pay $64.22 to the plaintiff and to several of the other defendants, including **John and Sally Kidd**.[312]
We cannot be sure that this is the same John Kidd, but there were no other John Kidds in this three-county area in the 1830s, so it most likely IS this John Kidd.

1833 – **John Kidd** again appears on the Dinwiddie County, VA PPTL, again taxed on one horse, and no other property.

1834 – in the April 1834 session of the Dinwiddie County, VA Chancery Court, there is a suit wherein the Commonwealth of Virginia (for the benefit of the Literary Fund) sues Beverly Anderson, **John Kidd** and Mary Kidd. According to this entry, **John Kidd** and Mary Kidd

---

[308] Although this would seem to imply that she was single (rather than widowed), the space on the form was titled "Consort of, or Unmarried." We suspect that she had been widowed decades earlier.

[309] "Virginia, Bureau of Vital Statistics, Death Records, 1853-1912",
database, *FamilySearch* (https://www.familysearch.org/ark:/61903/1:1:D91N-THMM : 23 September 2020), Jemima Whitmore, 1857. Retrieved from FHL #2056979, image 392 via familysearch.org (unrestricted access).

[310] Trent Harrison was in fact the husband of Mary C. Kidd, the daughter of Thomas J. Kidd. He was involved in several transactions with Thomas J. Kidd and James 6a Kidd, and this supports the hypothesis that they were all closely related.

[311] This is a rough estimate, based upon his age (50) at the time of his 1858 marriage record, his age (55) per the 1860 federal census (which may not be the same John Kidd, but likely is), and his age (51) on his two 1862 marriage records.

[312] FHL film #31107, item 1, Chancery Court Order Book 1, 1832-1852, pp. 35-36, reviewed and transcribed by RK on 3/29/2010. Scanned image in RK's Kidd files.

were no longer inhabitants of the Commonwealth. Mary Kidd was ordered to pay $200 to the Commonwealth, for the benefit of the Literary Fund, plus the costs of the suit. And the defendant Anderson was to pay "so much as shall not exceed the $220 in his hands" to satisfy this obligation, which he did.
I can't tell from the entry whether he paid the debt for Mary Kidd, or he was equally indebted, and paid his own debt. No mention is made of John Kidd in the settlement.[313]
He doesn't appear again in Dinwiddie County, to my knowledge, and has moved out of the state by 1834.
The Mary Kidd cited in this record is almost certainly Mary/Polly Kidd, the widow of Benjamin Kidd who died in 1821. See her section in this paper.

This **John Kidd** disappears from Virginia records for a time; I'm unable to find him on the 1840 and 1850 federal censuses. He reappears in 1858, evidently returning to Lynchburg by 1858 (see below).

1858 – On May 6, 1858, **John Kidd**, age 50 and a widower, married Mary J. Burks, age 40 and a widow, in Lynchburg, Virginia.[314] Both were residents of Lynchburg at the time. **John Kidd's parents are listed as Benjamin and Polly Kidd**, and his occupation was "tobacconist." John's birthplace is listed in this record as North Carolina, as was Mary J.'s. While the latter is not a fit, given the other information here, including the next marriage record, we believe that this is indeed **John Kidd**, the youngest son of Benjamin and Polly/Mary Kidd of Dinwiddie County, Virginia.

1860 – he *may* be the **John Kidd** found on the 1860 federal census in the Western District of Campbell County, Castle Craig post office, page 433, household 21/21:
John Kidd 55MW Laborer $800/$200 VA
Mary J. "   49WF   b.VA
(no others) (John's occupation doesn't match the earlier records, and their ages don't match the ones in the 1858 marriage record, but their names are identical.)

1862 – On February 12, 1862, **Jno. Kidd**, a widower age 51, born in Dinwiddie County to Benjamin and Polly Kidd, married Mary Frances Eads, widow age 21, born in Albemarle County to George & Elizabeth Eads, in Lynchburg. Jno.'s occupation is listed as "tobacconist." The marriage was performed by W. H. Kinckle.[315]

On November 12, 1862 in Lynchburg, **John Kidd**, age 31 (probably a clerical error, and actually 51, based upon the record above), a tobacconist and widower **born in Dinwiddie County to Benjamin and Polly Kidd**, married Mary F. Flowers, age 35, a widow born in

---

[313] FHL film #31107, item 1, Chancery Court Order Book 1, 1832-1852, pp. 42-43, reviewed and copied by WRK, February 2010. Scanned images of this record in the Dinwiddie Misc Records folder on Dropbox. The Commonwealth Literary Fund was established in 1810 to fund public education in Virginia and was and is funded by court fees, fines, and sale of unclaimed property, including unclaimed lottery winnings today.

[314] Lynchburg, Virginia Marriages, 1853-1887, p. 80, line 15, retrieved from FHL #2048488, item 3, image 406. Scanned image available upon request.

[315] Lynchburg, Virginia Marriage Register vol. 2, 1853-1881, found on FHL #32268, item 1, image 25. Image available upon request.

Campbell County to William and Patty Woolridge. The ceremony was performed by H. W. Dodge.[316]

This is the last known record found for this John Kidd that we're aware of. We do not know what became of him, or whether he had any surviving children.

JOHN B. KIDD – the son of James5a (George 4, Benjamin3, William2, Thomas1) Kidd
[A John B. Kidd descendant is a close Y-DNA match to both Reiley Kidd and William R. Kidd, two of the authors of this paper, and other descendants of George4 Kidd, sharing a distinctive Y-DNA marker.]
Born 26 February 1794[317] in Dinwiddie County, VA,[318] Warren County, NC,[319] or in Mecklenburg County, VA
Married Elizabeth M. "Betsy" Rainey in 1819 in Mecklenburg County, VA
Lived in Mecklenburg County, VA his entire adult life.
Died September 1862 in Mecklenburg County, VA.[320]

Although John B. Kidd spent most of his life in Mecklenburg County, VA, we have strong reason to believe that he is related to the Amelia County Kidds for these reasons:
1. a John B. Kidd descendent is a close Y-DNA match to Reiley Kidd and William R. Kidd, authors of this paper, and other descendants of George4 Kidd, sharing a distinctive Y-DNA marker.
2. a Copy Book belonging to John B. Kidd, containing birth and death dates of the family, includes dates of death for James Kidd's wife Elizabeth Beasley.[321]
3. a James Kidd appeared in Mecklenburg County, VA shortly before John B. Kidd did, and later sold land to John B. Kidd; and
4. John B. Kidd served as bondsman for the 1825 Mecklenburg County, VA marriage of one of this James Kidd's daughters Elizabeth Ann Kidd.[322]

(See James5a Kidd's section in this compilation for more details.)

1800 – James Kidd is listed on the 1800 Census in Warren County, North Carolina,[323] with his wife (Elizabeth) age 26-44, and one male child, less than 10 years old. This would be their son **John B. Kidd.**

---

[316] Lynchburg, Virginia Marriage Register vol. 2, 1853-1881, found on FHL #32268, item 1, image 27. Image available upon request.

[317] Transcript of John B. Kidd's Copy Book, Library of Virginia, Archives & Manuscripts Room, Manuscript call # 25295a, 1 leaf.

[318] His father MAY be the James Kidd that witnessed the marriage of Usle Kidd to John Brewer in Dinwiddie County, VA in 1794. This Usley would have been our James Kidd's sister.

[319] Although all his census entries list his place of birth as Virginia, his father was in Warren County, NC until after 1800, and it is most likely that he was born there, and not Mecklenburg County, VA.

[320] John B. Kidd Copy Book (see above).

[321] See earlier footnotes (above) pertaining to this Copy Book, evidently transcribed out of the family Bible. A transcript of this record is in Appendix Three of this compilation.

[322] On 20 July 1825, Elizabeth Ann Kidd (James Kidd's daughter) and Riddick Temple obtained a marriage bond in Mecklenburg County, VA. John B. Kidd was the surety for this bond, and consent was given by James L. Kidd.

[323] 1800 federal census, Halifax, Warren County, NC, p. 814: Kidd, James 10001-00010; no slaves. No other Kidd household heads there. This James Kidd is 45 or over in age, with a son 0-9, and a wife 26-44.

1810 – I have not found John B. Kidd or his parents on this census, but numerous other records around this time show that James and Elizabeth Kidd were still residents of Warren County until 1816.

1818 – On 16 February 1818, a marriage bond for the marriage of **John B. Kidd** and Betsy M. Rainey was obtained in **Mecklenburg County, Virginia**. [324] William Rainey was bondsman, and Williamson Rainey, [325] father of the bride, gave his consent because she was still a minor. John B. and Betsy were married on 19 February 1818.[326]

1820 – There is only one household in Mecklenburg County, VA with the surname of Kidd, that of James Kidd, on page 157A:
James Kidd: **1WM 16-25** and 1>44; 2F<10, 1 10-15, 1 16-25 & 1>44. Three slaves.
It appears that **John B. Kidd** and his young family are living with his father and mother.

1821 – On the evening of 17 June 1821, John B. Kidd's mother Elizabeth died.[327] The fact that **John B. Kidd** recorded the time as well as the date of his mother's death suggests that he was in her household when she died, and this is supported by the fact that he has yet to appear on his own on the Mecklenburg County PPTLs.

1823-1828 – **John B. Kidd** appears for the first time on the Mecklenburg County, VA Personal Property Tax Lists in 1823, with 2 slaves over 12, and 4 horses.[328] No other Kidds are listed on this PPTL.
Previously James Kidd was the only Kidd on this list, with 2 white male tithes (himself and son John B., presumably). In 1823, James drops from this list. (See James5a Kidd in this compilation for more information.)
Subsequently, **John B. Kidd** appears on the Mecklenburg County PPTLs as follows:
1824 - 2 slaves over 12, 2 horses. No other Kidds.
1825 - 3 slaves over 12, 4 horses. No other Kidds.
1826 - not on this list; the only Kidd is James Kidd, with 1 slave and 4 horses.
    John B. may be in this household.
1827 - 3 slaves over 12, 2 horses. No other Kidds.
1828 - 3 slaves over 12, 2 horses. No other Kidds.

1825 – On 20 July 1825, **John B. Kidd** was surety for the marriage bond for his sister Elizabeth Ann Kidd and Riddick/Roderick Temple's marriage. Consent was given by James L. Kidd, father of Elizabeth.[329] Roderick Temple is identified as Kidd's brother-in-law in an 1827 deed (see below).

---

[324] FHL #1870770, Mecklenburg County, VA Marriage Bonds F-P, 1800-1820, images 438 (bond) and 439 (consent), retrieved online via Familysearch.org. Digital images available from the author, or on Ancestry.com (author's family tree).

[325] Wayne Rainey, a Rainey researcher, has provided information on Elizabeth and has information on her ancestors. His email address is hwrainey@yahoo.com. He writes (Sept. 2006): "Elizabeth Rainey, daughter of Williamson Rainey who was brother of my 3rd great grandfather and a American Revolutionary War veteran. His land was just sold and we are trying to make sure nothing happens to the graveyard."

[326] The date of their marriage comes from John B.'s Copy Book.

[327] Recorded in John B.'s Copy Book.

[328] Mecklenburg County, VA Personal Property Tax Lists, 1806-1828, US/CAN Film 1854099, for Paula Kidd by Nancy G. Heuser, professional researcher. No other Kidds besides James and John B. on these lists, according to Nancy.

[329] FHL #1870779, Mecklenburg County, Virginia Marriage Bonds, 1841-1844, images 669-670, obtained online via familysearch.org by Reiley Kidd on Jan 19, 2017. Digital images available from author or on Ancestry.com.

1827 – On _ January 1827, Samuel Jones of Rutherford County, TN and Mary Jones his wife "who holds a life estate in the land" sold **John Kidd** a tract of 50 acres in Mecklenburg County, VA adjacent to William Jones and others for $50.
Both Samuel and Mary Jones signed by marks.[330]
This deed was recorded 20 August 1827.

On 3 March 1827 James Kidd of Mecklenburg County sold to (his son) **John B. Kidd** of Mecklenburg County for $500 a tract of 500 acres adjoining lands of Presly Hinton, James Carrol, Charles Jones, and estates of John Martain and William Jones. The deed was recorded in court the same day.[331]

On 25 August 1827, **John B. Kidd** and Betsy M. his wife of Mecklenburg County sold to Roderick Temple of Brunswick County "for and in consideration of the love and affection for our brother-in-law and for $1" a tract of land containing 198 ½ acres on Charles Jones' line, a sweet gum on Great Creek, along Jones' line to Hunter's pond, etc. James Kidd and Sally Griffith were witnesses.
Signed and sealed by **John B. Kidd**; Betsy M. Kidd signed with a mark.
On March 30 1833, the justices certified that John B. personally acknowledged the deed, and that Betsy M. Kidd relinquished her dower rights.[332]

1828-1830 – **John B. Kidd** first appears on the Mecklenburg County, VA Land Tax Lists in 1828, assessed for 500 acres on the east and west sides of Great Creek, deeded to him by James Kidd;
He was also taxed on 50 acres on Great Creek, land deeded to him by Mary Jones (or James).
Entries on the 1829 and 1830 LTLs were identical to that of 1828.[333]

1830 – John B. Kidd is found on the 1830 federal census in Mecklenburg County, VA; he's listed as **"John D. Kidd**," with one WM<5, 3 5-9, & 1 30-39; 1F 5-9, 1 10-14 & 1 30-39 and 1 60-69. Ten slaves. [334]
The identity of the older white woman is unclear. His mother & Betsy's mother both died in 1821.

1833 – On 30 August 1833, **John B. Kidd** and Elizabeth M his wife sold to Elizabeth Wall for $110 a tract of land containing 50 acres adjoining Barker, Z. Jones, and Robin Thomas. This deed was recorded the same date.[335]

1834 – In a deed dated 8 Dec 1834, Thomas Palmer of Northampton County, NC sold to **John B. Kidd** of Mecklenburg County for $852.50 a tract of land containing 310 acres and adjoining

---

[330] Mecklenburg County, VA Deed Book 22, p. 488.

[331] Mecklenburg County Deed Book 22, pages 342-343, found in FHL #32542, Mecklenburg County, VA Deed Books 22-23 (1825-1829), image 197, retrieved via familysearch.org. Images available from the author.

[332] Mecklenburg County, VA Deed Book 25, page 369.

[333] Mecklenburg County, VA Land Taxes, 1815-1830, researched for Paula Kidd by Nancy G. Heuser, professional researcher. No other Kidds besides James and John B. on these lists, according to Nancy.

[334] 1830 federal census, Mecklenburg County, VA, p. 58:
William Rainey 0010001-110001 (older male 40-49; older female 30-39)
John D. Kidd 130001-011001001 (older male and female both 30-39; elderly female 60-69

[335] FHL #32544, Mecklenburg County, VA DB 26, pages 10-11(image 11), retrieved online via familysearch.org.

John Griffin(?), Willis Kennon, Robert Kennon, Harris, Fowler and Puckett. Deed recorded 19 January 1835.[336]

1840 – **John B. Kidd** was the only Kidd household head on the federal census in Mecklenburg County, VA, , East District, p. 411:[337]
John B. Kidd: 2M <4, 1M 5-9, 1M 10-14, 2M 15-19, 1M 40-49, 1 60-69; 3F 5-9, 2F 15-19, and 1 30-39; eleven slaves; 25 total, with 11 in agriculture.
There is an older man in his household ; this man is 60-69 in 1840, and thus was born between 1770 and 1780. This is evidently John B.'s father, James, who died less than two years later, while living with John B. and his family.

1841 – On 12 January 1841, James M. Harwell, Commissioner, of Mecklenburg County sold to **John B. Kidd** of the same place for the sum of $1400 "or its equivalent"…"all the right, title and interest vested in him by a decretal order of the County Court of Mecklenburg to a certain tract of land in Mecklenburg County and known as the estate of John and Luraney Griffis(?), dec'd, supposed to contain 140 acres…" This tract was adjacent to land already owned by John B. Kidd, among others. This deed was acknowledged in Court on 15 Mar 1841 and ordered to be recorded.[338]

1846 – The Mecklenburg County will of William Rainey, signed on 8 Jan 1846, bequeaths two slaves and other property to his daughter Elizabeth M. Kidd [wife of **John B. Kidd**].[339]

1850 – On the 1850 federal census in Mecklenburg County, VA, 98th Regiment, p. 59A, HH 167/167:
John B. Kidd 58M farmer $5245 VA
Betsy   "   45F VA
Bartlett "   22M laborer VA
James   "   21M   " VA
William "   10M   VA
Allen   "   8M VA
Dick   "   6M VA
Elizabeth " 18F VA
Arminta   " 15F VA
Mary   "   13F VA
He was the oldest Kidd in the county on this census.

---

[336] Magazine of Virginia Genealogy, vol. 37(1), p. 36, citing Mecklenburg County DB 26, p. 240. Image retrieved online, FHL #32544, Mecklenburg County, VA Deed Books 26-27 (1834-1838), via Familysearch.org. Image available from author.

[337] 1840 federal census, Mecklenburg County, VA, East District, p. 411A:
John B. Kidd 211200101-030201 (oldest males 40-49 and 60-69; oldest female 30-39)

[338] FHL #32545, Mecklenburg County, VA Deed Books 28-29 (1838-1842), retrieved via familysearch.org (unrestricted access), image 436.

[339] Mecklenburg County, VA Will Book 16, pp. 374-376. Retrieved via familysearch.org, FHL #32524, Mecklenburg County, VA Will Books 16-17 (1843-1853), images 218, 219. Images available from author.

1860 – On the 1860 federal census in Forksville, Mecklenburg County, VA, Roll 1362 Book 1, Page
236, HH 29/29:
John B. Kidd 67MW $15,000/8,000   (places of birth all blank on this page)
Elizabeth "   57FW
Allen   "   20M farm laborer
Mary Dugger 22F domestic
Armstead   5M

1862 – **John B. Kidd** wrote and signed his will in Mecklenburg County, Virginia on 12 June 1862.
His will was proved in Court on 16 September 1862, so he died in this interval. The exact
date of his death and the place of his burial are not known.
His probate documents, listing all his heirs, are available online at this URL:
http://files.usgwarchives.net/va/mecklenburg/wills/kiddj.txt
Moreover, there are numerous Mecklenburg County Chancery Court records pertaining to
his heirs, viewable online at the Library of Virginia's online records site, Virginia Memory.[340]

More information about John B. Kidd and his descendants can be found in our Mecklenburg
County, Virginia compilation, as well as on his page in our Middlesex County Kidds family tree on
Ancestry.com (see this URL: https://www.ancestry.com/family-
tree/person/tree/37652986/person/19120499431/facts

<u>LODOWICK[341] KIDD</u> – son of George4 (Benjamin3, William2, Thomas1) Kidd
(This is Reiley Kidd's line, through Lodowick's eldest son William.)
Born about 1765 in Amelia County, VA
The name of his first wife (the mother of his first seven children) is unknown.
Was taxed in, owned property in, and is found on censuses in Amelia or Dinwiddie
County, VA until 1822, when he moved to Fayette County, TN, taking all his children
but his eldest son, William Kidd, with him; none of the others were over twenty and
out on their own at this time.
Married second Lucy A. ___, most likely in Dinwiddie County, VA[342]; she was the
mother of at least seven and possibly nine children.
Moved to Tippah County, MS in 1848, reuniting there with sons William and George
Kidd, who had migrated there a short time earlier.
Died in Tippah County, MS in June 1856.

Evidence for Lodowick being son of George4 Kidd is indirect, but persuasive:
1. George Kidd Sr. moved to Amelia County in 1762 (along with one of his brothers), and
all Kidds found in Amelia and adjacent counties in the subsequent 80 years can be traced to
him. That is, no *other* Kidd line is identifiable in Amelia County at this time.
2. Lodowick's PPTL tax in 1787-1791 was paid by George Kidd Sr., when Lodowick was
still in George Sr.'s household. The only other Kidd listed in the county was George Kidd
Jr., Lodowick's older brother. (See below).

____

[340] Virginia Chancery Records Index, at http://www.virginiamemory.com/collections/chancery/ ; Once there, click on
"Search the Index," select Mecklenburg as the county, and type "Kidd" into the space for Surname #1.
[341] Lodowick's given name is spelled many different ways in records for him; we have preserved the variations as they
appear in each record, denoting them by enclosing them in quotes in each instance.
[342] Some of his children born before 1822 left records that their mother's name was Lucy.

3. Lodowick Kidd witnessed a 1792 land purchase by George Kidd Jr., suggesting a family relationship.

4. Y-DNA test results show a very close Y-DNA match between Reiley Kidd, a documented descendant of Lodowick Kidd, and other proven descendants of George4 Kidd, who share a distinctive Y-DNA marker.

1787 – The first record for **Lodowick Kidd** is the 1787 Amelia County Personal Property Tax List, when he's listed by name as an additional white male over the age of 21, living in the household of George Kid Sr., Ladwick, and George Kid Jr.

Person paying tax	WM>21 (including taxpayer)
George Kid Sr.	George Kid Sr., **Ladwick Kid**, and George Kid Jr.

Below is an image of this entry:[343]

> 2 George Kid Sr. | George Kid, Ladwick Kid | 1 | | 3 | 10
> George Kidd | George Kid | | | 1 | 2

1788-1791 – he again appears in his father's household in each of these years on the Amelia County, VA PPTLs, with identical listings each year:

Person paying tax	WM>21 (including taxpayer)
George Kid Sr.	George Kid, **Lod. Kidd**, Jas. Kidd
George Kid Jr.	George Kid

1792 – **Loddick (sic) Kidd** appears on the **Dinwiddie** County, VA PPTL for the first time in 1792, on the list of William Watts, taxed for one horse and no slaves. His brother, Benjamin5 Kidd also appears on the Dinwiddie County PPTLs (the only other Kidd to do so), but Benjamin was in the other district, that of Braddock Godwin.
[Benjamin was the first Kidd to appear in Dinwiddie County records, appearing on the 1791 Dinwiddie PPTL.]

And on 1 September 1792, Daniel Coleman and Francis his wife of Amelia County sold to George Kidd of the same place for the sum of £96.10 a tract of land in Amelia County containing 96½ acres and adjoining Robert Tanner, William Hale, Thomas V. Brookings, and Andrew Waugh.[344] **Lodowick Kidd** is listed as a witness to this deed, along with Jesse Coleman and Ebenezer Coleman.

1793-1800 – Lodowick Kidd **drops** from the Dinwiddie County PPTLs in 1793 (despite being listed on the Dinwiddie LTLs during this period) and does not reappear until 1801. See below.

1795-1822 – **Lodowick Kidd** appears for the first time on the Dinwiddie County LTLs, taxed on 152 acres in **Dinwiddie** County, VA on Bowen's Branch (a tributary of Namozine Creek), 12 miles NW of Courthouse, conveyed by the Robert King estate. This listing recurs annually through 1822. [345], [346]

---

[343] Amelia County, VA PPTLs, 1782-1813, retrieved via familysearch.org from FHL #2024454, image 157.

[344] Amelia County Deed Book 19, pp. 217-218, retrieved from FHL #30438, image 312 via Familysearch.org.

[345] *Land Records, Dinwiddie County, Virginia, 1752-1820*, p. 106.

[346] Dinwiddie County Land Tax Lists, 1782-1785, 1787-1804, retrieved from FHL #0029920 via familysearch.org (unrestricted access), image 226, where he appears on Daniel Pegram's 1795 list.

No other Kidd male is taxed for land in Dinwiddie County until 1814, when Benjamin Kidd (Lodowick's older brother) appears on these lists, taxed for 218 acres on White Oak Branch, 13 miles NW of the Courthouse, land he acquired from H.B. Duvall.

In 1817, Jasper Kidd (Lodowick's youngest brother) first appears in Dinwiddie County Land Tax lists; he's joined by James Kidd in 1818. (The latter is most likely James6b, Lodowick's nephew.)

1801-1802 – a "**Lauderick Kidd**" is in the household of John McRea on the Dinwiddie PPTLs.[347]

1803-1822 – **Lodowick Kidd** appears almost annually[348] on the Dinwiddie County PPTLs, with various spellings of his unusual name.[349] In 1813 and 1815, he's listed as "**Ladwick and son William.**"

1810 – On the federal census in Dinwiddie County, VA, p. 151:
Kidd, Lodwick 11001-2111-5 (one M 0-9, 1 10-15 & 1>45; 2 females 0-9, 1 10-5, 1 16-25 and 1 26-44.) (There were no other Kidd households in Dinwiddie County in 1810.)

1820 – On the federal census in Dinwiddie County, VA, p. 13:
Kid, Lodwick 210001-1231, 4 in Ag (Two M 09, one 10-15 and one over 45 years old; 1 female 0-9, two 10-15, 3 16-25 and 1 26-44); 6 slaves.

1822 –In 1822, **Lodowick Kidd** conveyed 62 acres of his land to his son William, and deeded the balance of 125 acres to Rice Eanes.[350] He thereafter does not appear in Virginia records. At the age of 58, he left his eldest son William in Virginia,[351] and moved the rest of his family to the area that would soon become Fayette County, Tennessee.[352] In doing so, he was one of the early pioneers to settle in West Tennessee. This part of the state was not officially open to settlement until after it was purchased from the Indians in the Chickasaw Cession of 1818. Fayette County was formed in 1824 out of Shelby County and Hardeman County. A Tennessee State census taken in 1826 listed only 265 free male inhabitants in Fayette County.[353]

---

[347] "Dinwiddie County, Virginia Data 1752-1865" compiled and indexed by Thomas P Hughes, under probable kinships from personal property tax rolls 1782-1820 (page 97) Lauderick Kidd 1801-1802 in the household of McRea, John PRS. In this case, Lodawick is there not as a relative (unless he's married a McRae girl), but as a hired worker, for whom the landowner is paying the poll tax.

[348] No Personal Property Tax was collected in 1808, so no PPTL exists for that year. The only years Lodawick doesn't appear on the annual PPTLs are 1819 and 1820, which is peculiar, since he DOES appear in Dinwiddie County on the 1820 census. It isn't too unusual for the tax assessor to miss individuals from year to year, but usually they were individuals with no personal property to tax. However, Lodawick typically had 2-3 slaves and a similar number of horses each year. In 1815, the only year in this decade where they recorded the number of cattle, Lodawick had 9 cattle, more than most of the individuals on the list.

[349] Spellings include Lodowick, Ladowick, Ladwick, Laudwick, Lodwick and Loddick, in the course of these 19 years.

[350] Dinwiddie County, VA Land Tax Lists, 1805-1823, FHL microfilm #0029921, image 461 of 490: In 1823, Lodowick Kidd drops from the Dinwiddie LTLs, and the 1823 entry for Rice Eanes (image 461 on this reel)shows that he received 125 acres from Lodowick Kidd in the prior 12 months. No actual deeds from this era are extant, so the exact date on which Lodowick sold the land is unknown.

[351] William was by this time married and had young children; he evidently decided to stay behind).

[352] Lodowick was selected for jury duty on 7 December 1824 (Fayette County Court Minutes). This corresponds with Goodspeed's History of Tennessee (1888), page 808, which says that Lodowick Kidd settled in Fayette Co. in 1824.

[353] Beginnings of West Tennessee. Samuel Cole Williams.

1824-1828 – **Lodowick Kidd** was a resident of Fayette County by 7 December 1824, when he was selected for jury duty, according to Court minutes.[354] He continued to be selected as a juror there through at least 1828.

1830-1849 – Lodawick left numerous records in Fayette County in this period, including state and federal census records, road orders, tax lists, and land deeds.[355]

1849 – On December 1, 1849, **"Lodderwick" Kidd** sold 170 acres on the Wolf River in Fayette Co., TN for $1105 to William P. Butterworth.[356] This deed was witnessed by Jesse Butterworth, Henry L. Kidd (Lodowick's eldest son by his second marriage) and E. L. Allen.
Lodowick then left Fayette County, Tennessee and moved to Tippah County, Mississippi (which adjoins Fayette County, TN to the south). On 13 December 1849, Lodwick Kidd bought W 1/2 SE 1/4 of Section 16, R2T2E, for $27,[357] and the NE 1/4 of Section 21 (the Section on the southern border of Section 16), R2T2E, "North of the Wolf River", for $500.[358] Here he rejoined his son William, who brought his family west from Dinwiddie County, Virginia and had bought the adjoining land in 1848, one year earlier.[359]

1850 – Lodowick appears on the 1850 Tippah County MS census (**"Ludwick Kidd"**)[360] next door to Belotes on one side, and to George Kidd and William Kidd on the other.

1856 – Lodowick also appears on an 1856 Tippah County Tax List,[361] along with Henry Kidd.

Lodowick Kidd died testate in Tippah County, Mississippi in June of 1856, leaving behind a large family. Unfortunately, his will was among the records lost when Union troops burned the Tippah County Courthouse on 9 June 1864. However, some records related to his estate survived, including the final account of his estate's administration and the distribution of shares of his estate to his heirs.

An extensive write-up on Lodowick and his descendants is available from Reiley Kidd, one of the authors of this compilation. See also Lodowick's page on our Kidd family tree on Ancestry:
https://www.ancestry.com/family-tree/person/tree/37652986/person/19120498774/facts

---

[354] Fayette Co., TN Court Minute Book A, January 1836 – March 1840, p. 88, on FHL microfilm reel 1003137, image 794. Image available upon request from author

[355] A biography of Lodowick Kidd, including these records and much more, is available from Reiley Kidd, one of the authors of this compilation.

[356] "1 December 1849, Lodderwick Kidd for...$1105...paid by Wm. P. Butterworth...sold 170 acres lying in Fayette County on the waters of the Wolf River in the 10th surveyor's district, range 6 and section   1....being part of a tract bought by said Lodwick Kidd of Samuel Pickens" (Fayette Co. Deed Book P, page 22).

[357] Thomas and Mary Medlock deeded to "Lodderwick Kid" (Tippah County Deed Book I, page 403).

[358] John and Elizabeth M. Clark deeded to "Lodderwick Kidd" (Deed Book J, page 6).

[359] William had bought the SE 1/4 of Section 16 on 4 December 1848 from Thomas Medlock, for $200 (Deed Book H, page 377). And William's son, William George Kidd, obtained a land patent on 320 acres (N1/2 of Section 16) two days later from the Land Office at Pontotoc, Mississippi, for $40.05. He promptly sold the E 1/4 of NE 1/4 S16 to Thos. Medlock for $10 (Deed Book H, page 550).

[360] 3rd Division, page 562, 1000/1000, on 15 Nov 1850: Kidd, Ludwick 85M VA $500, CROW; Lucy 55F VA, Robert 33M VA, Sobrina 29F VA, Lucy 27F VA, Henry 24M TN, Samantha 22F TN, James 20M TN, Louisa 17F TN, Matilda 15F TN, Sylvester BELOTE 17M TN, Ludwick Kidd 9M TN, William Kidd 6M TN.

[361] Listed as "Ludwick Kidd," Hamilton's district, near Canaan, MS.

MARTHA (KIDD) YOUNG, the daughter of George5a Kidd, per his 1844 will
>**Born 17 November 1792**
>**married Elliott Young in 1816, Amelia County, VA**
>**Left Amelia County with her family and that of her brother, James6b Kidd in 1828 (see below)**

1816 – On 26 January 1816, **Martha Kidd** married Elliott Young in Amelia County, VA. **George Kidd** (this is George5a Kidd, son of George Sr.) was listed as father of the bride.[362]

1818 – In a deed signed 18 February 1818, George Kidd Senr. and Mary his wife sold for $800 to Elliott Young (their son-in-law who married their daughter **Martha**) a parcel of land containing 130 acres adjoining David Adams, Burwell Coleman, George Kidd, Herod T. Crowder, Jack Bevill and David Allen.[363]

1827 – In a deed signed 8 October 1827, **Elliott Young and Martha his wife**, and George Kidd and Robert Bevill & Frances his wife, all of Amelia County, for $800 sold to Elizabeth C. Tarborne 150 acres adjoining the lands of Wm. Scott, Bevill, **George Kidd**, Herod T. Crowder, Joel Bevill, the estate of Allen, Daniel Allen and Wm. B. Scott.

1828 – Following the sale of the land above, she and her husband, Elliott Young moved west, along with her brother James6b Kidd and his family. The Youngs stopped in Montgomery County, TN, while James Kidd and his family continued to Green County, KY.[364]

1844 – Martha is named (as Martha Young) in her father, George5a Kidd's will, which he signed on 19 November 1844 in Amelia County. See his section of this compilation for details.

MARTHA (TWEATT) KIDD, wife of Thomas J. Kidd[365] See his section of this compilation.

MARTHA (YOUNG) KIDD, wife of William R. Kidd

1844 – William R. Kidd married **Martha D. Young** on January 31, 1844 in Dinwiddie County, VA.[366] Martha died in June 1859 (see below).

1859 – **Martha Kidd**, wife of William R. Kidd, died in June 1859. She's listed on the 1860 mortality schedule for Amelia County, VA, which lists her age as 34. She died suddenly of a "disease of the heart."[367]

MARY (POLLY) KIDD, the wife of Benjamin5 Kidd. Maiden name unknown.

1822-1832 – **Mary Kidd** first appears on the Dinwiddie County PPTLs, "in place of Benjamin Kidd" and was his widow. She was taxed on 2 horses and a carriage, but owned no slaves.

---

[362] *Amelia County, Virginia Marriage Bonds, Consents, and Ministers' Returns, 1816-1852*, by T.P. Hughes.
[363] Amelia County DB 25, pp. 58-59 (scanned images available).
[364] Personal correspondence from Margaret Winders, a descendant of this family, 1982.
[365] The 1879 marriage record of their son, Stith J. Kidd names his parents as T. J. Kidd and Martha Thweat. The death record of Thomas J.'s eldest son, James Kidd, lists his mother's name as Jane Gent. We conclude that Martha was Thomas J. Kidd's second wife, and that they married sometime after the death of Jane Gent Kidd.
[366] *Some Marriages in the Burned Record Counties of Virginia.* Many Dinwiddie County marriages were recorded in Dinwiddie County Deed Books, including this one. It was retrieved from Dinwiddie County Deed Book 5, p. 390 from FHL #31094, image 551 (restricted access)
[367] Amelia County, VA 1860 Mortality Schedule at Ancestry.com, p. 40.

She continued to appear annually on these PPTLs through 1832.[368] Not found thereafter.
See Appendix Four for more details.

Mary Kidd also appears for the first time on the Dinwiddie County, VA Land Tax Lists in
1822, with the notation, "by way of Benjamin Kidd." A **Mary Kidd** continues to appear
annually through 1843, but disappears in 1844. This land was on White Oak Creek, 13 miles
NW of the courthouse.

1830 – On the VA census in Dinwiddie County (none in Amelia), along with Jasper, Mary, Thomas
J and William Kidd.[369]
Kidd, Jasper – 0200001-0020001 (oldest M & F both 40-49)
Kidd, Mary – 00111- 0020101 (males 10-14, 15-19 & 20-29; oldest F 40-49)
   This is Mary Kidd, widow of Benjamin.
Kidd, James – 001001-0001, 1F slave>55 (James 30-39; the only is female 15-19)
Kidd, William – 310001-00001, 1M & 1F slave 10-24 (oldest M 30-39; female 20-29)
Kidd, Thomas J. – 0010001- 000102, no slaves (oldest M 40-49; 2F 30-39).

1833, ff. – not found on Dinwiddie County, VA Personal Property Tax Lists.

1834 – in the April 1834 session of the Dinwiddie County, VA Chancery Court, there is a suit
wherein the Commonwealth of Virginia (for the benefit of the Literary Fund) sues Beverly
Anderson, John Kidd and **Mary Kidd**. According to this entry, John Kidd and Mary Kidd
were no longer inhabitants of the Commonwealth. Mary Kidd was ordered to pay $200 to
the Commonwealth, for the benefit of the literary fund, plus the costs of the suit. And the
defendant Anderson was to pay "so much as shall not exceed the $220 in his hands" to
satisfy this obligation, which he did.
I can't tell from the entry whether he paid the debt for Mary Kidd, or he was equally
indebted, and paid his own debt. No mention is made of John Kidd in the settlement.[370]
(See 1843, below.)

1840 – Mary Kidd is NOT found on the 1840 Dinwiddie, Amelia or Nottoway County census. But
a **Mary Kidd** DID continue to appear in the annual **Dinwiddie** County, VA **Land** Tax Lists
from 1822 through 1843, and not thereafter. She was taxed on 211 acres on White Oak
Branch, 13 miles NW of the courthouse, and her tax was "Life" rather than "Fee." This
means that she had a life estate in the property, to be sold or otherwise transferred upon her
death.

1843 – on 14 July 1843, a deed between Alexander Donnan, commissioner, and William Lewis was
created. A judgment against **Mary Kidd** had been rendered by the Dinwiddie Court of
Commissioners in the April 1843 term, in the case of Tucker vs. Kidd, evidently over a debt

---

[368] The Dinwiddie PPTL made by Louis P. Lanier in 1831 is not on the microfilm for PPTLs, BUT is on the Dinwiddie
County, VA Land Tax Lists, 1824-1835, FHL microfilm #0029922 microfilm reel, along with Lanier's 1831 Land
Tax List. Mary was taxed 12¢ for two horses.
[369] 1830 federal census, Dinwiddie County, VA. All but Thomas J. and William are on p. 390. William is on p. 392 and
Thomas J. is on p. 410.
[370] FHL film #31107, item 1, DCVA Chancery Court Order Book 1, 1832-1852, pp. 42-43, reviewed and copied by
WRK, February 2010. Scanned images of this record in the Dinwiddie Misc Records folder on Dropbox. The
Commonwealth Literary Fund was established in 1810 to fund public education in Virginia and was and is funded by
court fees, fines, and sale of unclaimed property, including unclaimed lottery winnings today.

owed by Mary (also referred to as **Polly** in this record) to Tucker; the Court decided in Tucker's favor. Donnan was appointed special commissioner to sell the 211 acres on White Oak Creek in Dinwiddie which was listed **as the same land Benjamin Kidd, deceased** seized and possessed, and which at this time stands charged in the name of **Polly or Mary Kidd** in the Commissioner of Revenues book in Dinwiddie County.[371]

This Mary/Polly is the widow of Benjamin Kidd. And the John Kidd mentioned in the 1834 record above likely was her son, living with her after husband Benjamin Kidd's death.

<u>MARY C. (KIDD) CLARK(E) HARRISON</u>, the daughter of Thomas J. Kidd and his first wife Jane Gent[372]
Born abt 1818, in Dinwiddie County, Virginia[373]
Died sometime after the 1870 federal census.

1835 – On 8 June 1835 in Dinwiddie County, VA, Samuel H. Clarke married **Mary C. Kidd**. Recorded 18 May 1840.[374] This record is a list of marriages performed by Rev. Russell B. Foster in Dinwiddie County in the year 1835. It is not clear why this list is being recorded 5 years later, but this Deed Book contains several such lists of marriages.

1838 – On 21 December 1838, Thomas J. Kidd of Dinwiddie County executed a deed of trust to P. W. Harper, for and in consideration of the natural love and affection that I bear toward P. W. Harper, as well as for the further consideration of $1 to me paid by the said Harper, …I do give and grant unto the said P. W. Harper …two feather beds and two bedsteads and clothing, one walnut table and one dressing ditto (sic), six rush bottom chairs, one loom and one spinning wheel, one pine chest, one hair trunk, and one pine cupboard, earthen ware and kitchen furniture, consisting of cups and saucers, dishes and plates, one iron pot, oven and lid, and one frying pan; To have and to hold for the special benefit of **my daughter, Mary C. Clark**, and the heir or heirs of her body …"

He signed the deed, and was able to write. On March 25 1839, he acknowledged the deed as his act and intention in Dinwiddie County Court, and it was admitted to record. [375]

1842 – **Mary C. Clarke** married Trent E. Harrison in Dinwiddie County, VA on 16 November 1842. As with her first marriage, Rev. Russell B. Foster performed the ceremony.[376]

---

[371] Dinwiddie County, VA DB 4, pp. 67-68, copied by WRK 6/29/09; scanned iages in the Dinwiddie County Deeds folder on Dropbox.

[372] This is conjectural, as we don't know the date of either of Thomas J. Kidd's marriages. We know that Jane Gent was the mother of Thomas's first child, James7 Kidd, born abt 1816. And we know that Thomas J's next known child (after Mary C.) was Stith J. Kidd, born abt. 1825, AND that Stith's mother was Thomas J.'s second wife, Martha Thweat, as his 1879 marriage record names his parents as T. J. Kidd and Martha Thweat. It seems more likely that, if Mary C. was born abt 1818, her mother was more likely Thomas J.'s first wife, given the gap between her birth and that of Stith J. Kidd.

[373] This estimated year of birth is based on her age at the time of the federal censuses: 35 in 1850; 39 in 1860; and 52 in 1870. Her first marriage was in 1835, and this would be more consistent with her birth before 1820.

[374] Dinwiddie County, VA. DB 2, page 517. From a list of marriages by Russel B. Foster. Deed book located at Dinwiddie County Courthouse. A scanned image of this record is in the Dinwiddie County Shared Folder on Dropbox.

[375] Dinwiddie County DB 2, p. 243.

[376] *Virginia Marriages, 1740-1850*, on Ancestry.com. This marriage was recorded in Dinwiddie County Deed Book 3, p. 609 (scanned image available).

1850 – On the federal census in the Northern District of Dinwiddie County, page 462, HH 431:
>   **Trent E. Harrison** 49MW farmer $0 Real Estate b.VA
>   **Mary C.** " 35FW b. VA
>   (no others)

1860 – On the federal census in District No. 1, Dinwiddie County, VA, page4, HH 23:
>   **Trent E. Harrison 59MW farmer $1,500 Real Estate/$573 personal estate b. VA**
>   **Mary C.** " ,   39FW b. VA
>   Martha F. Kidd   8FW b. VA (this is Martha, the orphan daughter of Mary's brother, Stanfield Kidd)
>   Next door is George Whitmore, a very wealthy farmer and nurseryman.

1870 – On the federal census in Dinwiddie County iin Darville township, 1st Revenue District, Dinwiddie C.H. P. O., page 483, HH 915/945:
>   **T. E. Harrison 69MW farmer $576/$330 b. VA**
>   **Mary C.** "   52FW keeping house b. VA
>   (and several others)

Mary's second husband, Trent E. Harrison played an important role for this branch of the Kidd family.

Mary's father Thomas J. Kidd, deeded 20 acres to him in 1851.

A year later, Thomas J. Kidd lost his land to foreclosure, and Trent Harrison was the highest bidder, regaining possession of that land for the family.

In March of 1857, he served as the informant for the Dinwiddie County death record of Jemima (Kidd) Whitmore, his wife's aunt and the daughter of Benjamin5 Kidd. In this record, his relationship is recorded as "friend."

In 1871, after the wife of James6a Kidd's died, James deeded all his real and personal estate to his brother-in-law Trent Harrison; he likely did so to assure that someone would take care of him in his final illness and death.

On 21 September 1874, T. E. Harrison presented to the Dinwiddie Court "satisfactory evidence to the (illegible) that Jas. Kidd is entitled to a certain (illegible) of pension, and that he died in the county of Dinwiddie on the 10th day of April 1874, leaving no widow or minor child, & without sufficient assets to defray the expenses of his last sickness and burial, and that the same was paid by Mr. Harrison."[377]

We have not found any subsequent records for Mary C. or Trent Harrison, and have no idea what became of them.

MATILDA (WELLS) KIDD – the presumed daughter of Harrison Wells Sr., and the wife of William Kidd of Chesterfield County
>   **Born abt. 1807, likely in Dinwiddie County, VA**
>   **Married William Kidd in Dinwiddie County, VA abt 1834**
>   **Died May 1876 in Chesterfield County, VA**

1810 – A **Harrison Wells** appears on the federal census in Dinwiddie County, on page 168:
>   Harrison Wells: 1WM 10-15, 1 16-25 & 1 >44; 2F<10, 2 10-15 & 1>44. No slaves.

---

[377] Dinwiddie County Order Book, 1873-1881, pages 81-82, retrieved by WRK at LoV, reel 171, in August 2011; digital images available upon request.

This man appears to be her father (and the father of Harrison Wells Jr., below); their birth years are consistent with the children in this household.

1817 – On 6 October 1817, **Harrison Wells** and Patsy his wife of Dinwiddie County, VA sold to George Crowder of the same place for $200 a tract of land in Dinwiddie County containing by estimation 35 acres more or less, adjoining Green, Drury Crowder, and others. This deed was witnessed by E. Worsham, Francis Wells and Jarrel (X) Scott (his mark). **Harrison Wells** signed with an X, as well.

This deed was not recorded until 21 January 1839.[378]

[A courthouse fire in 1832 destroyed nearly all their records to that point. We know of this deed only because it was not proved in court and recorded until 1839. We include it here as evidence that Harrison Wells was a landowner in Dinwiddie County by 1817.]

1820 – **Harrison Wells** is on the federal census again in Dinwiddie County, with 1WM>44, 2F 10-15, 1 16-25 and 1>44. Eight slaves.

1824-1831 – **Harrison Wells** is found annually on the Dinwiddie County LTLS (we have not searched the LTLs prior to 1824, but suspect that he's listed there as well), taxed each year on several parcels of land "near Cox Rd, 12 miles NW of the Courthouse. In 1832, he drops from these tax lists, and does not reappear.[379] See 1832, below.

1830 – **Harrison Wells** is again listed on the federal census in Dinwiddie County, with 1WM 15-19 & 1 50-59; 1F 20-29 (we think that this is Matilda) & 1 50-59.

Nearby on this census are households headed by James Kidd, Mary Kidd and Jasper Kidd.

1832-1834 – In 1832, **Matilda W. Wells** appears on the Dinwiddie County LTLs for the first time, taxed on 60 acres on Cox Rd, 13 miles NW CH. **A notation in the margin reads, "Deed from Harrison Wells."**[380]

She appears again on the Dinwiddie LTLs in 1833 and 1834, taxed on the same land. See next entry.

We suspect, but cannot be certain, that Harrison Wells Sr. died in this era.

1835-1850 – a "**William Kidd and wife**" appear on the Dinwiddie County, Land Tax List for the first time in 1835, taxed on 60 acres on Cox Rd., 13 miles NW of the Courthouse, and an added notation says "heretofore charged to Matilda W. Wells."

These entries strongly suggest that **Matilda W. Wells** was the daughter of Harrison Wells Sr., and that she married this William Kidd ca 1834-35.

They continue to be taxed on this land annually through 1857, the last year we've checked.

1850 – on federal census in Lower district of **Chesterfield** County, VA, p. 134, HH 338 (mis-indexed at Ancestry.com as "Ridd"):

Kidd, William 47MW "operator" VA cannot read or write

 " , **Matilda** 43FW VA cannot read or write

 " , Edward 18MW operator VA

---

[378] Dinwiddie County, VA Deed Book 2, pages 196-197, retrieved via familysearch.org from FHL #31093, image 107.

[379] Dinwiddie County Land Tax Lists, 1824-1835, retrieved from FHL #29222 via familysearch.org (unrestricted access), as follows: 1824 - image 16; 1825 - image 86; 1826 - image 175, 1827 – image 187; 1828 - image 320; 1829 – image 375; 1830 – image 386; 1831 – 479.

[380] Dinwiddie County Land Tax Lists, 1824-1835, examined on FHL #29922 via familysearch.org (unrestricted access), image 583.

" , James 15MW operator VA
" , Thomas 12MW VA
" , Ann E. 10FW VA (is this Sarah? We believe that she is)
HH 339
Wells, Harrison 37MW Machinist VA cannot read or write
" , Ann 35FW VA cannot read or write
" , Henry 14MW VA
" , Susan 12FW VA
" Lucy 11FW VA
We believe that this is Matilda's brother.

1853 – on Nov 1853, **Edward Kidd** sold to Robert H. Sydnor for $75 all his interest in a tract of
land (now in the possession of said Kidd's father and mother until their death) in Dinwiddie
County containing 60 acres bounded on the south and east by the land of Robert H. Sydnor,
west by the land of Upton Crow, and north by the land of Richard P. Pike.[381]

1855 – On 18 January 1855, a James Kidd sold all of his right in a certain parcel of land in
Dinwiddie County containing 60 acres "in the possession of **Mrs. Matilda Kidd** her life"
(estate?) to Robert H. Sydnor for $75. The land was bounded on the north by R. H. Sydnor,
on the west by Upton Crow, on the south by Cox Road and on the east by R. H. Sydnor.
This James Kidd appeared before a justice in Petersburg to acknowledge the deed. It was
admitted to record in Dinwiddie County Court on 19 November 1855.[382]
This is Matilda's son, James selling his interest in land that belonged to his mother.

This James died on Sept. 23, 1855 in Chesterfield County at the age of 20. This record
names his parents as William and **Matilda Kidd**, and his birthplace as Dinwiddie County.
The cause of his death was not known.[383]

1860 – on federal census in "Mattoaca Factory, southern district," **Chesterfield** County, VA, p. 60,
HH 432/442:
Kidd, William 45MW works in factory $300/30 VA cannot read or write
" , **Matilda** 40FW domestic VA cannot read or write
" , Sarah A. 16FW weaver VA
(no others, but nearby are several Traylor families.)

The Mattoaca Cotton Factory began operation in 1834 and the small village of Mattoaca
developed adjacent to the factory. In time it became a cotton mill. The mill ceased
operations about 1922.

1863 – In a Dinwiddie County, VA deed dated 20 October 1863, Sarah Ann Kidd of Chesterfield
County, VA sells to Robert Sydnor of Dinwiddie County for $75 "all her right, title and
interest to a certain parcel or tract of land on Cox Rd." in Dinwiddie, "left by the late
Harrison Wells to **William Kidd and wife**, during their natural life."[384] It seems from this

---

[381] Dinwiddie Court House, deed book 8, pages 17-18, viewed by WRK 14 Jan 2010, copies on file. Retrieved from
FHL #31096, images 14-15.
[382] Dinwiddie County, VA. DB 8, pages 395-396, retrieved from FHL #31096, images 224 & 225. Copies available upon
request.
[383] http://www.chesterfieldhistory.com/Chesterfield_Co_reg_of_deaths_1853--1896.pdf
[384] Dinwiddie County, VA DB 11, pp. 25-26, viewed by WRK Jan 2010, copies on file.

deed that her mother retained the land during their lifetime, given the later deed signed from them to Robert Sydnor. See below.

1864 – On 16 March 1864, **Sarah A. Kidd** married J.W. Williams in Chesterfield County, VA.[385]
This entry matches the informant for Matilda's death record in 1876 (see below).

1866 – On 20 Mar, 1866, **William Kidd** and his wife Matilda, both of **Chesterfield County,** deeded their life interest in a certain parcel of land containing 60 acres in Dinwiddie County, and bounded on the south by Cox Road, on the west by Upton Crow, on the north by William Sally (Lally?) and on the east by Joseph Crowder. to Robert H. Sydnor for $30.00. Recorded 20 Aug, 1866.[386]
Both William and Matilda Kidd signed with an X.

1870 – I am unable to find either William or Matilda Kidd on the federal census this year, despite the fact that Matilda didn't die until 1876 (see below). We do not know when or where William Kidd died.

1876 – **Matilda Kidd**, white female, died May 1876 in Chesterfield County of old age at 65. Born in Dinwiddie, husband **William Kidd, deceased**. Josh Williams, son-in law reporting.[387]

NANCY/ANN M. (SUTHERLAND) KIDD, the 2nd wife of James 6a Kidd
Born abt. 1800, probably in Dinwiddie County, VA
Married 1st Allen Thweatt in 1818, 2nd James 6a Kidd.
Died 13 June 1870 in Petersburg, VA.
See James 6a Kidd's section of this compilation.

1818 – On 1 December 1818, **Nancy M. Sutherland** married Allin (Allen) Thweatt in Dinwiddie County, VA.[388]

1820, 1830, 1840 – she's in the HH of her husband Allen Thweatt on the federal censuses in these years.

1841 – **Ann M. Thweatt** appears for the first time on the Dinwiddie County Land Tax Lists, taxed for the same two tracts of land that her husband Allen Thweatt had been taxed on in previous years: one parcel of 483 acres, and a second one of 4¾ acres, both "on the Great Branch, 5 miles west of the Courthouse. A notation in the margin adds "From estate of Allen Thweatt by will" for both of these parcels. Allen Thweatt evidently died in the prior 12 months, and she has inherited his land via his will.[389]
While earlier census records suggest that they had children, none apparently were named in this will. Nearly all Dinwiddie County wills were destroyed in courthouse fires, and no will for Allen Thweatt has been found, to our knowledge.

1842 – In a deed signed 11 January 1842, **Ann M. Thweatt** of Dinwiddie County sold a parcel or tract of land in Dinwiddie County containing 58 acres to William B. Scott for $174.

---

[385] Personal correspondence from WRK, an author of this paper, from old notes.
[386] Dinwiddie County, VA. DB 11, pages 269-270, retrieved from FHL #31097, images 571-572. Copy available upon request.
[387] Chesterfield County Death Registers, 1853-1896.
[388] *Virginia, Select Marriages, 1785-1940*, on Ancestry.com.
[389] Dinwiddie County, VA Land Tax Lists, 1841-1850, FHL #29924, image 59, retrieved via Familysearch.org. Scanned image available.

Neighbors and landmarks bordering this land included Wm. B Scott, Mayo, **Ann M. Thweatt**, Boisseau, the Great Branch, and Scott's Road. In the deed itself, she's referred to as **Ann M. Thweatt**, and she signed it using that name. She appeared in Dinwiddie Court on 12 January to acknowledge the deed as legitimate before two justices of the peace, and their certification names her as **Nancy Thweatt**.[390]

1842-1847 – **Ann M. Thweatt** appears annually on the Dinwiddie LTLs, taxed on the same land, in each of these years.[391]

1848 – a James Kidd appears for the first time in 9 years on the Dinwiddie County Land Tax Lists (as **"James Kidd & wife"**,[392] taxed on 425.5 acres "on the Great Branch," 5 miles NW of the courthouse. The notation for this entry says, **"deed from Ann M. Thweat."** This James is considerably more wealthy (judging from the value of his land and buildings, valued at $1382) than the earlier James Kidd was; it appears that his <u>has remarried in the prior 12 months</u>, and that his new wife has brought this property to the marriage.
James Kidd and his wife are also taxed on another parcel of 4.75 acres in the same location. This is the land that he evidently swaps with James Boisseau (see below).

1848 – On 27 July 1848, James Kidd and his wife **Ann M. Kidd** of the first part of Dinwiddie and sold to James Boisseau of the second part for $1.00 and a satisfactory consideration, a tract of land containing 430 acres bounded east by A. K. Boisseau and other, north and west by John W. Gilliam, south by **Dr. William B. Scott**. Signed James Kidd, Ann M. Kidd, who consents. James H. Boisseau and William B. Scott, justices. Recorded 19 Aug, 1848. [393]

On 19 August 1848 Boisseau and Scott sold 430 acres in Dinwiddie County to **James Kidd** for $1.00.[394]
He and James Boisseau have made some sort of land swap, trading the land previously owned by James' second wife, **Ann M. (Thweat) Kidd**.

1850 – On the federal census in the northern district of Dinwiddie County, VA, p. 454, HH 302:
Kidd, James 57MW farmer $3250 VA
 " , **Nancy M.** 49FW VA
Ellison, Betty 16FW   VA (apparently a domestic servant)
Pritchet, Washington 18 mulatto male laborer VA (apparently a free black male)
 " , David 30BM laborer VA cannot read or write (apparently a free black male)

1860 – On the federal census in the South Ward of Petersburg district, p 301, HH 418:
Kidd, James 65MW no occupation $1000/8000 VA

---

[390] Dinwiddie County, VA Deed Book 3, p. 228, retrieved from FHL #31093, item 2, image 442. Scanned image available upon request.

[391] Digital images of these entries are available upon request. The 1847 LTL was retrieved from FHL ##29924 – Dinwiddie LTLs, 1841-1850, image #354.

[392] FHL #29924, Dinwiddie LTLs, 1841-1850, image # 390. This listing is notable in that it, unlike nearly all the other entries, adds "and wife" and indicates that she's a property owner in her own right. She has brought this land into the marriage.

[393] Dinwiddie County, VA. DB5, page 599. Deed book located at Dinwiddie County Courthouse.

[394] Dinwiddie County, VA. DB 5, page 600. Boisseau and Scott sold back the same land they purchased from Kidd and wife on 27 Jul, 1848. The first sale was from James Kidd and wife to Boisseau and Scott. The sale back was only to James Kidd. Deed book located at Dinwiddie County Courthouse.

" **, Ann M.** 60FW VA

(no others)

1868 – The Petersburg Daily Index (newspaper of Petersburg, Virginia) on 6 Aug, 1868 contained a notice from **James Kidd** about a missing Bible, lost at the registration desk of the West Ward with the name Ann Thweatt inscribed, containing the family record of the Thweatt and Kidd family. Since James is taxed on land in 1848 that is noted as received from Ann M. Thweatt, this appears to be their family Bible.[395]

1870 – On the federal census in Petersburg, VA, 4th Ward, p. 326, HH 836, apparently a duplex:

Kidd, James 75MW no occupation VA

" **, Nancy M.** 68FW keeps house VA cannot read or write

1870 – a Nancy Kidd, age 75, died in Petersburg, Virginia on 13 June 1870.[396]

Her funeral notice appeared in the Petersburg Index on 14 June 1870:

> FUNERAL NOTICE.—THE FU-
> neral of the late Mrs. ANN M., wife of James
> Kidd, will take place at the High Street Metho-
> dist Church THIS (Tuesday) MORNING, at 10
> o'clock. The friends and acquaintances of the
> family are respectfully invited to attend.

She is buried in Blandford in James Kidd's plot but apparently there is no marker.[397]

RICHARD L. KIDD, the son of Joseph Kidd of Brunswick County, Virginia.
b. July 1845, VA, d. 1906, Petersburg, VA
See our Brunswick County, VA compilation for much more information on this man and his ancestors.

1868-1871 – **Richard L. Kidd** appears on the annual PPTLs in Petersburg (independent city in Dinwiddie County), VA in these years.

1870 – On the federal census in Petersburg (3rd ward), VA, p. 253, HH 199/212:

Kidd, Richd. L. 25MW Com. House Clerk VA

1880 – On the federal census in Petersburg (3rd Ward), VA, ED 92, sheet 24D, p. , HH 185/298:

Kidd, R.L. 35MW single merchant VA VA VA

1900 – On the federal census in Petersburg city, Dinwiddie County, VA, ED 100, sheet 7B, p. 128A, living at 28 Guarantee St., HH 134/162:

Kidd, Richard L. head WM July 1845 54M marr.17yr. VA VA VA bookkeeper

" , Nettie wife WF Aug 1862 38M marr.17yr. 8 children/8 living VA VA VA

" , Lewis L. son WM Feb 1884 16S VA VA VA asst. bookkeeper

" , Mary E. dau WF Jan 1886 14S VA VA VA in school

" , Richard L. son WM Nov 1887 12S VA VA VA in school

" , Marvin R. son WM Sept. 1889 10S VA VA VA in school

" , Nettie F. dau WF Dec 1891 8S VA VA VA in school

" , William D. son WM Dec 1893 6S VA VA VA in school

---

[395] Personal correspondence from William R. Kidd.

[396] Virginia, Deaths and Burials, 1853-1917, on Ancestry.com, citing FHL #33443, Peterburg, Virginia Deaths, image. A scanned image of this record is available in the Dinwiddie County Shared Folder on Dropbox.

[397] Personal correspondence from William R. Kidd.

" , John M. son WM April 1885 5S VA
" , Sallie P. dau WF Jan 1898 2S VA

ROBERT KIDD (see Stanfield T. Kidd)

1851 – In March of 1851, John T.S. Young presented an account of his guardianship of one Robert (middle initials are difficult to read, but appear to be S.T) Kidd. The account included expenditures for 1850-1851, and included a bill paid to Thomas J. Kidd for about $10. This Robert Kidd was an adult, as the record also stated that Henry Worsham was the guardian of Robert Kidd's wife; this record referred to the Lunenburg county court.[398]
We cannot find a Robert Kidd on any other records in Dinwiddie, Amelia, or Lunenburg county, and are confident that this is indeed Robert Stanfield T. Kidd, who married Missouri Smithson of Lunenburg County. See Stanfield Kidd's section in this compilation.

SARAH ANN (KIDD) WILLIAMS, the daughter of William and Matilda (Wells) Kidd
Born abt 1844 in VA
Married Joseph (Josh) Williams in Chesterfield County, VA in 1874

1850 – On the federal census in Lower district of Chesterfield County, VA, p. 134, HH 338 (mis-indexed at Ancestry.com as "Ridd"):
Kidd, William 47MW "operator" VA cannot read or write
 " , Matilda 43FW VA cannot read or write
 " , Edward 18MW operator VA
 " , James 15MW operator VA
 " , Thomas 12MW VA
 " , **Ann E.** 10FW VA (**is this Sarah A.**? We think that's most likely.)

1860 – On the federal census in "Mattoaca Factory, southern district," Chesterfield County, VA, p. 60, HH 432/442:
Kidd, William 45MW works in factory $300/30 VA cannot read or write
 " , Matilda 40FW domestic VA cannot read or write
 " , **Sarah A.** 16FW weaver VA
(no others, but nearby are several Traylor families.)

1863 – In a Dinwiddie County, VA deed dated 20 October 1863, **Sarah Ann Kidd** of Chesterfield County, VA sells to Robert Sydnor of Dinwiddie County for $75 "all her right, title and interest to a certain parcel or tract of land on Cox Rd." in Dinwiddie, "left by the late Harrison Wells to William Kidd and wife, during their natural life."[399] It seems from this deed that her parents retained the land during their lifetime, given the later deed signed from them to Robert Sydnor. See William Kidd's notes.
Sarah Ann Kidd signed this deed with an X. It was admitted to record in Dinwiddie County Court on Feb. 15, 1864.

---

[398] Dinwiddie County, VA Guardian Accounts, 1844-1856, LDS microfilm #31108)on permanent loan at the Bellevue, WA FHC), pp. 326, 374, reviewed and abstracted by RK 4/6/10.
[399] Dinwiddie County, VA DB 11, pp. 25-26, viewed by WRK Jan 2010, copies on file. Retrieved from FHL #31097, images 447-448.

In this deed, Sarah A. Kidd is selling her interest in the parcel of land deeded to her mother, Matilda Wells Kidd, by Matilda's father. See Matilda's section of this compilation.

1864 – On 16 March 1864, **Sarah A. Kidd** married J.W. Williams in Chesterfield County, VA.[400]

1870 – She is likely the woman below, on the federal census in Chesterfield County, Matoaca township, 2nd Revenue District, page 110, living in a tenement house,
HH 744/870
Williams, Joseph H. 27MW carpenter $0/$125 VA
  " , **Sarah A**. 24FW keeps house VA
  " , Annie N. 3FW VA
  " , George 1/12MW VA

1876 – Matilda Kidd, white female, died May 1876 in Chesterfield of old age at 65. Born in Dinwiddie, husband William Kidd, deceased. **Josh Williams**, son-in law reporting.[401] This is Sarah A. Kidd's husband.

We have not traced Sarah Ann (Kidd) Williams further.

<u>STANFIELD T. KIDD</u>, also known as Robert S.T. Kidd, the third son of Thomas J. (ThomasJ6, Benjamin5, George4, Benjamin3, William2, Thomas1) Kidd
Born abt. 1831, VA
Married Missouri E. Smithson (date uncertain, but by June of 1850), likely in Lunenburg County, Virginia
Drops from records after 1853

1850 – On the federal census in Dinwiddie County (southern District), VA, p. 471, HH 23:
Kidd, Thomas J. 64WM Wheelright $100 VA
Whitmore, Jemima 54WF VA cannot read or write (likely Thomas's sister)
Kidd, Stanfield 19WM wheelright $0 VA married within the year
  " , Missouri E. 17FW VA married within the year (Stanfield's wife)

1850 – He appears on the Dinwiddie PPTL, listed as **Stanfield T. Kidd**, with no property other than one horse.

1851 – He appears on the Dinwiddie PPTL, listed as **Robert S.T. Kidd**, again with no property other than one horse.

1851 – At a County Court held for **Dinwiddie** County on the 17th day of March, 1851, John T. S. Young, guardian of **Robert S. T. Kidd** appeared in Court and presented his report (below).[402]

<table>
<tr><td>John T. S. Young }</td><td>Commissioner Hargrave's Office</td></tr>
<tr><td>Guardian of   }</td><td>Dinwiddie March 1851</td></tr>
<tr><td>Robt. S. T. Kidd }</td><td></td></tr>
</table>

---

[400] Personal correspondence from WRK, an author of this paper, from old notes.
[401] Chesterfield County Death Registers, 1853-1896.
[402] Dinwiddie County Guardian Account Book, 1844-1865, pp. 326-327, viewable online on the Dinwiddie County website: https://www.dinwiddieva.us/747/Archives-and-Historical-Documents ; scroll down to find Guardian Book, 1844-1865, where you'll find a PDF of the entire book; you can view it online and download selected pages.

To the County Court of Dinwiddie:

Your Commissioner respectfully reports to the Court that on the 17th day of March 1851, John T. S. Young, the guardian exhibited before your Commissioner a statement of all the monies which he the said Young had received or become chargeable with, or had disbursed, together with the vouchers for such disbursements. That the Commissioner embraced the said guardian in the list of fiduciaries whose accounts were before him for settlement, which was posted at the front door of the Courthouse of said County, on the first day of March Court last, and on the date of this report (ten days having elapsed since the said account was mentioned in the said list) made up and completed the following guardianship account of the said John T. S. Young, of the said Robert T. S. Kidd, and on the 31st day of December 1850, finds a balance of Four hundred and one dollars and five cents, principal and interest, due from the said John T. S. Young in his character of guardian of which sum $13.56 is interest. The account is supported by satisfactory vouchers, (the most of which were made by the said ward himself before his marriage and after and requested his guardian to settle them) and is herewith returned – see statement on page 2nd.

Your Commr. further reports to the Court, that he has examined whether the said guardian has given such bond as the Law requires, and whether it is in a penalty, and with security sufficient, & finds the same to be unobjectionable and fully sufficient. All which is respectfully submitted. Given under my hand the 5th day of April 1851.

(signed) J. E. Hargrave Commr.

Robert S. T. Kidd, In account current with John T. S. Young, his guardian

1850

June 1st   By amt. recd. Of Dr.(?) Henry C. Worsham, guardian }
              of said Kidd's wife, this day per acct.   }
              and report of Commr. GHargrave, returned   }
              to Lunenburg County Court.   }

1850				$670.31
June 1	To paid	Dr. Henry C. Worsham	$12.03	
July 15	" "	Commr. Hargrave	12.50	
August	" "	Clerk of Lunenburg - tickets	.64	
Oct. 22	" "	Burton & Draper	30.41	
" "	" "	William F. Thompson - bond	15.97	
" 25	" "	Young, Baldwin & Co.	40.97	
Nov. 11	" "	Sheriff of Dinwiddie - tickets	.60	
" 11	" "	Clerk of Lunenburg - tickets	.36	
Dec. 20	" "	Thos. J. Kidd - Bond	16.92	
" 31	" "	Perry L. Derby	2.63	
" "	" "	Perry L. "	1.50	
" "	" "	Charles Young	7.00	
" "	" "	Charles Young & Son	86.85	

"	"	To	Amt. due guardian for corn, wheat, fodder, etc. furnished ward per acct. acknowledged by said Kidd	20.93	
"	"	To	5 per cent Commissions on $670.31	33.51	
"	"		Amt. of disbursements	$282.82	
Dec. 31		To	Balance per Contra	387.49	
				$670.31	$670.31
Dec. 31		By	Balance to Debit		$387.49
		By	Int. on $387.49 from June 1, 1850 to Dec. 31, 1850		13.36
			Balance due by John T. Y. Young in his character of guardian Dec. 31st, 1850, principal and interest		$401.05

J. E. Hargrave, Gn.

At a County Court held for Dinwiddie County on the 21st day of April, 1851, this account current of John T. S. Young, guardian of **Robert S. T.Kidd**, was returned and ordered to be recorded.

Teste

Jno. P. Crump, C. C.

1851 – On 3 December 1851, Robert Allgood and his wife Eliza C. Allgood of Dinwiddie County, VA sold to **Stanfield Kidd** of the same place for $250 a tract of land in the upper part of Dinwiddie County containing 100 acres, bounded by George Whitmore, Archer Bevel and others. This deed was recorded 19 January 1852. [403]

1852 – On 17 September 1852, **Stanfield Kidd** and his wife Missouri sold to Jemima Whitmore and Thomas J. Kidd, all of Dinwiddie for the sum of $1, 5 acres of land in Dinwiddie adjoining the lands of George Whitmore on the road at the southeast corner of the said Stanfield Kidd, to have and to hold the said Jemima Whitmore and Thomas J. Kidd and at the death of Jemima and Thomas J, the said land reverts back to the former owners and their heirs and Stanfield and Missouri. This deed was recorded 18 October 1852.[404]

1853 – **Stanfield Kidd** appears on the Dinwiddie County, VA PPTL this year, but not thereafter.

---

[403] Dinwiddie County, VA. DB 7, page 151. Retrieved from FHL #31095, image 362. Copy available upon request.
[404] Dinwiddie County, VA. DB 7, page 259, retrieved from FHL #31095, image 416. Copy available upon request.

1853 – On 31 Aug 1853, **Stanfield Kidd** and his wife Missouri sold 160 acres in Dinwiddie for
$250.00 to Susan V. Jackson, bordered by George Whitmore on the east and William
Ferguson, deceased, and others. This deed was recorded 17 Oct 1853.[405]

We have found no subsequent records for Stanfield or Missouri Kidd, and do not know what
became of them.

<u>STITH J. KIDD</u>, **the second son of Thomas J. (ThomasJ6, Benjamin5, George4, Benjamin3,**
William2, Thomas1) Kidd and his wife, Martha Thweatt[406]
Born abt. 1825 in Dinwiddie County, VA
Occupation: wheelwright, as was his father
Married(1) Mary/Minna Helen Platt/Plate in 1848 in Henrico County, VA
Lived much of his life in Petersburg, Virginia
Divorced by Minna in 1875 in Petersburg
Married (2) Lucy G. Ragsdale in Dinwiddie County in 1879
Died October 1, 1883 in Brunswick County, VA

1844-1846 – **Stith Kidd** appears these three years on the Personal Property Tax Lists in the city of
Petersburg, an independent city in Dinwiddie County. Each year he's taxed for himself, the
only white male over 16 in his household, and he has no taxable property (slaves, horses,
etc.). In 1844, there is also a William Kidd on the Petersburg PPTL.[407]

1847 – "**Stith J. Kidd**, age 23, born Dinwiddie County, fair complexion, black eyes, light hair, 5'11",
occupation – carpenter" was one of the men listed on the Roster of the Virginia Public
Guard as of Sept. 30, 1847.[408]

1848 – **Stith J. Kidd** married Minnie Helen Plate (or Platt) on 22 December 1848 in Henrico
County, VA.[409] According to descendants, she was born in Bremen, Germany, and came to
America in 1844 at the age of 16. Census records name her birthplace as Germany (1860)
and Bremen (1870).

1849 – **Stith J. Kidd** appears on the **Dinwiddie** County, VA PPTL this year, but not before or
after. He has no property.

1850 – He appears again on the **Petersburg** PPTL ("Stith J. Kidd"), taxed only for himself.[410]

---

[405] Dinwiddie Court House, deed book 7, page 434, reviewed Jan. 14, 2010 by WRK. Retrieved from FHL #31095,
image 508. Copy available upon request.
[406] Per his 1879 marriage record in Dinwiddie County, VA.
[407] Petersburg PPTLs, reviewed by William R. Kidd at the Library of Virginia, 2009.
[408] http://www.newrivernotes.com/va/vapg1847.htm   The Virginia Public Guard was organized in 1802 as the
Commonwealth's standing army. It was authorized to have 69 enlisted men, 14 non-commissioned officers and
musicians and three officers. Their principal duties were ceremonial, to guard the public property and state officials
in Richmond and to guard the Commonwealth penitentiary.
The Public Guard was also charged with maintenance of the Public Armory and the weapons contained therein.
Barracks were built near the Armory to house the men and their families. The Virginia Public Guard continued in
existence until 1869, when it was abolished. The functions of the Guard were assumed by the Virginia State Police.
[409] Henrico County, VA Marriage Bonds, cited on Ancestry.com. I haven't confirmed this source, but its given as
Marriage Bonds of Henrico County, VA, 1782-1853, p. 94.
[410] Ibid, WR Kidd, 2009.

1850 – On the federal census in Petersburg, VA, page 337B, HH 245/265, either living in a duplex,
or sharing a house with a John & Frances Mann and his family, a grocer from Ireland:
Kidd, S.J. 24MW blacksmith VA
   " , Mary 21FW VA [Minna]
   " , T.H. 6/12MW VA

1854-1856 – He appears annually on the Petersburg PPTL, listed as "**S.J. Kidd**, "taxed only for
himself, and $45-50 of personal property.[411]

1859 – He again appears on the Petersburg PPTL as "**S.J. Kidd**," taxed only for himself and
furniture worth $75.

1860 – On the federal census in the West Ward of Petersburg (independent city within Dinwiddie
County), VA, pages 225-226, enumerated 20 July 1860, HH 2073/1230:
Kidd, S.J. 35MW wheelwright VA
   " , M.H. 30FW b. Germany
   " , Lewis E. 7WM VA attended school within year
   " , James   9MW VA attended school within year
   " , Theodore F. 5MW VA
   " , Thomas 10MW VA attended school within year
   " , Benj. M. 3MW VA
   " , Frederick 7/12MW VA

1860-1863 – He appears on the Petersburg PPTLs annually as "**Seth J. Kidd**," taxed for himself and
similar property and income as in the past.

1863 – On 1 September 1863, **S.J.** (Stith Jones) **Kidd** and his wife entered into a Deed of Trust with
John Jackson and his wife, Ann Jackson, as outlined below.
This deed, made this the 1st day of September A.D. 1863 between John Jackson and Ann E.
Jackson his wife of the first part, Alexander Dorman of the second part, and Mina Helen
Kidd, the wife of Stith J. Kidd, and the said Stith Kidd in his own right, and their children,
Thomas Henry, James Alfred Jones, Lewis Edward, Theodore Franklin, Benjamin Marion,
Frederick Orlando and Josephus Charles Kidd, and any other children to them born, of the
third part –
Witnesseth, that the said Jackson and wife, for and in consideration of the sum of five
hundred dollars cash in hand paid to them, the receipt whereof is hereby acknowledged,
they, the said Jackson and wife do by these presents grant, bargain, sell and convey to the
said Alexander Dorman in Trust for the purposes hereafter declared, with general warranty
that certain lot or parcel of land…on the east side of Halifax Street in the City of
Petersburg…
And the said Dorman, as Trustee, is to hold the said property for the benefit and use of the
said Stith J. Kidd, his wife and children, & any after born child or children, free from all
debts and contracts of said S. J. Kidd, in such way as he may deem best, and so to be held
during the lives of S. J. Kidd and his wife, at their deaths then the said property is to be sold
and the proceeds divided equally [between] all their children and their descendants of any
who may have died, per stirpes. Should the said Mina Helen Kidd desire it and the Trustee
approve of it, he is authorized to sell this property and invest the proceeds in such other
property as may be deemed best; the said property so purchased to be held precisely in the

---

[411] Ibid, WR Kidd, 2009.

same way, upon the same conditions and restrictions and to go as this now conveyed. It is further understood that in the event that the said Mina Helen Kidd, the wife of S. J. Kidd, should survive him and she shall request it and the Trustee approve it, and the said M. H. Kidd desire to move away from this state, the said Trustee may sell the said property and pay the proceeds over to her.

John Jackson {seal}

Ann E. Jackson {seal}

This deed was acknowledged in Petersburg Court on 1 September 1863 by both John Jackson and his wife. It was admitted to record in Hustings Court in Petersburg on 17 October 1863.[412]

It is clear in this record that Mina was a strong, independent woman, perhaps with some wealth of her own, and she's trying to secure her children's economic future from her husband's debts.

1866 – Residence in Petersburg VA: **Kidd, Stith J.,** wheelwright, h Halifax nr the line.

1868-69 - Residence in Petersburg VA. **Kidd, Stith J.,** wheelwright, Halifax n R Road h do.[413]

1868-1872 – He appears on the Petersburg PPTLs annually, as **S.J. Kidd** or **Seth J. Kidd**. In this interval, he was never taxed for another white male over 16 or 21, other than himself. He was poorer after the Civil War, but gradually acquired more property.

1870 – On the federal census in Petersburg (6th Ward), VA, p. 418, enumerated 17 Aug. 1870, HH ??/9:

Kidd, Stith J. 45MW wagon-maker $500/100 VA
 " , Minna H. 39FW   keeps house Bremen
 " , Thos. H. 20MW printer's apprentice VA
 " , James A. 18MW wks. minl water VA
 " , Lewis E. 17MW printer's apprentice VA
 " , Theodore F. 15MW wks tob(acco?) fact VA
 " , Benjamin 13MW at school VA
 " , Frederick 11MW at school VA
 " , Joseph 9MW at school VA
 " , Jno. C. 6MW VA
 " , Alexander 3MW VA
 " , Minnie 1FW VA

1870-71 – Residence in Petersburg VA. **Kidd, Stith J.,** wheelwright, Halifax nr Butterworth Bridge.[414]

1872-73 – Residence in Petersburg VA. **Kidd, Stith J.,** wheelwright, Halifax nr Butterworth Bridge.[415]

---

[412] Petersburg City Deed Book 28, pages 19-20, retrieved from LoV reel 16. Scanned images available upon request.
[413] Petersburg City directory 1868-69, page 48, located at LVA, reviewed 2-22-03.
[414] Petersburg City directory 1870-71, page 116, located at LVA, reviewed 2-22-03
[415] Petersburg City directory 1872-73, page 83, located at LVA, reviewed 2-22-03

1875 – **Stith H. Kidd** was divorced by his wife Minnie on the charge of adultery, in Petersburg, VA.[416]

1876-77 – **Stith Kidd** is not mentioned in the Petersburg directory, but based on the divorce in 1875, the following people, listed as residing in Petersburg, VA in 1876-77, appear to be his divorced wife and two of their children:
Kidd, Alfred butcher h 556 Halifax,
Kidd, Franklin gas-fitter h 556 Halifax,
Kidd, Minnie Mrs. h 556 Halifax.
George F. Kidd was also listed in the same directory, see George F.'s notes in this document.[417]

1879 – **Stith Kidd**, age 51, born Dinwiddie County, obtained a marriage license for his marriage to Lucy Goode Ragsdale, age 34, born Lunenburg County, on 22 April 1879 in Dinwiddie County, VA.[418] According to the Dinwiddie County marriage records, the marriage occurred on 30 April 1879 in Dinwiddie County.[419] The bride's marital status was 'single' and the groom's was listed as widowed (despite the divorce record above for Stith). His parents are listed as T. J. Kidd and Martha Thweatt; hers as Edward and Sally Ragsdale. His occupation is "coachmaker." They were married at the residence of W.A. Snead of Dinwiddie.

1880 – On the federal census in Darvilles district (south [of?]Butterwood Creek), Dinwiddie County, VA, ED 81, sheet 9A, page 131A, HH 69/71:
Kidd, Seth J. WM head 53M wheelright VA VA VA
  " , Lucy G. WF wife 38M keeping house VA VA VA
  " , Charles J. WM son 18S VA VA VA
  " , John C. WM son 15S blacksmith VA VA VA
Washington, Martha BF 16S servant cannot read or write VA VA VA

1882 – Said by descendant Thomas K. Bernard in his information on Ancestry.com to have died after 1882, citing *"A History of the Kidd family in Virginia,"* at the Virginia State Library. He has information on most of Stith's children, and their descendants.
According to him, Stith J. Kidd had twelve children, eleven of them sons.
William R. Kidd has found birth records for several of Stith J. Kidd's children (by his first wife, Minna Helen Platte):
Robert A(lexander). Kidd, b. 22 January 1867, in Petersburg, VA[420]
Minnie C. Kidd, b. 19 January 1869 in Petersburg, VA[421]

Stith J. Kidd was alive in 1882, because he is listed in a Dinwiddie County deed dated 11 September 1882, as a leaseholder and head of a family. He is making a claim using the Homestead Exemption claiming livestock (1 horse, 1 cow, 1 hog), crops (corn, tobacco and cotton) , and household furnishings worth over $800.00. In this claim he declares his intentions to add to this claim from time to time until it reaches the amount allowed by law

---

[416] Chancery Order Book 2 of Hustings Court, pp. 12-13; Drawer 32-35 had the actual reports of the witnesses.
[417] Petersburg City directory 1876-77, page 96, located at LVA, reviewed 2-22-03 by WRK.
[418] Dinwiddie County, VA Marriage Register, 1850-1880, reel #20 (cited on Ancestry, not personally reviewed by RK). WRK provided their ages at the time of the marriage, citing p. 125 of the Marriage Index.
[419] Dinwiddie County Marriage Register, p. 89. WRK has images of the marriage records.
[420] Virginia Birth Index at the State Library of Virginia, p. 71. Parents were listed as SJ and MN Kidd.
[421] Virginia Birth Index at the State Library of Virginia, p. 90. Parents were listed as Stith R and Minnie Kidd.

under the Homestead Exemption law. S. J. Kidd signed this document and it was admitted to record on this date.[422]

Evidently this law protected (and still does – it is in existence today) certain property up to a set amount from seizure, garnishment, etc., in the case of debts.

1883 – **Stith J. Kidd** died on 1 October 1883 in Brunswick County, VA due to "malarial fever."[423] This record lists his wife as Lucy, his occupation as "mechanic," and his age as 55. It also states that he was born in Dinwiddie County. Unfortunately, the informant for this record (W. W. Howerton, "friend") evidently did not know the names of his parents; the space on the form was left blank.

<u>THOMAS J. KIDD</u> – Most likely the son of Benjamin5 (George4, Benjamin3, William2, Thomas1) Kidd, and the brother of James6a Kidd. This is the authors' working hypothesis.[424], [425]
Born abt 1786 in VA
Probably married twice: first to Jane Gent,[426] and second (by the birth of Thomas's second son, Stith J., circa 1825) Martha Thweatt [427], [428]
Died abt 1858 in Dinwiddie County, VA

Because Thomas J. Kidd deeded 20 acres of land to his son-in-law, Trent Harrison in 1851, and then a James Kidd deeded all his real and personal property in 1871, Ann Andrews[429] and William R.

---

[422] Dinwiddie County Court House, deed book 16, page 44, viewed 1-14-2010, copies on file, reviewed by WRK. Scanned image available upon request.

[423] *Virginia, Deaths and Burials, 1853-1917*, on Ancestry.com, citing FL #2056974, item 2, Brunswick County Deaths and Burials, 1853-1896. A scanned image of this record is in the Brunswick County Shared Folder on Dropbox (image 487 on this microfilm reel).

[424] Bill writes (Nov. 2009): Here is part of what I think links Thomas and James as brothers:

1. War of 1812-A James Kidd and a Thomas Kidd both served in the 83rd Regiment of WM in the War of 1812 from Jul 1 to Jul 6 1813, different companies but same Regiment and dates. My James Kidd and a Thomas Kidd served in the 1st Regiment of the VM in the War of 1812, service dates both started at 28 Aug 1814, end dates were 5 Dec 1814 for James and 30 Nov 1814 for Thomas. I think the James listed first may be my James, even though this is not in his service record. Same counties, same basic dates of enlistment. - WRK

2. Mary C Kidd, daughter of Thomas J Kidd. Samuel H Clarke married Mary C Kidd 8 Jun 1838, then Mary C Clark married Trent E Harrison 16 Nov 1842. 24 Dec 1854 William R Kidd wins a suit against Samuel Clarke, a business partner in a saw mill. This always made me think William and Mary may have been close cousins if he went into business with her husband. Can't be sure it was the same Samuel Clark but that's most likely.

3. Trent E Harrison. Both Thomas and James left their property to Trent E Harrison in their wills. Also, Trent E Harrison was listed as a witness in the pension record of James Kidd. There was a Benjamin Harrison (relationship unknown) living at South Pine near Smiths Lane in the 1870's, which looks like the same address for James Kidd in the mid to late 1860's.

[425] He could *possibly* be the son of James5a Kidd, son of George Kidd Sr., for reasons explained here. However, James5a was born in 1767, and this would make him less than 20 years of age at the birth of Thomas J. Kidd. While not unheard of, this was not typical in this era.]

[426] The death record of Thomas J. Kidd's first son, James7 Kidd, lists his mother's name as Jane Gent; it left blank the name of his father.

[427] The 1879 marriage record of their son, Stith J. Kidd names his parents as T. J. Kidd and Martha Thweat.

[428] Her given name comes to us in the 1838 deed cited here (see under 1838, in Thomas's section), and this coincides with the 1879 marriage record for their son, Stith J. Kidd's marriage to Lucy Goode, which names the groom's mother as Martha Thweatt. See his section of this paper.

[429] Ann Andrews was the wife of Preston H. Andrews; her husband was a descendant of Thomas J. Kidd, and she was an avid researcher until her death. Preston Andrews died in 2018.

"Bill" Kidd believe that he's the son of James5a Kidd, or at least the son of A JAMES KIDD. Reiley Kidd, the other author of this paper, believes that it's more likely that both Thomas J. Kidd and James6a Kidd were the sons of Benjamin5 Kidd.

[The Descendants Chart for George4 Kidd, found in Appendix Two, may help the reader visualize the relationships being hypothesized here.]

Whoever his father was, Thomas J. Kidd was almost certainly the father of Stith J. Kidd, Stanfield Kidd, and one other son, probably the man listed in this paper as "James7 Kidd." His only known daughter was Mary C. Kidd, who married (as her second husband) Trent Harrison in 1842. See their sections in this compilation for more details.

Ca. 1786 – We estimate 1786 as his year of birth, based on his entry in the 1850 federal census (see below), where his age is listed as 64. This corresponds reasonably well with his first appearance on the Dinwiddie County PPTLs in 1810.

1810-1851 – A **Thomas Kidd** first appears on the Dinwiddie County, VA personal property tax lists in 1810, with one white over 16 (himself); he is listed annually thereafter through 1851; beginning in 1817, he is listed as **Thomas J. Kidd** (and no other Thomas Kidd is listed). In 1818 for the first time he was taxed for one horse. In 1810-1815 and 1826, he is listed as **Thomas**; in all the other years he is listed as **Thomas J.** All these references appear to be to the same man, since there is never a year where two Thomas Kidds appear on the same Dinwiddie PPTL.

1814 – Private **Thomas Kidd** is listed on the pay roll of Captain William H. Cousin's Company of Rifleman 1st Regiment Virginia Militia for the pay roll of the 28th of August 1814 to the 30th of November 1814, and his dates of service were for the same dates; time of service was 3 months and 5 days. Rate of pay was $8.00 per month. Pay and muster roll includes 2 days for returning home 40 miles. Pay roll dated 4 Dec 1814. Thomas was present for the Muster roll dated 30 Nov 1814 at Camp Powell's Creek, Prince George County. This **Thomas Kidd** appointed William Worsham his attorney in an enclosure with the service record which reads as follows; Know all men by these present that I **Thomas Kidd** of the County of Dinwiddie have made ordained constituted and appointed William Worsham of the County aforesaid my true and lawful Attorney for me and in my name to receive all of my wages which is due me (except one month's pay) and give a receipt (?) in my name for the same as a soldier in the service of the Virginia Militia, under the command of Genl. Chamberlayne, in the first Regt under Col. Byrnes and in Captain William H. Cousin's Company of the said Regt hereby ratifying whatsoever my said Attorney shall do therein by virtue hereof in witness whereof I have hereunto set my hand and seal this 23rd day of January Eighteen hundred and fifteen. Signed by his mark, **Thomas Kidd**, witnessed by William Mason. The last page in the service record simply states "Cousins-Thos Kidd-paid in full."[430]

A James Kidd also served in this unit, serving 6 days (July 1-6, 1813), according to pension claims made by both men.

We believe that these men were brothers.

---

[430] Thomas Kidd service record, War of 1812, card numbers 38579077, 9184, original at NAB, viewed 8/7/2009, WRK has copy.

1815 – On 23 January 1815, he appointed attorney William Worsham as his representative in a Dinwiddie County, VA court document, to pursue wages owed to him for his service in the Virginia militia during the War of 1812.[431]

1820 – **Thomas J. Kidd** appears on the 1820 federal census in Dinwiddie County:
Kidd, Thomas J.: one male 0-9, one 10-15, one 16-25, & one 26-44; one female 0-9, and one 16-25, 1 in agriculture, 3 slaves.[432]
He's also listed among those in the county involved in manufacturing; his occupation is listed as "gig-maker" and he has one employee.[433]

1820-1824 – **Thomas J. Kidd** appears yearly on the Dinwiddie County, VA PPTLs in these years. In 1820, for the first time, he has another white male over 16 in the HH. This is probably an apprentice or laborer living with Thomas, because his oldest son was still a child, born about 1820, and not old enough to be listed.
Unfortunately, in 1821, these PPTLs stopped listing the number of free white males in a household. So we can't get any idea about his sons from the PPTLs.

1826-1828 – He appears yearly on the Dinwiddie County, VA PPTLs. See Appendix Four for more details about his entries on these annual tax lists.

1830 – On the VA Census in Dinwiddie County (p. 410), 20 pages from other Kidds:
Thomas J. Kidd: 1M 5-9, 1M 10-15, and 1M 40-49; 1F 15-19, and TWO F 30-39; no slaves.

1836 – On 20 December 1836, Albert H. Reames of Dinwiddie County, Virginia sold to **Thomas J. Kid** (sic) of the same place for $100 a tract of land containing 143⅓ acres in the upper part of Dinwiddie County, bounded by Perry S. Derby, William B. Thompson, Peterson W. Harper, Claudius P. Bevill and Mack Wainwright. Recorded 17 Mar, 1837. [434]

1836-1850 – **Thomas J. Kidd** is taxed on the above land annually on the Dinwiddie County Land Tax Lists from 1836 through 1850. The land is "on Butterwood Road, 16 miles SW from the courthouse." Butterwood Creek and Butterwood Road are both due west of the county seat.
The amount of land changes over the years, as he sells some land, and buys other parcels (itemized below). See Appendix Five for more details about his listings on these LTLs.

1835-1852 – **Thomas J. Kidd** also appears on the Dinwiddie County, VA PPTLs every year in this span.[435]

1838 – On 9 March 1838, **Thomas J. Kidd** and Martha T. Kidd his wife of Dinwiddie County sold for $100 to Sally Whitmore and Jemimah Whitmore of the same place "all that tract or parcel of land located in the upper part of Dinwiddie County and containing 72 acres, and bounded by the lands of William B. Thompson, Perry L. (S.?) Derby, and Peterson W. Harper **Thomas J. Kidd** signed this deed; Martha signed with an X. They each

---

[431] RK has a photocopy of this document, provided by the late Jane Andrews, wife of Preston Andrews of Altavista, VA, a descendant of this man.
[432] Dinwiddie County 1820 federal census, p. 12 A, 110110-10100.
[433] Dinwiddie County 1820 federal census, p. 30A.
[434] Dinwiddie County, VA. DB 1, page 522. Deed book located at Dinwiddie County Courthouse.
[435] Dinwiddie County, VA Personal Property Tax Lists:
1837-1841, FHL US/CAN Film 0031114, personally viewed by Reiley Kidd at the Bellevue WA FHC May 29, 2009; (Lewis P. Lanier's list each time), with no slaves and one horse.

acknowledged the deed in Dinwiddie County Court on 9 March 1838. It was admitted to record on 2 April 1838. [436]

He bought this land (and a bit more, evidently) back a year later. See 1839, below.

On 21 December 1838, **Thomas J. Kidd** of Dinwiddie County executed a deed of trust to P. W. Harper, for and in consideration of the natural love and affection that I bear toward P. W. Harper, as well as for the further consideration of $1 to me paid by the said Harper, …I do give and grant unto the said P. W. Harper …two feather beds and two bedsteads and clothing, one walnut table and one dressing ditto (sic), six rush bottom chairs, one loom and one spinning wheel, one pine chest, one hair trunk, and one pine cupboard, earthen ware and kitchen furniture, consisting of cups and saucers, dishes and plates, one iron pot, oven and lid, and one frying pan; To have and to hold for the special benefit of **my daughter, Mary C. Clark**, and the heir or heirs of her body …"

He signed the deed, and was able to write. On March 25 1839, he acknowledged the deed as his act and intention in Dinwiddie County Court, and it was admitted to record. [437]

[Mary C. (Kidd) Clark was the wife of Samuel H. Clark/Clarke.,[438] and after his death, the wife of Trent E. Harrison. See her section of this compilation.]

1839 – On 27 April 1839, Jemima & Sally Whitmore sold to **Thomas J. Kidd**, all of Dinwiddie County, a tract of land containing 80 acres in the upper part of Dinwiddie for $100, adjoining P.W. Harper, Perry S. Derby, and William B. Thompson. The deed was recorded 11 May 1839. [439]

1840 – **Thos. J. Kidd** is on the 1840 federal census, in Dinwiddie County, with 1WM 5-9, 1 15-19 & 1 50-60; 1F 20-29, 2 40-49; one free colored female 24-36, and one male slave, 24-36; 2 in mfg and trade. [440] Thomas was a wheelwright, according to the 1850 census (see below). The other individual involved in Mfg and Trade is probably his eldest son, possibly James7 Kidd, but it could be one of his slaves.

1843 – On 20 May 1843, **Thomas J. Kidd** entered a Deed of Trust with P.W. Harper, putting up his land of 143⅔ acres, the land on which he lived, to secure a debt of $250. Thomas J. signed the deed; his wife Martha T. Kidd signed with an X.[441]

1844 – On 13 February 1844, P.W. Harper sold to **Thomas J. Kidd** for $100, plus the further sum of $100 a tract of land containing 20 acres by late survey, adjoining the land of P.W. Harper west and north, Claudius P. Bevill and Laban? Reames on the east. Recorded 1 Mar, 1844.[442]

1849 – **Thomas J. Kidd**, being indebted to Archer I. Bevill for $75.41 due by bond on demand on 25 December 1849, in order to secure the bond, sells in trust to John T. I. Young the tract of land on which the said Kidd is now residing, containing 20 acres, but Kidd remains in

---

[436] Dinwiddie County, VA Deed Book 2, pp. 52-53, viewed on FHL #31093, image 33. Scanned image available from the authors.

[437] Dinwiddie County DB 2, p. 243:

[438] Their marriage certificate is found in Dinwiddie County, VA Deed Book 2, p. 517. Copy available upon request.

[439] Dinwiddie County, VA. DB 2, page 269. Deed book located at Dinwiddie County Courthouse.

[440]. Dinwiddie County, VA 1840 census, Geo. Rose's division, p. 19. Nearby are William Kidd (2), George Stell and Robert T. Stell.

[441] Dinwiddie Court House, deed book 4, pages 70-71, viewed 14 Jan 2010, WRK. This deed can be viewed online via familysearch.org, FHL #31094, image 41.

[442] Dinwiddie County, VA. DB 4, pages 267-268, retrieved via familysearch.org from FHL # 31094, images 139-140.

possession of the land, unless he defaults on said bond. Deed of Trust dated 30 March 1849, recorded 16 April 1849.[443]

[In fact, he did default, and his land was sold by T. I. Young to Trent Harrison. See 1852 deed, below.]

1850 – On the federal census in Dinwiddie County (southern District), VA, p. 471, HH 23:
Kidd, Thomas J. 64WM Wheelwright $100 VA
Whitmore, Jemima 54WF VA cannot read or write (likely his sister)
Kidd, Stanfield 19WM wheelwright $0 VA married within the year
 " , Missouri E. 17FW VA married within the year (Stanfield's wife)

1852 – This indenture made on 8 May 1852, between John T. I. Young, trustee **of Thomas J. Kidd** of the first part and Trent E. Harrison of the second part … whereas by a certain deed (of trust) bearing date of 30 March 1849 and duly recorded in Clerk's office of Dinwiddie County – Thomas J. Kidd did convey to the said Young, his heirs and assigns, a certain tract or parcel of land in the county of Dinwiddie, and by which deed the said Young was empowered to sell the said land, and whereas the said Young, in the exercise of the said power did sell the said land to the said Harrison, with the consent of the said Kidd, evinced by his signature to this deed. Now therefore this indenture, witnesseth that in consideration of the premises and the sum of $100 paid or secured to be paid before the sealing and delivery of these presents, has bargained and sold… to the said Harrison the said land. Both Young and Thomas J. Kidd signed this deed, and acknowledged it in Court on 8 May 1852. It was admitted to record 16 August 1852.[444]
This sale confirms that Thomas J. Kidd did indeed default on this deed of trust, resulting in the sale of the land that he had owned since 1838; moreover, it was bought by Trent Harrison, who had married Mary C. Kidd, Thomas J. Kidd's daughter, in 1842. In 1871 a James Kidd deeded Trent Harrison his real and personal property; this suggests a relationship between James and Thomas J. Kidd.
We believe that this James Kidd was Thomas J. Kidd' s brother.
See his section in <u>Appendix Five</u> for a full listing of his annual entries on the Dinwiddie LTLs, 1838-1852.

1852 – On 17 September 1852, Stanfield Kidd[445] and his wife Missouri sold to Jemima Whitmore and **Thomas J. Kidd**, all of Dinwiddie for $1 a tract of land containing 5 acres in Dinwiddie, adjoining the lands of George Whitmore on the road at the southeast corner of the said Stanfield Kidd. To have and to hold the said Jemima Whitmore and **Thomas J. Kidd** and at the death of Jemima and Thomas J, the said land reverts back to the former owners and their heirs and Stanfield and Missouri. Recorded 18 Oct, 1852. [446]

1853-1857 – **Thomas J. Kidd** and Jemima Whitmore paid land taxes on the above 5 acres of land in Dinwiddie County, "near Beaver Pond Creek," 16 miles west of the Courthouse. A notation

---

[443] Dinwiddie County, VA Deed Book 6, 1846-1850, p. 184, US/CAN film number 31095, image 4109, reviewed by RK at the Bellevue FHC Jan. 5, 2010. Digital image available on request.
[444] Dinwiddie County Deed Book 6, page 184, retrieved from FHL #31095, image 109. Copy available upon request.
[445] Thomas J. Kidd's son.
[446] Dinwiddie County, VA. DB 7, page 259. Deed book located at Dinwiddie County Courthouse. This deed is viewable online via familysearch.org, on FHL #31095, image 416 (unrestricted access).

in the right margin of her entry says, "5 acres formerly charged to Jemima Whitmore and Thomas J. Kidd."[447]

1853 – On 31 Aug 1853, **Stanfield Kidd** and his wife Missouri sell 160 acres in Dinwiddie for $250.00 to Susan V. Jackson, bordered by George Whitmore on the east and William Ferguson, deceased, and others. This deed was recorded 17 Oct 1853.[448]

1857 – **Jemima Whitmore** died in Dinwiddie County, Virginia in March of 1857 at the age of 68. The cause of death was "consumption." Her death record lists her marital status as "unmarried."[449] The space on the form for the names of her parents was left blank. The informant was Trent E. Harrison, "Friend."[450, 451]

1858 – In 1858, Thomas J. and Jemima both drop from the Dinwiddie County LTLs; presumably the above 5 acres of land reverted to Stanfield and Missouri Kidd or their successor, Susan V. Jackson, according to the provisions of the 1852 deed above. However, the amount of land that Susan V. Jackson was taxed on did not change in 1858 or 1859. We are not sure what became of that land.

Nevertheless, we believe that Thomas died circa 1858. We have found no further records for him, or for Jemima Whitmore, whom we believe was Thomas J.'s sister. See her section of this compilation.

<u>USLEY (KIDD) BREWER NEAL</u> – the daughter of George4 Kidd, AKA George Kidd Sr., named in his 1797 will in Amelia County, VA

The name "Usley" appears to be a shortened version of "Ursula", according to responses to my query on several mail lists. Though it sounds Nordic or Germanic, several respondents said their Scottish or English ancestors included an Usley.

1793 – Usley Kidd is specifically named in her father, George4 Kidd's will, which he signed on 4 March 1793.[452]

1794 – On 16 April 1794, an **Usley Kidd**, daughter of George Kidd, married John Brewer in Amelia County, VA. [453] Witnesses to consent were Stephen Southall and George Kidd.

---

[447] Dinwiddie County Land Tax Lists, 1858-1863, retrieved from FHL #29926 via familysearch.org (unrestricted access), image 40.

[448] Dinwiddie Court House, deed book 7, page 434, reviewed Jan. 14, 2010 by WRK. Retrieved from FHL #31095, image 508. Copy available upon request.

[449] Although this would seem to imply that she was single (rather than widowed), the space on the form was titled "Consort of, or Unmarried." We suspect that she had been widowed decades earlier.

[450] "Virginia, Bureau of Vital Statistics, Death Records, 1853-1912", database, *FamilySearch* (https://www.familysearch.org/ark:/61903/1:1:D91N-THMM : 23 September 2020), Jemima Whitmore, 1857. Retrieved from FHL #2056979, image 392 via familysearch.org (unrestricted access).

[451] Trent Harrison was in fact the husband of Mary C. Kidd, the daughter of Thomas J. Kidd. He was involved in several transactions with Thomas J. Kidd and James 6a Kidd, and this supports the hypothesis that they were all closely related.

[452] Amelia County, Virginia Will Book 5:359-360.

[453] *Amelia County Virginia Marriages from 1735-1850*, page 16. Also from *Amelia County Marriages 1735-1815*, by Wright, p. 17.

1798 – This John Brewer of Dinwiddie County died about 1798; his will was recorded 4 Oct. 1798 in Dinwiddie, and was witnessed by James Kidd, James Clay, and Robert McBean.[454]

1812 – On 17 November 1812, a marriage bond was issued for the marriage of Joel Neal and **Usley Kidd**. George Kidd gave the consent for Usley; witnesses to the consent were Thomas Neal and Herod Crowder. Surety was Thomas Neal. Witness to the bond was Thomas W. Powell. John Neal consents for Joel Neal. They were married on 24 November 1812 by Rev. James Chappell.[455]

This Usley could be a different person, but there are so few Kidds in this area that we believe both records belong to Usley, the daughter of George4 Kidd..

WILLIAM KIDDs

William was a very popular given name in these Kidd families. In fact, two of the authors of this work trace back to DIFFERENT William Kidds who lived in Dinwiddie County at the same time.

This compilation includes data elements for the following <u>seven</u> William Kidds:
1. **William, son of Lodowick,** ~1797-1883
2. **William "the younger,"** of Dinwiddie & Chesterfield counties, ~1813 – bet. 1866-1876
3. **William Kidd, "miller,"** born in Chesterfield County, VA, ~ 1827; died in Darvilles Twp, Dinwiddie on 21 March 1873.
4. **William Archer Kidd,** grandson of William "the younger," ~1858 - ~1935
5. **William Haley Kidd,** son of Archer Kidd, 1869-1918
6. **William R. Kidd,** most likely the son of James6a Kidd, ~1819 – bet. 1870-1880
7. **William W. Kidd** (ancestry unknown), ~1819 – 1850?

WILLIAM KIDD, the son of Lodowick5 (George4, Benjamin3, William2, Thomas1) Kidd

Kidd, and the ancestor of Reiley Kidd, one of the authors of this paper.
Born abt. 1797 in Dinwiddie County, VA
Died in 1883 in Tippah County, MS

1813-1816 – This **William Kidd** first appears in the household of his father Lodowick on the 1813 Dinwiddie County, VA PPTL:[456]

Kidd Lodwick & son Wm	2	1	—	3				1	7
Kidd Thomas	1			1					16
Killard Buckner	1	1		1					75
Kidd Benjamin	1	1		1					75

In 1814, the entry says "Lodwick and son" but doesn't name William.
In 1815, their entry says "**Kidd, Lodwick and son Wm.**"

---

[454] *Some Wills from the Burned Counties*, by William L. Hopkins, p. 26: cites VGS Quarterly 10:3, Acc. 27293-15 and Acc. 28657-2.

[455] *Marriages of Amelia County, Virginia, 1735-1815*, by Wright, p. 80.

[456] Binn's Genealogy, Dinwiddie County, Virginia, Personal Property Tax Lists, 1782-1819, available online (paid membership) at http://www.binnsgenealogy.com/MembersOnlyArea/Dinwiddie.php
CDR-000440, PPTL 1813A, image 7.

In 1816, it again says "Lodwick and son" but doesn't state that son's name.

In 1817 (see below) Lodwick pays only 1 white male tithe (his own), and **William** appears next on the PPTL, responsible for his own tithe.

1814 – This **William Kidd** served in the War of 1812 as a private in the Company commanded by A.B. Conway, in the 39th Regiment of the Virginia Militia, commanded by Col. James Byrne (?). His application says he entered the service on 28 August 1814 in Petersburg, VA and that he served until discharged at Camp Powells Creek (?) on Nov 30, 1814.[457]

1817 – **William Kidd** first appears on his own on the Dinwiddie County, VA 1817 Personal Property Tax List; he has no slaves or horses.

Name								
King John	1							
Kidd Bartholomew	1							
Kidd Lodowick	1	1	1	4				2	12
Kidd William	1							
Hegs Peterson	2	2		2				1	76
Kidd Jasper	1							
Kidd Thomas J.	1	1							70
King Henry	1	3	3	1	50			3	14
Kidd Benjamin	1	2	4	1	30			2	62
Kilpatrick Abner W.	1	2	1	1	180			2	88
Lee John	1							

1818 – On June 15, 1818, **William Kidd** obtained a marriage bond for his marriage to Elizabeth A. Southall, daughter of James Southall in Amelia County, VA. Barnett Southall served as witness or security.[458] They were married the same day.[459]

1818-1820 – **William Kidd** is on the Dinwiddie County PPTL each of these years, taxed on 1WM>16 (himself), and 1 horse.

1820 – **William Kidd** is on the Dinwiddie County, VA federal census (1001-001; one male under 9, one male 16-25 and one female 16-25), no slaves. He is living next to or with his father, Lodowick Kidd.[460]

1822 – On 13 April 1822, **William Kidd** purchased a tract of land containing 62 acres in Dinwiddie County on Bowens branch, a tributary of Namozine Creek from his father and step-mother, Lodowick and Lucy A. Kidd.[461]

---

[457] This information comes from his application for bounty land, filed on June 30, 1855 in Tippah County, MS for his service in the War of 1812, BLW #43985-160-55. He received a pension for this service (Sur. Orig. 27753, Sur. Ctf. 20126. Copies available upon request.

[458] Virginia, Marriage Records, 1700-1850, a database created by Ancestry.com, 2012, citing "Marriage Bonds in Amelia County.

[459] The George Stell Almanac, a tiny pocket almanac containing the notes of George Stell, the father of Mary Ann Stell, William Kidd's first wife, and evidently added to later by Mary Ann Stell after her marriage to William Kidd, because it contains the birth dates of William Kidd's children, by both his wives, up to 1830 (at which time the entries stop).

[460] 1820 Dinwiddie County, VA federal census, p. 13.

[461] All Dinwiddie County deeds prior to 1833 are no longer extant; but the 1848 deed in which William SELLS the land provide the specifics. See that deed in this chronology.

With this sale, Lodowick Kidd was liquidating his holdings in Dinwiddie County, in preparation for his move to western Tennessee.

1823 – **William Kidd** is appears for the first time on the Dinwiddie County, VA Land Tax Lists, taxed on 62 acres on Bowan's Branch, 12 miles NW of the courthouse, conveyed by deed from Lodowick Kidd (his father).[462]

Abt. 1825 – **William Kidd's** first wife Elizabeth A. Southall died about 1825.

1826 – On June 14,1826, **William Kidd** married Mary Ann Stell, the daughter of George Stell.[463]

1826-1848 – at least one **William Kidd** appears each year on the Dinwiddie County, VA Personal Property Tax Lists. He's not found on these lists after 1848 (the year that he moved with his family to Tippah County, Mississippi).
The other William Kidd on these lists appears to have been two different Williams. One was William R. Kidd, but RK doesn't believe that he alone can account for all the mentions of the other William. See the section for "William the younger" that follows in this paper.
At no time were more than two William Kidds in Dinwiddie County on these PPTLs; however, for many of these years, there was also a William Kidd on the Nottoway County PPTLs (Nottoway is just south of Dinwiddie, and these families moved back and forth between these two counties, and also Amelia County, to the northwest).
SEE APPENDIX FOUR for a complete listing of Kidd entries on the Dinwiddie County PPTLs, 1782-1858.

1830 – **William Kidd** appears on the VA census in **Dinwiddie** County (George5a was the only Kidd in Amelia in 1830), along with James, Mary, Thomas J. and Jasper Kidd.[464]
Kidd, Jasper – 0200001-0020001 (oldest M & F both 40-49)
Kidd, Mary – 00111- 0020101 (males 10-14, 15-19 & 20-29; oldest F 40-49)
   This is evidently Mary Kidd, widow of Benjamin.
Kidd, James – 001001-0001, 1F slave>55 (James 30-39; the only is female 15-19)
Kidd, William – 310001-00001, (3WM<5, 1 5-9 & one 30-39; one WF 20-29. One male and one female slave, each age 10-24)
Kidd, Thomas J. – 0010001- 000102, no slaves (oldest M 40-49; 2F 30-39).

1830, 1831 – a **William Kidd** appears on the **Amelia** County, VA Personal Property Tax Lists these two years, a free male over 16, by himself, with no slaves. This may be a different William Kidd, such as the William W. Kidd discussed later in this paper.

1832-1841 – Starting in 1832, there are two William Kidds on the annual **Dinwiddie** County Personal Property Tax Lists, distinguished by "Jr." and "Sr." This designation most likely indicates "the elder" and "the younger," rather than indicating a father-son relationship. Reiley Kidd's William Kidd did have a son, William G. Kidd, but he was born in 1824, and would not have been of age to appear on these lists.
We believe that the one usually referred to in these lists as **"William Sr."** is Reiley Kidd's ancestor. The other William, usually referred to as "William Jr." is probably William W.

---

[462] Dinwiddie County, VA Land Tax Lists, 1805-1823, FLH microfilm #0029921, reviewed by RK, Aug. 2009.
[463] Per the almanac of George Stell, Mary Ann Stell's father.
[464] 1830 federal census, Dinwiddie County, VA. All but Thomas J. and William are on p. 390. William is on p. 392 and Thomas J. is on p. 410.

Kidd, or another, yet unknown William Kidd. See William W. Kidd's section for a fuller explanation.

1834 –   On 5 February 1834, Frances Eanes of Dinwiddie County entered into a Deed of Trust with **William Kidd** of Dinwiddie County in order to secure the payment of debts owed to Archer J. Bevill and others. Eanes owed Bevill $68 as security for bonds to M.B. Grigg (29 Jan, 1834), Charles S. Browder (1 Nov, 1834 & 5 Jan, 1834). In this Deed of Trust, Eanes sells to Kidd for $1.00 6 head of cattle, 25 head of hogs, 3 feather beds and furniture and loom, 2 horses and all household & kitchen furniture & plantation utensils & 1 cart, as well as title and interest in the property, containing 150 acres. This property was to be held in trust by **William Kidd** until debt of $68 is satisfied or until sale of all property is undertaken to satisfy the debt. [465]

1837-1839 – There are two William Kidds on the Dinwiddie County, VA personal property tax lists (Lewis P. Lanier's list each time), listed each year as follows:[466]
William Kidd Senr. – no slaves, 1 horse, and 1 2-wheel carriage.
William Kidd Jr. – no slaves, 1 horse.

1838 – On 2 April 1838, **William Kidd** entered into a deed of trust with Robert H. Jones and James Clay, all of Dinwiddie County. Kidd was indebted to Daniel Clay of Dinwiddie in the sum of $30 due by bond, with James Clay as his security. In this deed of trust, Kidd used as collateral "one horse, two cows and their increase, one feather bed and furniture, six Windsor chairs, and all my household and kitchen furniture." **William Kidd** signed this document with an X.[467]

1840 – Only **William Kidd Sr.** is found on the Dinwiddie County, VA personal property tax list this year (Lewis P. Lanier's list), with no slaves and two horses, but no carriage.[468]

1840 – There are two William Kidds on the Dinwiddie County, VA federal census
#1, on page 9
Wm Kidd 1031001-220001 (one male 0-4, 3 males 10-14, one 15-19 & one 40-49; 2 females 0-4, two 5-9 and one 30-39 – this William fits with RK's ancestor.
#2, on the prior page, page 8:
Wm Kidd 1200010001-000001 (one male 0-4, 2 males 5-9, 1 male 30-39, and one 70-79; one female 30-40. This William Kidd would have been born between 1801 and 1810, too old to be William R. Kidd, and too young to be William Kidd Sr., RK's ancestor. For now, we're calling him "William the younger," and do not know where he fits in.

1841 – Again there are two William Kidds on the Dinwiddie County, VA personal property tax list (Lewis P. Lanier's list):[469]

---

[465] Dinwiddie County, VA. DB 1, pages 75-76, retrieved from FHL #31091, images 56-57 via familysearch.org.

[466] Dinwiddie County, VA Personal Property Tax Lists, 1837-1841, FHL US/CAN Film 0031114, personally viewed by Reiley Kidd at the Bellevue WA FHC May 29, 2009.

[467] Dinwiddie County Deed Book 2:56, retrieved from FHL #31093, image 35. Digital image of this deed available from the author.

[468] Dinwiddie County, VA Personal Property Tax Lists, 1837-1841, FHL US/CAN Film 0031114, personally viewed by Reiley Kidd at the Bellevue WA FHC May 29, 2009.

[469] Dinwiddie County, VA Personal Property Tax Lists, 1837-1841, FHL US/CAN Film 0031114, personally viewed by Reiley Kidd at the Bellevue WA FHC May 29, 2009.

Kidd, William Sr. – no slaves and 2 horses.
Kidd, William Jr. – no slaves, one horse.

1843 – On 7 Mar 1843, Mary Pentecost of Dinwiddie County sold to **William Kidd** , also of Dinwiddie for $49 a tract of land in Dinwiddie containing 14 acres on the waters of Bowings Branch, a tributary of the Namozine Creek, and being a part of a tract of land that Pentecost bought from Pleasant Akin of Petersburg, bounded as follows: east by Bowings Branch, north by said Kidd's spring branch, a tributary of said Bowings Branch, west by said Kidd's land. This deed was recorded 20 Mar 1843.[470]

In a Circuit Superior Court of Law and Chancery held for Dinwiddie County on 6 April 1843, **William Kidd and Mary Ann** his wife and the other heirs of George Stell, dec'd were the plaintiffs in a suit against Hambleton Williamson, administrator of George Stell, dec'd, defendant. After reviewing the records, including the 1821 will of the deceased, the Court ruled that the defendant render an account of his administration of the estate of the deceased before a commissioner of the Court, who is directed to examine, state and settle the same, and make report thereof to this Court, with any matters specially stated, deemed pertinent by himself, or which may be required to be so stated.[471]

1848 – On 30 October 1848, **William Kidd and Mary A**. his wife sold to William P. Clarke for $266 a tract of land on the waters of "Bowings Branch, a tributary of Namozine Creek," and made of two separate tracts or parcels, one containing 62 acres, <u>purchased from Lodowick Kidd and Lucy A. his wife on 13 April 1822,</u> and the second of 14 acres, purchased from Mary Pentecost and recorded 7 March 1843.[472]

Circa 1848 – **William Kidd** moved his large family from VA to northern Mississippi in 1848 or 1849, most likely in 1848, since he's not on the Dinwiddie PPTL in 1849, and these lists were created in the late winter or early spring.

1850 – On the Federal census in Tippah County, MS, p. 562:
HH 1002/1002
Kidd, William 53M VA Blind
  " , Mary A. 43F VA
  " , Camillus 21M VA
  " , Rufus 20M VA
  " , Charity 17F VA
  " , Mary 15F VA
  " , Olivia 14F VA
  " , Kinchin 12M VA
  " , Letitia 10F VA
  " , Fletcher 8M VA
  " , Altamira 5F VA
  " , Utemius 3M VA

---

[470] Dinwiddie County, VA. DB 3, page 564. Deed book in Dinwiddie County Courthouse.
[471] Dinwiddie County Chancery Order Book 1, 1832-1852, p. 332, reviewed by WRK and photocopied at the Dinwiddie CH on 23 February 2010.
[472] Dinwiddie County, VA DB 6, 1846-1850, p. 28, FHC microfilm #31095, reviewed by RK Jan. 5, 2010 at the Bellevue, WA FHC. Deed recorded Nov. 11, 1848.

1855 – **William Kidd** applied for Bounty Land on June 30, 1855 in Tippah County, MS for his service in the War of 1812 as a private in the Company of commanded by A.B. Conway, in the 39th Regiment of the Virginia Militia, commanded by Col. James Byrne (?). His application says he entered the service on 28 August 1814 in Petersburg, VA and that he served until discharged at Camp Powells Creek (?) on Nov 30, 1814. Judging from his application, he had not previously applied for Bounty Land. His application was witnessed by Lodawick Kidd (his father) and Rachael Kidd (his sister); both signed with "X"s.

He appears in Tippah County and later in Benton County (a daughter county formed from part of Tippah County in 1870), MS in the 1860, 1870, and 1880 federal censuses. He died 2 July 1883 in Benton County, MS and is buried there.

More information on him is available from Reiley Kidd, one of the authors. See also his pages in our MSX Kidds family tree on Ancestry.com:

https://www.ancestry.com/family-tree/person/tree/37652986/person/19120498754/facts

WILLIAM KIDD (the younger) of Dinwiddie & Chesterfield County, VA, married Matilda Wells

It is difficult to calculate his date of birth, particularly since we're not certain that all the citations below belong to one man, though we believe that they do.

It seems likely that he was born by 1813,[473] and perhaps as much as a decade earlier. He married Matilda W. Wells about 1834 (see below), and died before she did, sometime between 1866 and 1876.

We've not been able to determine who his parents were.

1830, 1831 – a **William Kidd** appears on the Amelia County, VA PPTLs these two years, but not following. This is not Reiley Kidd's William Kidd, as he is in Dinwiddie County, on the census and the 1830 Dinwiddie PPTL that year. No William Kidd appears on the Dinwiddie County PPTLs for 1831.[474]

This William was over 16, and had no taxable property.

He is too old to be William R. Kidd (below), who was born about 1819, and represents a third, as yet unplaced William Kidd. He most likely is the William Kidd whose wife was Matilda, and whose descendants were later in Chesterfield County, VA, though at this point we aren't certain of that. But for the time being, we're assuming that they all are the same William Kidd, and the data fits with this hypothesis, in terms of ages, known children, etc.

1832-1845 – Starting in 1832, there are two William Kidds on the annual Dinwiddie County Personal Property Tax Lists, distinguished by "Jr." and "Sr." This designation most likely indicates "the elder" and "the younger," rather than indicating a father-son relationship. Reiley Kidd's William Kidd did have a son, William G. Kidd, but he was born in 1824, and would not have been of age to appear on these lists. Just who is the second, younger William Kidd?

Comparing the two entries each year for these two Williams, one always has more property than the other, and their entries are consistent from year to year. The William referred to on most lists as "William Sr." is consistent with RK's ancestor, William, the son of Lodowick

---

[473] He had to be at least 16 years old when he appeared on the Amelia County, VA PPTL in 1830, for instance. His wife, Matilda's age is equally difficult to guestimate, from the census entries, where her ages are inconsistent with each other. If her death record is more accurate, she was born abt. 1811.

[474] SEE APPENDIX FOUR for a complete listing of Kidd entries on the Dinwiddie County PPTLs, 1782-1858.

Kidd, for several reasons. First and foremost, William Sr. is listed annually through 1848, and not thereafter, and RK's ancestor William moved to Tippah County, MS in 1848. And his property and other white males in the household match the known facts about this William Kidd.

The other William is too old to be William R. Kidd, and William R. Kidd appears on the **Nottoway** County, VA PPTLs for most of these years.

This **younger William Kidd's** personal property varies from year to year, as follows:

Year	Slaves	Horses	2-wheel carriage (value)
1832	0	2	0
1833	1	2	0
1834	0	1	0
1835	0	1	0
1836	0	1	0
1837	0	1	0
1838	0	1	0
1839	0	1	0
1840	not on the Dinwiddie PPTL		
1841	0	1	0
1842	not on Dinwiddie PPTL		
1843	not on Dinwiddie PPTL		
1844	0	1	0
1845	not on Dinwiddie PPTL? William R. Kidd appears for the first time, with much more property than this William Kidd had.		

1840 – There are two William Kidds on the Dinwiddie County, VA federal census
#1, on page 9
Wm Kidd 1031001-220001 (one male 0-4, 3 males 10-14, one 15-19 & one 40-49; 2 females 0-4, two 5-9 and one 30-39 – this William fits with RK's ancestor.

#2, on the prior page, page 8:
Wm Kidd 1200010001-000001 (one male 0-4, 2 males 5-9, 1 male 30-39, and one 70-79; one female 30-40. RK and WRK cannot identify this William Kidd. He appears too old to be William R. Kidd (WRK's ancestor), and too young to be William Kidd Sr. (RK's ancestor).

1835-1850 – a **"William Kidd and wife"** appear on the Dinwiddie County, Land Tax List for the first time in 1835, taxed on 60 acres on Cox Rd., 13 miles NW of the Courthouse, and an added notation says "heretofore charged to Matilda W. Wells."
He and wife continue to be taxed on this land annually through 1850, the last year we've checked.
Looking at earlier Dinwiddie LTLS, we find that a Harrison Wells first appears on these tax lists in 1828, taxed on 3 parcels on Cox Road (parcels of 30 acres and 44½ acres, 12 miles NW of the Courthouse, and an 18½ acre parcel 14 miles NW CH), along with a 108 acre tract on Winterpock Creek, 8 miles NW CH.[475] This Harrison Wells is listed annually through 1831, then drops from the Dinwiddie LTLs. In 1832, Matilda W. Wells appears on

---

[475] Dinwiddie County Land Tax Lists, 1824-1835, retrieved from FHL #29222, image 320 via familysearch.org (unrestricted access), Lewis P. Lanier's List, 1828.

the Dinwiddie LTLs for the first time, taxed on 60 acres on Cox Rd, 13 miles NW CH. She appears again in 1833 and 1834.

These entries suggest that Matilda W. Wells was the daughter (or sister) of Harrison Wells, and that she married this William Kidd ca 1834-35.

1850 – On the federal census in the Lower district of Chesterfield County, VA, p. 134, HH 338 (mis-indexed at Ancestry.com as "Ridd"):
Kidd, William 47MW "operator" VA cannot read or write
 " , Matilda 43FW VA cannot read or write
 " , Edward 18MW operator VA
 " , James 15MW operator VA
 " , Thomas 12MW VA
 " , Ann E. 10FW VA (is this Sarah? Or is she in another HH?)
Slaughter, George 19MW operator VA
(Next door is Harrison Wells and family, whom we believe is Matilda's brother, given deed naming their daughter Sarah A. Kidd – see her section)

1855 – William and Matilda's son James died on Sept. 23, 1855 in Chesterfield County at the age of 20.[476]

1860 – On the federal census in "Mattoaca Factory, southern district," Chesterfield County, VA, p. 60, HH 432/442:
Kidd, William 45MW works in factory $300/30 VA cannot read or write
 " , Matilda 40FW domestic VA cannot read or write
 " , Sarah A. 16FW weaver VA
(no others, but nearby are several Traylor families.)

The Mattoaca Cotton Factory began operation in 1834 and the small village of Mattoaca developed adjacent to the factory. In time it became a cotton mill. The mill ceased operations about 1922.

1863 – In a Dinwiddie County, VA deed dated 20 October 1863, Sarah Ann Kidd of Chesterfield County, VA sells to Robert Sydnor of Dinwiddie County for $75 "all her right, title and interest to a certain parcel or tract of land on Cox Rd." in Dinwiddie, "left by the late Harrison Wells to **William Kidd** and wife, during their natural life."[477] It seems from this deed, that her parents retained the land during their lifetime, given the later deed signed from them to Robert Sydnor. See below.

A Harrison Wells lived next to William and Matilda Kidd in Chesterfield County in 1850. He was similar in age to them, and was probably Matilda's brother.
As noted above, an older Harrison Wells, likely Matilda's father, appeared on Dinwiddie County LTLs as early as 1828. He's also found in Dinwiddie on the 1810, 1820 and 1830

---

[476] http://www.chesterfieldhistory.com/Chesterfield_Co_reg_of_deaths_1853--1896.pdf
This source lists his parents as William and Matilda Kidd, and his birthplace as Dinwiddie County. The cause of his death was not known.
[477] Dinwiddie County, VA DB 11, pp. 25-26, viewed by WRK Jan 2010, copies on file.

federal censuses.[478] He drops from the LTLs in 1832, and we suspect that he died in the preceding year.

We looked for a will or other probate record for Harrison Wells, but found nothing. Similarly, a search for Chancery Court records for him was negative. Any records for him that might have existed would likely have not survived the extensive record losses that Dinwiddie County endured.

1864 – On 16 March 1864, Sarah A. Kidd married J.W. Williams in Chesterfield County, VA.[479] This entry matches the informant for Matilda's death record in 1876 (see below).

1866 – On 20 March 1866, **William Kidd** and his wife Matilda, both of **Chesterfield County,** deeded their life interest in a certain parcel of land containing 60 acres in Dinwiddie County, and bounded on the south by Cox Road, on the west by Upton Crow, on the north by William Sally (Lally?) and on the east by Joseph Crowder. to Robert H. Sydnor for $30.00. Recorded 20 Aug, 1866.[480]
Both William and Matilda Kidd signed with an X.

1870 – I am unable to find either William or Matilda Kidd on the federal census this year, despite the fact that Matilda didn't die until 1876 (see below).

1876 – Matilda Kidd, white female, born in Dinwiddie County, died May 1876 in Chesterfield of old age at 65. Her husband **William Kidd**, is listed as deceased prior to Matilda's death. The informant for this record was "Josh Williams, son-in law."[481]
We don't know the date or place of this William Kidd's death.

WILLIAM KIDD, "MILLER," b abt. 1827 in Chesterfield County, died 1873 in Dinwiddie County
All information at this time for this William Kidd comes from his 1873 death record.[482]

1827 – This **William Kidd** was born ca 1827, since he was 46 years of age at his death in 1873. His death record states that he was born in Chesterfield County, VA. The informant evidently did not know the names of his parents, since this box was left blank.

1873 – He died of pneumonia on 21 March 1873 in Darvilles Twp, Dinwiddie County, VA. He was a widower at the time of his death. His occupation was listed as "miller." The informant was H. Pursells, listed as a friend of the deceased. Pursells was also the assessor of Dinwiddie county at the timeand the official who filled out this Death Register, signing the page on which this death record appears.

He does not appear to be any of the other William Kidds listed here. He was born a decade or more later than William R. Kidd, and the occupation of miller does not fit with William R. Kidd.

---

[478] 1810 census: 1M 10-15, 1 16-25 & 1>44; 2F<10, 2 10-15 & 1>44.
    1820 census: 1M>44; 2F 10-15, 1 16-25 and 1>44. Eight slaves.
    1830 census: 1M 15-19 & 1 50-59; 1F 20-29 & 1 50-59. Four slaves.
[479] Personal correspondence from WRK, an author of this paper, from old notes.
[480] Dinwiddie County, VA. DB 11, pages 269-270, retrieved from FHL #31097, images 571-572. Copy available upon request.
[481] Chesterfield County Death Registers, 1853-1896.
[482] *Dinwiddie County Virginia, Deaths and Burials, 1853-1896*, FHL #2056979, image 451, retrieved via Familysearch.org. Scanned image available.

Perhaps he is related to the James Kidd who died at the age of 80 in Darvilles District on August 1874, another person whom we have not been able to identify.

WILLIAM ARCHER KIDD, **the son of Edward Kidd of Chesterfield County, VA, and grandson of William "the younger" Kidd.**
    Born in 1858, Chesterfield County, VA,
    Married Louisiana C. (Waltriss or Waltrip), born 15 January 1855, died 30 October 1939.[483]
    Died in 1935, Chesterfield County, VA.
    WRK, one of the authors of this paper, found a William Archer Kidd listed as father of the following children on the Chesterfield County, Virginia Births index.[484] Though two different names are listed for mother, census records suggest Louisian(n)a and Susanna were the same woman:
    Kidd, Rebecca Susan, b. Nov 1879, Chesterfield, Parents: **William Archer** & Susanna, p. 219
    Kidd, Rebecca, b. Feb 1880, Chesterfield, Parents: **William Archer** & Susanna, p. 230
    Kidd, Morles Edward, b. 2 Feb 1882, Chesterfield, Parents: **William Archer** & Susanna, p. 262
    Kidd, Elverine (twin), b. 5 Oct 1884, Chesterfield, Parents: **William Archer** & Louisiana, p. 297.
    Kidd, Kerosine (twin), b. 5 Oct 1884, Chesterfield, Parents **William Archer** & Louisiana, p. 297; she died two days after birth.[485]
    Kidd, James William, b. Sept 1886, Chesterfield, Parents **William Archer** & Susanna, p. 327[486]
    Kidd, (S.B.), b. Aug 1889, Chesterfield, Parents **William Archer** & Louisiana, p. 381
    Kidd, Pearl Gertrude, b. 25 Sep 1890, Chesterfield, Parents **William Archer** & Louisiana, p. 392
    Kidd, Ruby Florence, b. 14 Jul 1893, Chesterfield, Parents: **William Archer** & Louisiana C., p. 454

1870 – He is possibly this **William Kidd**, on the federal census, Petersburg P.O., Manchester township, Chesterfield County, VA, p. 378, HH 801/948 (evidently in an apartment building or tenement of some sort, with 3 families, 18 individuals, in the same building):
Vaughan, Francis L. 53WM carpenter   VA cannot write
  " , Mary 56FW keeps house VA Can read and write
Hunt, Martha A. 46WF works in cotton factory VA cannot write
  " , Ann 17FW weaver VA cannot write
Brown, Elizabeth 26FW weaver VA cannot write
Deshman, Mary J. 10FW works in cotton factory VA cannot read or write
Kidd, William A. 12MW works in cotton factory VA cannot read or write

---

[483] From her headstone at Findagrave.com, where a photo of her headstone can be found.
[484] Chesterfield births, 1853-1888, retrieved from reel 33 at the Library of Virginia (not available via familysearch.org).
[485] Chesterfield County Death Registers, 1853-1896.
[486] He is buried in the East Matoaca cemetery in Chesterfield County, VA (found on Findagrave.com). His headstone lists his DOB as June 9, 1886, and his date of death as July 2, 1969. His wife, buried in the same plot, was Minnie H. Kidd.

1878 – On 23 December 1878, a **William A. Kidd**, age 21, married L. (Louisiana?) Waltress, age 22, in Chesterfield County, VA.[487]

1880 – **William A. Kidd** appears on the federal census in the city of Manchester, Chesterfield County, VA, ED 70, sheet 15C, p. 130, HH 144/159:
Smith, George C. WM 45M retail grocery England England England
  " , Martha A. wife FW 42M keeps house NC NC NC
  " , Frederick W. son MW 18S clerk in factory NC England NC
  " , Mattie dau FW 11S at school NC England NC
  " , Kate dau FW 8S   NC England NC
Kidd, William (H. or A.) boarder WM 24M plumber VA VA VA
  " , Louisa boarder WF 26M at home VA VA VA
  " , Mary E. boarder WF 3S VA VA VA

1900 – We haven't been able to find him in this census. We scanned the entire 7th revenue district in Matoaca twp., and didn't find them.

1910 – He is on the federal census in in Matoaca, Chesterfield County, VA with wife Louisiana and several children, ED 8, sheet 8A, p. 163, HH 146/157:
Kidd, William A. head MW 52M1 VA VA VA laborer, cotton mill
  " , Louisana wife WF 54M1 marr.33y 12children/7living VA VA VA no occ.
  " , Ruby dau WF 16S VA VA VA laborer, cotton mill
  " , ?Gayle dau WF 12S VA VA VA no occupation
Mann, Aldridge boarder WM 19S VA VA VA laborer, trunk factory

(next door on one side is Ralph B. and Pearl Mann (Pearl could be William A.'s daughter, age 20 on this census and married just a year; on the other side is James Kidd, William A.'s probable son, and his young family.)

1920 – On the federal census in in Matoaca, Chesterfield County, VA with wife Louisiana and daughter (?) Doris, age 14.

1930 – On the federal census in Matoaca, Chesterfield County, VA with wife Louisiana and no others in the household.

1935 – died in Chesterfield County, VA, and was buried in East Matoaca Cemetery, alongside his wife, Louisiana.[488]

---

[487] Personal correspondence from WRK, from his old notes, citation not certain at this time.
[488] https://www.findagrave.com/memorial/39515554/william-archer-kidd

<u>**WILLIAM HALEY KIDD**</u>, **the son of Archer/Archibald Kidd**
>   **The ancestor of Rebecca Starr of England.**
>   **Born April 1870[489] in Greensville County, VA.**
>   **Lived in Greensville and Sussex County, VA, where he married twice, before moving to Warrenton, Warren County, NC in 1916.**
>   **Married Martha A. Hawkins about 1907, by whom he had two children: Bertha, born 1909 and a son George, born 1911. Martha died in Sussex County after childbirth in 1914.**
>   **Married second Rebecca L. High in September 1914 in Halifax County, NC; they were the parents of two sons Benjamin Harold (born in 1915) and Amos (born in 1917).**
>   **Died by his own hand in Warrenton, Warren County, NC on 23 August 1918, at the age of 48.[490]**
>   **Buried in an unmarked plot in the Old Warrenton Cemetery in Warrenton, Warren County, NC.[491] His death certificate lists his parents as Archie Kidd and May Williams.**

His widow Rebecca gave their two boys up after the death of her husband, according to Rebecca Starr. Son Benjamin was adopted by Vernon A. Kirk and his wife in Guilford County, NC in 1920; son Amos was adopted by William A. and Lula E. McCullough in 1920 in Guilford County, NC, and his name was changed to Raymond Allen McCullough. Amos/Raymond died in 1995 in Rowan County, NC.

For more information on William Haley Kidd and his descendants, please see his page in our Kidd family tree on Ancestry.com at: https://www.ancestry.com/family-tree/person/tree/37652986/person/19120499496/facts .

<u>**WILLIAM R. KIDD**</u> **(the ancestor of William R. "Bill" Kidd of Newport News, VA, one of the authors of this compilation)**
>   **Most likely the son of James6a Kidd of Amelia and Dinwiddie County.**
>   **See James6a's notes in this compilation.**
>   **Born abt. 1818 in Dinwiddie County, VA[492]**
>   **Married (1) Martha D. Young in 1844 in Dinwiddie County, VA; she died June 1859**
>   **Married (2) Martha E. A. Phillips in July 1861 in Amelia County, VA**
>   **Was a lumber dealer and farmer, who left records in Dinwiddie, Nottoway, Amelia and Chesterfield Counties, and was later in Petersburg City, then in Sussex County in 1870.**
>   **The date and place of his death are presently unknown.**

---

[489] His federal census entry in 1870 lists his age as "1/12" year, and specifically indicates that he was born in April. His 1918 death certificate lists his age at death as 51 years, but this is not likely, given this 1870 federal census entry. The informant was his younger brother, who likely did not know the year of his brother's birth.

[490] Rebecca Starr provided a copy of his death certificate. The informant for this death certificate was a John Kidd (his brother) of Jarratt (spelled Jarritt on the certificate) (Greensville County), VA.

[491] Findagrave.com; see https://www.findagrave.com/memorial/109175764 for more information.

[492] this estimated year of birth comes from his census entries in 1850 and 1860. No birth record has been found for him.

1839-1840 – He appears on the **Nottoway** County, VA Personal Property Tax Lists, listed as **William Kidd** (no middle initial). The only other Kidd there is a James Kidd, presumably his father.[493]

1840 – We have been unable to find him on the 1840 federal census. He's not in the household of his parents in Nottoway County.

1842 – **William R. Kidd** appears this one year on the **Amelia** County, VA PPTL, taxed only for his own tithe and one horse.[494]

1843-1844 – **William R. Kidd** is found on the annual PPTLs back in **Nottoway** County, VA.

1844 – **William R. Kidd** married Martha D. Young on January 31, 1844 in **Dinwiddie** County, VA.[495] Martha died in June 1859 (see below).

1845 -1852 – He appears on the **Dinwiddie** County, VA Personal Property Tax Lists for these years, listed annually as **William R. Kidd** (unlike the earlier listings for William Kidd Sr. [RK's ancestor] and William Kidd Jr. [as yet unplaced]).

YEAR	Slaves	Horses	2-wheel Carriages (value)
1845	2	1	1 ($50)
1846	1	1	0
1847	0	2	0
1848	0	1	0
1849	0	1	0
1850	2	1	0
1851	0	1	0
1852	0	2	0

1845 – 7 August 1845, **Nottoway** County Court: **William R Kidd** against John N Tucker and Philip Jackson. This suit abated at rules as to defendant Tucker and the defendant Jackson, his attorney pleaded payment to which the plaintiff replied generally the office/offer? In this case is set aside and cause continued for the defendant.[496]

6 November 1845. **Nottoway** County Court. **William R Kidd** is listed as a juror in Varnum et al vs. Thomas Wilson, and also as a juror in George B McKay for Robert Bolling vs. Joel Morty.[497]

6 November 1845. **Nottoway** County Court. **William R Kidd** against John W Tucker & Philip Jackson. The suit abated at rules as to defendant Tucker this day came as the ____ the plaintiff by his attorney as the defendant Jackson in his proper person ______. Defendant Jackson relinquishes his former plea whereby the plaintiffs action against him remains altogether ______ (unchanged?) Therefore it is considered by the court that the plaintiff

---

[493] In 1839 and 1840, he's listed only as William Kidd. He's not found there in 1841 or 1842, but reappears in 1843 through 1847, listed each time as William R. Kidd.

[494] Amelia County PPTLs, 1836-1853, retrieved from FHL #2024256, image 179.

[495] *Some Marriages in the Burned Record Counties of Virginia.* Many Dinwiddie County marriages were recorded in Dinwiddie County Deed Books, including this one. It was retrieved from Dinwiddie County Deed Book 5, p. 390 from FHL #31094, image 551 (restricted access)

[496] Order book 13, Nottoway County, VA. Page 413. Located in Nottoway County, VA Circuit Court.

[497] Order book 13, Nottoway County, VA. Page 423. Located in Nottoway County, VA Circuit Court.

recover against the defendant Jackson $32.25 with legal witness therein from the 5th day of December, 1844 the ___said deed in trust in the declaration maintained and his costs by him about his suit in his behalf expended.[498]

1850 – On the federal census in **Dinwiddie** County, VA, page 456A, HH 344:
    Kidd, Wm. R. 31MW farmer $0 VA
    " , Martha F. 24FW VA
    " , George W. 4MW VA

    William R. Kidd is also on the 1850 slave schedule, with six slaves:
    one 40 year old female black
    one 24 year old female black
    one 10 year old male black
    one 3 year old male mulatto
    one 2 year old male black
    one 1 year old female mulatto

    He is on the agricultural schedule of the 1850 census, which lists him as a tenant farmer, with one horse, 2 oxen, 1 cow, 12 swine. The use of the term "tenant" suggests he rents rather than owns his land.

1853 – **W. R. Kidd** reported the birth of Jim, a male slave born to Sally, his mother, 2 December 1853 in **Dinwiddie** County. W. R. Kidd listed as owner and master.[499]

1854 – **Wm. R. Kidd** is found on the **Chesterfield** County, VA PPTL this year.

    24 December 1854. **Chesterfield** County Court – **William R. Kidd** and Samuel Clarke became partners in the business of sawing timber for sale. Clarke was to furnish the mill and material and Kidd would provide the labor for cutting the timber at the Fenley water station on the Clover Hill railroad, near where the mill is located. Kidd states that he fulfilled his part of the agreement, but that Clarke has failed in his. Kidd also claims that lumber dealers in Richmond owe him $173.52, and that Clarke is insolvent. Court rules in favor of Kidd.[500]

1855 – Ida V. Kidd, the daughter of **W. R.** and M. F. **Kidd**, was born 16 January 1855, in Chesterfield County, VA.[501]

    William R. Kidd appears again on the **Chesterfield** County Personal Property Tax List in 1855.
    Also in 1855, **William R. Kidd** was the plaintiff in a Chancery Court suit against Samuel Clarke in Chesterfield County.[502]   See 1854, above.

---

[498] Order book 13, Nottoway County, VA. Page 423. Located in Nottoway County, VA Circuit Court.
[499] *Dinwiddie County, VA Births, 1853-1868*, microfilm #19 reviewed by WR Kidd at Library of Virginia.
[500] Personal correspondence from WR Kidd, 2003, citing "Court Order, Chesterfield County, VA, Library of Virginia Archive Room, letter."
[501] Chesterfield births, 1853-1888, reel 33 at the Library of Virginia (not available via familysearch.org).
[502] Found in the on-line index to Chancery Court records(Case 1855-033); no scanned images available. We've not obtained images of this record yet.

Maria Kidd, a 1-year-old girl, daughter of **W.R.** and M.F. **Kidd**, was born in **Dinwiddie** County; she died 6 August 1855 in **Chesterfield** County, VA of scarlet fever.[503]

1857 – In an **Amelia** County deed dated 26 February 1857, **William Kidd** entered into a Deed of Trust with Charles Lumsden and James Kidd, as follows: William Kidd and Charles Lumsden had formed a partnership under the name Lumsden and Kidd for the purpose of cutting and sawing timber and grinding corn on a piece of land in Amelia County called the Brown tract, which they recently bought from A. H. Burke. They also bought a saw mill engine. Both Kidd and Lumsden agreed to share equally in all expenses. William Kidd wished to indemnify and secure Lumsden against any payment Lumsden may make on behalf of Kidd's part with a negotiable note of $595.51, made by William Kidd and held by W. L. Watkins, trustee of Samuel Clarke, which will be due 1 January 1859. Charles Lumsden and James Kidd paid William Kidd $5.00 for five Negroes, currently residing in Petersburg. Signed by William R. Kidd, James Kidd and Charles Lumsden on 2 March 1857. Recorded in Amelia County Court 28 January 1858.[504]

1857-1867 – In these years **William R. Kidd** appears on the **Amelia** County, VA Personal Property Tax Lists.[505]

1859 – William R. Kidd's wife, Martha, died in June 1859 in Amelia County. She's listed on the 1860 mortality schedule for Amelia County, VA, which lists her age as 34. She died suddenly of a "disease of the heart."[506]

1860 – **William R. Kidd** is on the federal census in 5th Magisterial district, Mannboro P.O., Amelia County, VA, p. 77, (mis-indexed at Ancestry.com as RIDD), HH 606/581:
Kidd, W.R. 40MW lumberman $2000/5914 VA
  " , George W. 13MW VA
(No others; Martha F., his first wife, died in the prior year.)

The Slave Schedule for the 1860 census shows that **William R. Kidd** owned 4 slaves, and was renting a fifth from Mary Gilliam of Dinwiddie County.

On 26 July 1860, **William R. Kidd** and William C. Lumsden bought 200 acres in **Amelia** County from Abner H. Burke and his wife Mary for $1,500. The land was bounded north by the Appomattox River, east by the lands of Abner H. Burke, and south by Greens road and west by the lands of Joseph Wilson. The deed was recorded on the same day. [507]

Wm C. Lumsden sold his half of the 200 acres in Amelia County to J. L. Gilbert of Bridgeport Connecticut on 6 December 1860 for $800 including the buildings and interest in the Steam Engine Saw Mill and Grist Mill in Amelia County. This deed was not recorded in Amelia Court until a decade later, 8 Feb 1870. [508]

---

[503] Chesterfield County Death Registers, 1853-1896.
[504] Amelia County, Virginia DB 39:492, WRK, 2003.
[505] Personal correspondence from William R. Kidd, (details not given).
[506] Amelia County, VA 1860 Mortality Schedule at Ancestry.com, p. 40.
[507] Deed book 40:174, Amelia County, VA, Amelia County Courthouse, Amelia County, VA, book.
[508] Deed book 41, Amelia County, VA, Amelia County Courthouse, Amelia County, VA, book.

On 6 December 1860, J. S. Gilbert sold to **William R. Kidd** for $800 one half of the 200 acre tract of land, bought by Kidd and Lumsden from A. H. Burke in Amelia County, including one half interest in the Steam Engine Saw and Grist Mill, being the same property sold by Lumsden and wife to Gilbert. This deed was also not recorded in Amelia Court until 8 February 1870. [509]

1861-1870 – **William R. Kidd** appears on the Amelia County, VA, PPTLs in these years [510]

He also appears on the Amelia County, VA, Land Tax Lists in these years, taxed on 200 acres on the Appomattox River each year.[511]

On 31 July 1861, **William R. Kidd** married Martha E.A. Philips in Amelia County, VA. He is listed as a widower, and his occupation was "lumber merchant." [512]

1863 – On 6 February 1863, Joseph B. Williams and Mary Ann his wife sold to James Kidd (residence not specified for either the sellers or the buyer) for $1000 a certain tract of land in the county of Amelia containing 100 acres and bounded by the following lines, viz., beginning at **William Kidd's** corner (we believe that this is William R. Kidd, this James Kidd's son, and that this is the site of his lumber and grist mill venture) on the Petersburg Road, thence with his line …to the Appomattox River, thence up the river 159 poles to a small stream near a large red oak, thence a new line to the Petersburg Road, thence along the road to the beginning. Joseph B. Williams and Mary Ann Williams both signed this deed. The deed was acknowledged by the sellers before a notary public on 11 August 1866 in Amelia County, but wasn't entered into record in Amelia County until 16 March 1868.[513]

1866 – **Kidd's** Mill appears on the 1866 Jedediah Hotchkiss map, which shows the mill on Wintercomack Creek at the Appomattox. [514]

1866 Orders, Amelia County, VA. Rule vs. **Kidd** discharged. [515]
25 Oct 1866 Orders: **Wm R Kidd** appointed surveyor of the road in the place of Daniel Robertson with the usual hands. [516]

1867 – A son, John Kidd, was born 10 March 1867 in the City of Petersburg, VA to **William R Kidd,** occupation – Lumber Dealer, and Martha Kidd. The person giving the information was "Jas. Kidd, grandfather."[517]

1868 – **William R. Kidd**, lumber merchant, is listed in the 1868-1869 Petersburg City directory, living on Washington Street, near South Street. [518]

---

[509] "Deed book 41," Amelia County, VA, Amelia County Courthouse, Amelia County, VA, book.
[510] "Personal property tax record," Amelia County, VA, microfilm, LVA.
[511] Amelia County land tax records.
[512] "Register of Marriages," Amelia County, VA, book, Amelia County Courthouse.
[513] Amelia County Deed Book 40, p. 608, retrieved by WRK at LoV, reel 18, in January 2003. Image available upon request.
[514] Historical notes on Amelia County, VA," page 368.
[515] *Order Book 45 1856-66*, Amelia County, VA, 1866, Amelia County Courthouse.
[516] *Order Book 45 1856-66*, Amelia County, VA, 1866, Amelia County Courthouse.
[517] Petersburg, Virginia Register of Births, 1853-1871, page 111, retrieved from FHL #33443, image 92 of 450, via familysearch.org (unrestricted access).
[518] Petersburg City directory 1868-69, page 48, located at LVA, reviewed 2-22-03.

On 3 January 1868, the *Petersburg Daily Index* published an article titled "Mayor's Court yesterday morning, His Honor Mayor Collier presiding":[519]
"On Saturday evening last a difficulty occurred Mr. **W. R. Kidd** on the one part, and Thomas Pryor and Edward Pryor, colored, on the other, at the house of the former – having its origin in the settlement of some accounts. Blows were passed and some damage inflicted on either side. Mr. Kidd received a cut on the head, and both the Pryors slight injuries. The case was carefully investigated by the Mayor, who after reviewing the evidence of witnesses, reprimanded all the parties concerned and discharged them."

On 24 May 1868, Ida V. Kidd, daughter of **William R. Kidd**, died in Petersburg, VA.[520]

1869 – **William R. Kidd** appears on the Petersburg, VA, PPTLs in this year.[521]

A son, James Kidd, was born January 1869 in Sussex County, VA, to **William** (a farmer) and Martha **Kidd**; he died 26 October 1869 from diarrhea, aged 9 months. [522], [523]

On 16 September 1869, **William R. Kidd** and Martha A. his wife sold for $2,000 a tract of land containing 200 acres in the county of Amelia to William G Verrell, originally purchased by Kidd and Lumsden from A. H. Burke. Recorded in Amelia County, VA 8 February 1870.[524]

1870 – He is likely the William Kidd living in the HH of his son George W. Kidd on the federal census in Stony Creek P.O., Sussex County, VA, p. 9, HH 80:
Kids, George 25MW farmer VA
" , Robert 7MW VA
" , John 3MW VA
" , **William** 53MW farmer VA
Harvel, Manerva 16BF domestic servant VA cannot read or write
The two young boys, Robert and John, are William R. Kidd's sons by his second wife, Martha Phillips, who evidently has died in the past 12 months.[525]

6 October 1870, listed in Sussex County, VA, PPTLs, with 2 white males over the age of 21 in the house, taxed $2.93. [This is likely William R. Kidd and son George W.].[526]

No further records have been found for this William R. Kidd. We believe that he died in the decade following this entry, but his date and place of death are at present unknown.

---

[519] Retrieved from NewspaperArchive.com via Ancestry.com, page 3, column 1, Aug. 22, 2018.
[520] Death record 1853-1892, Petersburg VA, reel 34, LVA.
[521] Personal property tax record, reel 817, 1869, page 70, line 23, on microfilm at LVA, 3-14-03.
[522] Sussex COUNTY, VA. Death records, 1853-1896, reel 29. Microfilm at LVA.
[523] "Birth Records," 1867-1879, Sussex County, VA, reel 11, microfilm, LVA.
[524] Amelia County Deed Book 41, page 196, reviewed by WRK at Amelia Courthouse.
[525] At the time of the 1880 federal census, both Robert and John are in the household of John Phillips (Martha's widowed father) in Amelia County, Virginia, listed has his grandsons on this census.
[526] "Personal Property Tax Books," Sussex County, VA, district 1 of L. P. Hargrove, 1865-1870, microfilm, reel # 774, LVA.

1888 – **Kidd's Mill** is shown on the LaPrade Map of Chesterfield County, VA, published in 1888.[527]

For more information on **William R. Kidd**, see his page in our Kidd family tree on Ancestry.com, at https://www.ancestry.com/family-tree/person/tree/37652986/person/19120499471/facts

WILLIAM W. KIDD – We are unable to identify this William Kidd, or to associate him with other known Kidds
> **Born about 1819 in Dinwiddie County**
> **Married Delitha A. Williams before September 1841**
> **Drops from VA records in 1850; wife Delitha listed as a widow by 1859**
> **Apparently had no surviving children**

1840 – Despite the record below, we've been unable to find him on the 1840 census in Dinwiddie County or surrounding counties.
On 18 Nov 1840, Thompson Stewart, acting as a commissioner of the County of **Dinwiddie** under a decree made September term 1840 in the Chancery court suit of Frederick Mayes heirs vs. Frederick Mayes heirs, sold to **William W. Kidd** for $100.25 a tract of land from the estate of Frederick Mayes deceased containing 89 ¼ acres and lying in Dinwiddie County on Cox Road. This deed was recorded on 8 December 1840.[528]

1840-1858 – Despite the records cited here, this William W. Kidd never appears on the Dinwiddie County PPTLs.

1841 – **William W. Kidd** appears on the 1841 Dinwiddie County Land Tax List, taxed for 89¼ acres on Cox Rd 11 miles NW of the Courthouse.

On 25 September 1841, **William W. Kidd** and Delitha Ann Kidd his wife sold 90 acres to Joseph F. Williams for $100.25, the same amount they paid for it.[529]

1842 – The 1842 Dinwiddie Land Tax List shows that this land was deeded by **William Kidd** & wife to Joseph F. Williams.[530]
William W. Kidd then drops from the Dinwiddie County LTLs, and does not reappear.

1850 – **William W. Kidd** was an enlisted U.S. Army soldier during the War with Mexico. Information gives age as 31 (born abt. 1819), born in Dinwiddie VA., brown eyes, black hair, fair completion, height 5'11", occupation was painter. Enlisted on 20 Nov 1850. [Where he enlisted looks like Newport, but I can't be sure and I also am unsure of who it is he enlisted with; it looks like Capt. Maorne.] The only other note is that he deserted 16 Dec 1850, no other information.[531]

1855 – Delitha A. Kidd entered into a deed with Prussian Frazier et al in Dinwiddie County, VA, buying land, livestock and furniture.[532] The deed made no mention of William W. Kidd, who may have been deceased by this time.

---

[527] "Map of Chesterfield County, VA," 1888, LaPrade, Chesterfield County Historical Society.
[528] Dinwiddie County, VA. DB 2, page 595. Deed book located at Dinwiddie County Courthouse.
[529] Dinwiddie County Court House, Deed Book 3, page 154, retrieved fro FHL #31093, image 405 via familysearch.org (unrestricted access).
[530] List of Louis P. Lanier, 1842, "90 acres on Cox Road, 11Miles NW of Courthouse, valued at $2 per acre, no added value, valuation = $180, tax = $0.20.
[531] Personal correspondence, William R. Kidd.
[532] Deed Book 8, p. 253. See Delitha's section in this paper. No mention of William. Did he desert her? Die in Mexico?

1859 – On 3 June 1859, Delitha A. Kidd, a 36-year-old widow, married Alexander Hogwood, a 28-year-old farmer, single, in Dinwiddie County, VA.[533] Both were born in Dinwiddie County. His parents are listed as (Charles? Illegible) and Sarah Hogwood, and hers as Robert and Mary Williams.

1860 – Delitha is on the federal census in the west ward of Petersburg, VA, p. 194, HH 1816/1777:
Hogwood, Alex[r] 26MW laborer $0/25 VA cannot read or write
" , **Delitha** 36FW seamstress VA   evidently can read and write

1864 – On 12 September 1864, **Alexander Hogwood** and **Delitha** his wife sold to George S. Williams for <u>one cow and calf</u> "twenty-five acres of land with general warrantee, it being one-half of a tract or parcel of land given by a deed of gift to Joseph F. Williams by the late David Williams and admitted to record on the 18th day of March 1844, the said land lying in the county of Dinwiddie …bounded by the lands of Stephen Reams, F. C. Gittman and others. The above Joseph F. Williams sold the said land to Prussian E. Frayser being fifty acres as given him by David Williams, the said Frayser selling one-half that is twenty-five acres to **Delitha A. Kidd** …who has since intermarried with Alexander Hogwood." Alexander Hogwood signed this deed with an X, while Delitha apparently signed her name.[534]

We could find no other mentions of Delitha after 1864. Since there were no Kidd children in her household in 1860, we conclude that She and William W. Kidd most likely had no children that survived.

This ends our compilation of data. We welcome all constructive criticism, corrections, suggestions.

See our website at <u>www.kiddroots.org</u>

---

[533] Dinwiddie County, VA Marriage Register, 1853-1861, p 13, from LDS #1929644, item 1, reviewed and transcribed by RK 4/6/2010..
[534] Dinwiddie County Deed Book 11, pages 106-107, retrieved from FHL # 31097, image 488 via familysearch.org.

APPENDIX ONE: SOURCES INCLUDED IN THE CREATION OF THIS BOOK

We have made a concerted effort to identify every primary and secondary source record for each of these three counties, and to examine as many of them as we could. WorldCat, the online catalog of the Library of Virginia and the catalog of FamilySearch.org were our three main sources in this endeavor.

I. AMELIA COUNTY SOURCES

PRIMARY
U.S. Federal censuses, 1810-1850 (and later)

Amelia County Personal Property Tax Lists
http://www.lva.virginia.gov/public/guides/pptax.htm
1782-1813 – LoV reel #15 or FHL #2024454 (restricted access)
1814-1835 – LoV reel #16, or FHL #2024455 (restricted access)
1836-1853 – LoV reel #17 or FHL #2024456 (restricted access)
(Other, later PPTLs are available via LoV, if desired, via interlibrary loan)

Amelia County Land Tax Lists
http://www.lva.virginia.gov/public/guides/landTax.asp
1782-1818 – LoV reel #14 via interlibrary loan
1819-1841 – LoV reel #15 via interlibrary loan
1842-1850 – LoV reel #16 via interlibrary loan
(Other, later LTLs are also available via LoV, if desired, via interlibrary loan)

Amelia County Land Records
General Index to Deeds, 1734-1953, Grantees, surnames A, B (p.1-66) – FHL #1902598
General Index to Deeds, 1734-1953, Grantees, surnames B, C-E, & F (p. 1-24) – FHL #1902599
General Index to Deeds, 1734-1953, Grantees, surnames F (p. 25-end, G-K, L (p.1-88) – FHL# 1902600
General Index to Deeds, 1734-1953, Grantees, surnames L (p. 87-end), M-R – FHL#1902601
General Index to Deeds, 1734-1953, Grantees S-Z- FHL #1902602
General Index to Deeds, 1734-1947, Grantors, A-D – FHL #30422
General Index to Deeds, 1734-1953, Grantors, surnames B (p. 121a-end), C-E – FHL 1902593
General Index to Deeds, 1734-1953, Grantors, surnames E-J – FHL #1902594
General Index to Deeds, 1734-1953, Grantors, surnames K-Q – FHL #1902595
General Index to Deeds, 1734-1953, Grantors, surnames R-V - – FHL #1902596
General Index to Deeds, 1734-1953, Grantors, surnames W-Z – FHL #1902597
Deed Books available from 1734, ff. available via Familysearch.org or LoV via interlibrary loan.
Marriage Records and Vital Records
Index-Transcript of Marriage Bonds, 1735-1854 – LoV reel #54, item # ??
Register of Deaths, 1853-1871 (unpaged) – LoV reel #54. item 2??

Amelia County Wills
General Index to Wills, 1734-1926 – LoV reel 338 or FHL #30449, item 1
Will Books available from 1734, ff. available via Familysearch.org or LoV via interlibrary loan.
Amelia County Court Order Books
(Early Order Books covered by abstracts – see Secondary Sources)

Order Book 3, 1751-1755 (internal index) - LoV reel #40, item 1

Order Book 4a (Minutes), 1754-1758, unpaged, probably no index, LoV reel #40, iem 2

Order Book 4, 1755-1757, internal index – LoV reel #40, item 3

Order Book 5, 1757-1760, internal index – LoV reel #40, item 4?

Order Book 6, 1760-1763, internal index – LoV reel #41, item 1?

Order Book 7, 1763, internal index, but missing pages LoV reel #41, item 2?

Order Book 8, 1764-1765, (no index?) – LoV reel #41, item #3?

Order Book 9, 1765-1767, internal index – LoV reel#42, item 1?

Order Book 10, 1767-1768, internal index – LoV reel #42, item 2?

Order Book 11, 1768-1769, internal index – LoV reel #42 item 3?

Order Book 12, 1769-1771, internal index – LoV reel #43 item 1?

Order Book 13, 1772-1778, (internal index?) – LoV reel #43, item 2?

Order Book 14, 1776-1780, internal index – LoV reel #43, item 3?

(Order Books 15-22, below, have been abstracted and compiled by others – see Secondary Sources)

Order Book 15, 1780-1782, internal index – LoV reel #43, item 4?

Order Book 16, 1782-1785 IS MISSING

Order Book 17, 1785-1786, internal index – LoV reel #44, item 1?

Order Book 18, 1786-1788, internal index – LoV reel #44, item 2?

Order Book 19, 1788-1791, internal index – LoV reel #44, item 3?

Order Book 20, 1792-1795, internal index – LoV reel #44, item 4?

Order Book 21, 1795-1797, internal index – LoV reel #45, item 1?

Order Book 22, 1797-1800, internal index – LoV reel #45, item 2?

Order Book 23, 1800-1801, internal index – LoV reel #45, item 3?

Order Book 24 (Minutes), 1800-1804, unpaged – LoV reel #46, item 1?

Order Book 25, 1801-1802, internal index – LoV reel #46, item 2?

Proceedings from November 1804-April 1810 MISSING

Order Book 26, 1810- 1812, internal index – LoV reel #46, item 3?

NO Order Book 27

Order Book 28, 1812-1814, internal index – LoV reel #47, item 1?

Order Book 29, 1814-1817, internal index – LoV reel #47, item 2?

Order Book 30, 1817-1819, internal index – LoV reel #47, item 3?

Order Book 31, 1819-1821, internal index – LoV reel #48, item 1?

Order Book 32, 1821-1823, internal index – LoV reel #48, item 2?

Order Book 33, 1823-1825, internal index – LoV reel #48, item 3?

Order Book 34, 1825-1827, internal index – LoV reel #49, item 1?

Order Book 35, 1827-1828, internal index – LoV reel #49, item 2?

Order Book 36, 1828-1829, internal index – LoV reel #49, item 3?

Order Book 37, 1830-1832, internal index – LoV reel #50, item 1?

Order Book 38, 1832-1834, internal index – LoV reel #50, item 2?

Order Book 39, 1834-1837, internal index – LoV reel #50, item 3?

Order Book 40, 1837-1841, internal index – LoV reel #51, item 1?

Order Book 41, 1841-1845, internal index – LoV reel #51, item 2?

Order Book 42, 1846-1850, internal index – LoV reel #51, item 3?

Other, later Order Books also available.

Amelia County Superior Court of Law

Common Law Order Book No. 1, 1809-1821, internal index – LoV reel #94, item 1?

Common Law Order Book No. 2, 1822-1831, internal index – LoV reel #94, item 2?

Amelia County Circuit Superior Court of Law and Chancery
Chancery Order Book #1, 1832-1835 (no internal index??) – LoV reel 62, item ?
Common Law Order Book No. 3, 1831-1843, internal index – LoV reel 95, item ?
Common Law Order Book No. 4, 1843-1852, internal index – LoV reel 95, item ?

Amelia County Circuit Court
Chancery Orders No. 1, 1832-1855, (no internal index??) – LoV reel 62, item ?
(Other, later Circuit Court Chancery Order books)
Amelia County Index to Chancery Causes, A-Z. 1830-1847 – LoV reel #67, item ??

Virginia Chancery Records Index, online at
http://www.virginiamemory.com/collections/chancery/
Because of the loss of early records, this database covers 1844-1954, and the earliest entry for the
surname Kidd is in 1867.

Virginia Lost Records Digital Collection, 1674-1894, viewable online
at www.virginiamemory.com/collections/lost (no Kidds in Dinwiddie County in this database)

SECONDARY SOURCES
Those with regular text have been abstracted and all Kidd entries in them have been added to this
book; those in **bold font** have not been examined and mined yet.

1. *Virginia 'Publick' Claims, Amelia County,* compiled and transcribed by Janice L. **Abercrombie** and
   Richard Slatten, Iberian Publ. Co., Athens, GA, (no copyright date shown). (RK owns a copy)

2. *Amelia County militia list, 1781,* transcribed by Susan B. **Chiarello,** *Magazine of Virginia Genealogy,*
   49(1):ibc1, February 2011.

3. *Cemetery Records of Amelia County, Virginia,* compiled by the Amelia Historical Society, Dorothy
   Meek **Eppes,** editor, Gateway Press, Baltimore, MD, 2001.

4. *Amelia County, Virginia: marriage bonds, consents and ministers' returns, 1816-1852,* by Thomas Proctor
   Hughes, Memphis, TN, 1974.

5. *Amelia County, Virginia Order Books 17-18,* by Reiley **Kidd,** Colonial Roots, 2015. (SPL)

6. *Amelia County, Virginia Order Book 19,* by Reiley **Kidd,** Colonial Roots, 2015. (SPL)

7. *Tithe Lists for Amelia County, Virginia, 1765-1766, 1769-1771 & 1778,* by Reiley **Kidd,** Colonial
   Roots, 2015. (SPL)

8. *Wills in the Clerk's Office of Amelia from 1734-1811,* by James **Leach,** 1900 (LoV- ILL)

9. *Some Amelia County marriage records,* transcribed by Frankie **Liles,** Magazine of Virginia genealogy,
   vol. 48(3):247-249, August 2010.

10. *Deed Books, Amelia County, Virginia,* abstracted and compiled by Gibson Jefferson
    McConnaughey, Mid-South Publishing Co., 1985. (All at SPL)
    v. 1. Deed Book 1, 1735-1743, Bonds, 1735-1841. (SPL) viewed; no Kidds
    v. 2. Deed Book 2, 1742-1747 (SPL) viewed; no Kidds
    v. 3. Deed Books 3 and 4, 1747-1753 (SPL) viewed; no Kidds
    v. 4. Deed books 5 and 6, 1753-1759 (SPL) viewed; no Kidds
    v. 5. Deed books 7 and 8, 1759-1765 (SPL) viewed; no Kidds
    v. 6. Deed books 9-11, 1766-1773 (SPL) Geo. Kidd, 1771 deed from Clardy, in BD
    v. 7. Deed books 12-14, 1773-1778 (SPL) viewed; 1 Kidd, p 12, Geo Kidd's land one of

neighbors in 1773 deed from Hezekiah Bevill to Thos. Tucker; others were Francis Coleman, Abraham Coleman and George Worsham.

v. 8. Deed books 15-17, 1778-1786 (RK owns a copy) several Kidds: 12, 29, 120

11. *Will Book 1, Amelia County, Virginia. Wills, 1735-1761, Bonds, 1735-1754*, abstracted and compiled by Gibson Jefferson **McConnaughey**, Mid-South Publishing Co., 1978. (SPL) viewed; no Kidds

12. *Will Book 2X, Amelia County, Virginia, 1761-1771*, abstracted and compiled by Gibson Jefferson **McConnaughey**, Mid-South Publishing Co., 1979. (SPL) viewed; no Kidds

13. *Will Book 2, Amelia County, Virginia, 1771-1780*, abstracted and compiled by Gibson Jefferson **McConnaughey**, Mid-South Publishing Co., 1980. (SPL) viewed; no Kidds

14. *Court Order Book 1, 1735-1746, Amelia County, Virginia*, by Gibson Jefferson **McConnaughey**, Mid-South Publishing Co., 1985. (SPL) viewed; no Kidds

15. *Court Order Book 2, 1746-1751, Amelia County, Virginia*, by Gibson Jefferson **McConnaughey**, Mid-South Publishing Co., 1985. (SPL) viewed; no Kidds

16. *Amelia County, Virginia Miscellaneous Records, 1735-1865*, by Gibson Jefferson **McConnaughey**, Mid-South Publishing Co., 1995. (SPL) viewed

17. *Unrecorded Deeds & Other Documents, Amelia County, Virginia, 1750-1902*, by Gibson Jefferson **McConnaughey**, Iberian Publishing Co., 1996. (SPL) viewed; several Kidds

18. ***Daily Account Journals of Stirling Ford, MD, Amelia County, Virginia for 1829, 1830 & 1831***, abstracted by Gibson Jefferson **McConnaughey**, Mid-South Publishing Co., 1982.

19. *Index to Virginia Estates, 1800-1865. v. 7. Counties of **Amelia**, Brunswick, Cumberland, Goochland, Lunenburg, Mecklenburg, Nottoway, Powhatan, and Prince Edward*, by Wesley E. **Pippenger**, Virginia Genealogical Society, Richmond, VA, 2001 (KCLS, Bellevue – RK)

20. *Amelia County, Virginia Deeds, 1759-1765*, by **T. L. C. Genealogy**, Miami Beach, FL, 1990.

21. *Amelia County, Virginia Deeds, 1765-1768*, by **T. L. C. Genealogy**, Miami Beach, FL, 1990.

22. *Amelia County, Virginia, Court Orders (Order Book 2), 1746-1751: An every-Name Index*, by **T. L. C. Genealogy**, Miami Beach, FL, 1995.

23. *1815 Directory of Virginia Landowners, Amelia County*, by Roger G. **Ward**, New Papyrus Co., Inc., Athens, GA, (RK owns a copy)

24. *Marriages of Amelia County, Virginia, 1735-1815*, by Kathleen Booth **Williams**, Alexandria, Virginia, 1961. (SPL - done)

25. *Amelia County, Virginia Will Book 3, 1780-1786 (with additional deaths and heirs from Order Books 15 and 17)*, abstracted by Bel Hubbard **Wise**, Mountain Press, Signal Mountain, TN (no copyright date listed). (RK owns a copy – no Kidd entries)

26. *Amelia County, Virginia Will Book 4, 1786-1792 (with additional deaths and heirs from Order Books 18 and 19)*, abstracted by Bel Hubbard **Wise**, Mountain Press, Signal Mountain, TN (no copyright date listed). (RK owns a copy – no Kidd entries)

27. *Amelia County, Virginia Will Book 5, 1793-1799 (with additional deaths and heirs from Order Books 20, 21, and 22)*, abstracted by Bel Hubbard **Wise**, Mountain Press, Signal Mountain, TN (no copyright date listed). (RK owns a copy)

II. DINWIDDIE COUNTY SOURCES (INCLUDES PETERSBURG CITY)

Dinwiddie County was formed in 1752 from Prince George County. Nearly all of the early records for both of these counties have been lost: Deed Books dating from 1714 to 1728 in Prince George County, and a single Order Book for 1789-1791 in Dinwiddie County are the only county records surviving, following a Dinwiddie Courthouse fire in 1835, *and* both county courthouses being burned or pillaged during the Civil War.[535] In addition, there are two local plat books, and the original land patents in these counties, which may be found in the Library of Virginia.
Also surviving are the Personal Property Tax Lists and Land Tax Lists for these counties, since these were kept at the state level, not in the county courthouse.

Petersburg was established as an Independent Town in 1784, when the towns of Blandford, Pocahontas and Ravenscroft were added to it, and as an Independent City in 1850. Since that time, it has maintained its own records, separate from the rest of Dinwiddie County, including Land and Personal Property Tax Lists, Deeds, etc.

PRIMARY SOURCES

U.S. Federal censuses, 1810-1850

Virginia Chancery Records Index, online at
http://www.virginiamemory.com/collections/chancery/

Virginia Lost Records Digital Collection, 1674-1894, viewable online
at www.virginiamemory.com/collections/lost (no Kidds in Dinwiddie County in this database)

Dinwiddie County Deeds:
General index to Dinwiddie County Deeds, 1833-1889 – FHL #31092 (indexes DBs 1-18)
Dinwiddie County Deed Books 1-13 are available online at Familysearch.org, at Family History Centers and affiliated libraries (restricted access).

Dinwiddie County Wills:
General Index to Wills, 1830-1975 – FHL #1929701, item 2 (Item 1 is index, 1930-1975),
OR FHL #31099, item 1: General Index to Wills, 1830-1949
Will Book 1, 1830-1835 – FHL #31099, item 2
Circuit Court Will Book 1-A, 1830-1897 – FHL #31099, item 3
Will Books 2-3, 1835-1845 – FHL #31100
Will Books 4-5, 1845-1853 – FHL #31101

Dinwiddie County Loose Wills, ca. 1758-1869. FHL #1929708:
Item 2: will fragments (dates not known)
Item 3: Loose wills, ca. 1758-1799
Item 3: Loose wills, ca. 1800-1869

---

[535] Jones, Richard L., *Dinwiddie County. Carrefour of the Commonwealth*, Whittet & Shepperson, Richmond, VA, 1976, p. 32., and p. 315. In fact, a smattering of other Dinwiddie County records prior to 1833 also survived (listed on page 315), including Chancery Order Book No. 1, 1832-1852, Record Book Circuit Court of Law & Chancery, 1819-1841, and miscellaneous unbound wills.

Dinwiddie County, Virginia Land Tax Lists:
http://www.lva.virginia.gov/public/guides/landTax.asp
Land Tax Lists 1782-1785, 1787-1804 – FHL #29920, viewable online at Familysearch.org
Land Tax Lists 1805-1807, 1809-1823 – FHL #29921, viewable online at Familysearch.org
Land Tax Lists 1824-1835 [includes both land and personal tax ledgers of Lewis P Lanier – FHL #29922, viewable online at Familysearch.org
Land Tax Lists 1836-1840 – FHL #29923, viewable online at Familysearch.org
Land Tax Lists 1841-1850 – FHL #29924, viewable online at Familysearch.org
Land Tax Lists 1851-1857 – FHL #29925, viewable online at Familysearch.org
Land Tax Lists 1858-1863 – FHL #29926, viewable online at Familysearch.org

The Dinwiddie County Tax Books, 1782-1875 are ALSO now available online from the County website: https://www.dinwiddieva.us/978/Land-Tax-Books-1782-1875
On this website, one will find downloadable PDFs of each tax book for each of these years.

Dinwiddie County, Virginia Personal Property Tax Lists:
http://www.lva.virginia.gov/public/guides/pptax.htm

Dinwiddie County, Virginia Court Order Book, 1789-1791
FHL #31090, Item 2 (begins on image 108 of this microfilm), viewable online at Familysearch.org
(Restricted Access) (see below for an index for this order book)

Dinwiddie County Chancery Order Book 1 (1832-1852) (reviewed and Kidd entries photocopied by WRK, February 2010)

Record Book of Circuit Superior Court of Law and Chancery (1819-1841)

Sheriff's Fee Book (1763-??) (in Clerk's office, Circuit Court of the City of Petersburg, Virginia)

Surveyor's Plat Book, 1755-1865, viewable online at Familysearch.org (Restricted Access)
FHL #31090, item 1

PETERSBURG
Petersburg Deed Books, 1784-1901
General Index to <u>Petersburg</u> Deeds, 1784-1869 (indexes Deed Books vols. 1-31) – FHL #33407, item 1, viewable online at Familysearch.org (Restricted Access)
Petersburg Deed Book 1 (1784-1790), FHL #33707, item 2 - viewable online at Familysearch.org (Restricted Access)
(The rest of the Petersburg Deed Book microfilms have NOT been digitized as of February 2018, and are not available except by visiting the Family History Library at Salt Lake City.)

Petersburg Land Tax Lists

Petersburg Personal Property Tax Lists, 1787-1850[536] – now viewable online at Familysearch.org (Restricted Access)
FHL #1905759, item 2 – (1787/1788-1799) (1787-1794 includes Land Tax Lists)
FHL #1905760 (1800-1833)

------

[536] These have been reviewed by WRK, one of the authors, in 2009. See his summary in the Dinwiddie County Shared Folder.

FHL #1905761 (1834-1849)
FHL #1905762, item 1 (1850)

SECONDARY SOURCES (The brevity of this list reflects the dearth of surviving records for
Dinwiddie County.)
Those with regular text have been abstracted and all Kidd entries in them have been added to this
book; those in **bold font** have not been examined and mined yet.

1. *Virginia 'Publick' Claims, Dinwiddie County,* compiled and transcribed by Janice L. **Abercrombie**
   and Richard Slatten, Iberian Publ. Co., Athens, GA, (no copyright date shown). (RK owns a
   copy)
2. *Graveyards, Dinwiddie County, Virginia,* by the Margaret Lynn Lewis (Roanoke) Chapter, **DAR**,
   Petersburg, VA, 1945. (LoV)
3. *Some early settlers of Dinwiddie County, Virginia,* Genealogical Records, Genealogical Records,
   Glendale, CA, 2000. (obtained via ILL; 1 Kidd mention – Lodowick Kidd, 1810 census)
4. *Bath Parish register (births, deaths & marriages) 1827-1897 of Dinwiddie County, Virginia and St. Andrews
   Parish vestry book 1732-1797 of Brunswick County, Virginia,* by William Lindsay **Hopkins**,
   Richmond, VA, 1989. No Kidd or Kid entries.
5. *Land records, Dinwiddie County, Virginia, 1752-1820,* **Hughes, Thomas P**. and Jewel B. Sandefer,
   Memphis, TN, 1973
6. *Dinwiddie County. Carrefour of the Commonwealth,* **Jones, Richard L.**, Whittet & Shepperson,
   Richmond, VA, 1976.
7. *Index to Virginia Estates, 1800-1865. v. 8. Counties of Charles City, Chesterfield,* **Dinwiddie***, Greensville,
   Henrico, James City, Prince George, Surry and Sussex, cities of* **Petersburg***, Richmond, and Williamsburg,* by
   Wesley E. **Pippenger**, Virginia Genealogical Society, Richmond, VA, 2001
8. *Dinwiddie County, Virginia Surveyor's Platt Book, (1755-1796) and Court Orders, (1789-1791): An
   Every-Name Index,* **TLC Genealogy**, Miami Beach, FL, 1995 (Reviewed for Kidd, and Stell; not
   for other lines – out of print and available only via interlibrary loan.
9. *1815 Directory of Virginia Landowners, Dinwiddie County,* by Roger G. **Ward**, New Papyrus Co., Inc.,
   Athens, GA, (RK owns a copy)
10. *Marriage references and family relationships of Charles City, Prince George, and Dinwiddie Counties, Virginia,
    1634-1800,* by F. Edward **Wright**, Colonial Roots, Millsboro, Delaware, 2015. (LoV, SPL) No
    Kidds, Leaches; several Stills/Stell.

III. NOTTOWAY COUNTY SOURCES

U.S. Federal censuses, 1810-1850

Virginia Chancery Records Index, online at
http://www.virginiamemory.com/collections/chancery/
Nominally, this database begins with records in 1818, but the bulk of records in it are from 1866-
1932.

Virginia Lost Records Digital Collection, 1674-1894, viewable online
at www.virginiamemory.com/collections/lost (no Kidds in Nottoway County in this database)

Nottoway County Wills

- Will book 1   1789-1802   (no index found)
- Will book 2   1803-1809   no Kidd's listed
- Will book 3   1809-1816   no Kidd's listed
- Will book 4   1815-1822   no Kidd's listed
- Will book 5   1822-1827   no Kidd's listed
- Will book 6   1827-1834   no Kidd's listed

  (Date written on book is 1834-1839, which is actually book 7)
- Will book 7   1834-1839   no Kidd's listed
- Will book 8   1836-1845   no Kidd's listed
- No will books for 1845-1865, at least via FHL microfilms

Nottoway County Deeds

- Deed book 1   1789-1797   no Kidd's listed
- Deed book 2   1798-1805   one deed, Benj. Kidd
- Deed book 3   1805-1809   two deeds, Benj. Kidd
- Deed book 4   1788-1816   no Kidd's listed
- Deed book 5   (no book)
- Deed book 6   (no book)
- Deed book 7   1809-1827   no Kidd's listed
- Deed book 8   1827-1829   no Kidd's listed
- Deed book 9   (should have covered 1829 to 1836-during the Civil War, the Yankees removed the deed books. After the war, many were returned, but deed book 9 was not. There is a note in the back of one of the deed books from one of the Yankee soldiers written to "Johnny Reb", stating that they should thank him for returning what books he did. This was shown to me by the Circuit Court Clerk, 12-30-02. – WRK
- Deed book 10   1836-1842   no Kidd's listed
- No Deed Books survived for the period 1842-1865, another Civil War loss.

Nottoway County Land tax records

The Library of Virginia catalog[537] lists the following Land Tax List microfilm reels

1789-1813 LoV reel 221 – reviewed by RK November 2018; only Benjamin Kidd,
  listed 1805-1807. See his section of this paper.

1814-1836 reel 222 – reviewed by WRK

1837-1850 reel 223 – reviewed by WRK

1851-1861 reel 514 – reviewed by WRK

(The only Kidd found on these 1814-1861 Nottoway LTLs was James Kidd, found here from 1836 through 1847.)

Nottoway County Personal Property Tax Lists (PPTLs)

1789-1822 FHL #1870184, item 2

1823-1850 FHL #1870185, item 1

Wm R Kidd reviewed these years' PPTLs; see Excel spreadsheet of his findings in the Nottoway Shared Folder.

---

[537] Virginia Land Tax Lists, 1782-1927 on Microfilm, at http://www.lva.virginia.gov/public/guides/landTax.asp

Nottoway County Court Order Books (reviewed by WRK)

- Order book 1   1793-1797   no Kidd's listed
- Order book 2   1797-1799   no Kidd's listed
- Order book 3   1792-1808   one entry (incorporated in this compilation)
- Order book 4   1801-1806   one entry (incorporated in this compilation)
- Order book 5   1806-1809   one entry (incorporated in this compilation)
- Order book 6, 1809-1812   no Kidd's listed
- Order book 7, 1814-1817   no Kidd's listed
- Order book 8, 1817-1820   no Kidd's listed
- Order book 9, 1823-1827   no Kidd's listed
- Order book 10, 1827-1832   no Kidd's listed
- Order book 11 1832-1836   one entry (incorporated in this compilation)
- Order book 12 (no book)
- Order book 13 1837-1846   several entries, all incorporated in this compilation
- Order book 14 1846-1854   one entry (incorporated in this compilation)

SECONDARY SOURCES

Few books are available for Nottoway because of the extensive loss of courthouse records in the Civil War.

Those with regular text have been abstracted and all Kidd entries in them have been added to this book; those in **bold font** have not been examined and mined yet.

1. ***Some Early Landowners in Southern Nottoway and Northern Lunenburg Counties, Virginia and the Cocke (Coke) family who once lived there***, by Ben H. Coke, Iberian Publishing Co., Athens, GA, 1997. (LoV)

2. ***Nottoway County, Virginia: Founding and Development with Biographical Sketches***, by A. B. Cummins, W. M. Brown and Son, Printers, Richmond, VA, 1970. (LoV, VHS)

3. *Index to Virginia Estates, 1800-1865. v. 7. Counties of Amelia, Brunswick, Cumberland, Goochland, Lunenburg, Mecklenburg, **Nottoway**, Powhatan, and Prince Edward,* by Wesley E. Pippenger, Virginia Genealogical Society, Richmond, VA, 2001 (no hits for Nottoway Kidds)

4. *Nottoway Parish, Southampton County, tithables, 1778,* abstracted by Stephen W. Worrel, in *Magazine of Virginia Genealogy,* vol. 48, no. 1 (Feb. 2010), p. 59-62.

APPENDIX TWO: The Known MALE Descendants of George4 Kidd of Amelia County, Virginia

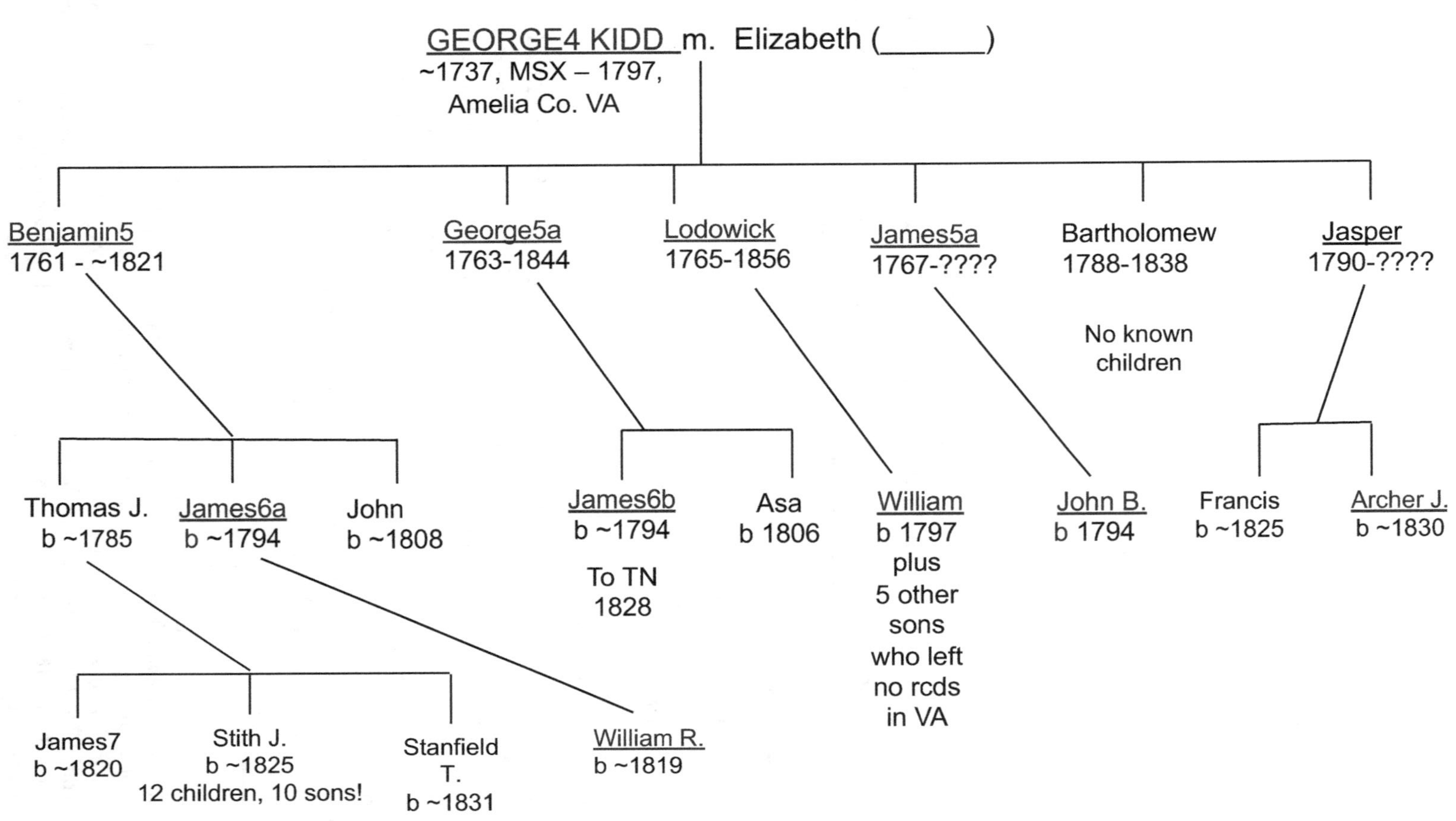

Individuals with underlined names have one or more descendants participating in the Kidd Y-DNA Project

APPENDIX THREE: TRANSCRIPT OF THE COPY BOOK OF JOHN B. KIDD[538]

John B. Kidd married to Betsey Raney 19th February 1818
John B. Kidd was born February they 26 – 1794
Betsey M. Kidd was born they 15th of May 1794
John B. Kidd married to Betsey M. Raney 19th February 1818

Rebekah I. (J.) Kidd was born the 10th of December 1818
Juley Ann Kidd was born they 5th of March 1820
Edward R. Kidd was born they 5th of July 1822
Bartt M. Kidd was born they 16th of August 1826
James L. Kidd was born they 11th of August 1828
Elizabeth E. Kidd was born they 8 of October 1830
Arrimintor Derman Kidd was born August the 14th 1832
William F. Kidd was born November the fifteenth 1836
Allen B. Kidd was born the 7t of May 1839
Richard J. Kidd was born 13 of July 1841

June they 17th – 1821 was they Day that Elizabeth Kidd died in the evening
March 31 – 1842 was the day that Lames [James] L. Kidd died 10 a clock in the night

Taken from the Copy Book of John Basey,[539] now in the possession of Mr. John M. Hall, LaCrosse, Va., started Tuesday July 1813, pasted inside the cover of the notebook.

Miles Hall was born January the 11 1823
Mary L. Hall was born September the 24, 1857
Edward J. Hall was born August the 25 1858
Cattie Hall was born July the 21 1867
Ella Hall was born July the 24 1874

Taken from the Copy Book of John Kidd, now in the possession of Mr. John M. Hall, Lacrosse, Va., Started in 1808. This is the same book that Judy Tudor refers to as the Baisey Book, because it was passed down to Etta Gertrude "Gertie" Kidd, the great-great-granddaughter of John B. Kidd; she married Dillard B. Baisey, and the Copy Book then went to her daughter, who married a Hall. An alternative provenance of this Copy Book is that it went to John B. Kidd's daughter, Elizabeth Kidd, who married Miles Hall. This is actually a better explanation for the passing down of the Copy Book, although it doesn't explain why Judy calls it the Baisey Book. Her note on the large scroll she prepared says that this book was "left at Hunt Club in 1992."

---

[538] The dates of James L. Kidd's birth and death are recorded in a Copy Book, apparently copied from the John B. Kidd family Bible. A typed transcript from this Copy Book , entitled "Kidd family Bible record, 1794-1842" is available on-line at the Library of Virginia, Archives and Manuscripts Room, Manuscript call #25295a, I leaf. Go to http://ajax.lva.lib.va.us/F/?func=file&file_name=find-b-clas05&local_base=CLAS05, and Search for "Kidd family Bible record, 1794-1842". When I search like this, it is record 14 among the bible records that come up. The citation reads: "March 31 – 1842 was the Day that James L. Kidd died10 o'clock in the night."

[539] The actual transcript reads just as listed here. However, since the copy book belonged to John B. Kidd, perhaps this notation (i.e., Basey) indicates what his middle initial stood for. I believe instead that the copy book was passed down to the Hall and Basey/Baisey families, which intermarried with the Kidd family.

APPENDIX FOUR: KIDD LISTINGS ON DINWIDDIE COUNTY PERSONAL PROPERTY TAX LISTS,1782-1858

Unlike Amelia County's Personal Property Tax Lists (PPTLs), the earliest PPTL extant for Dinwiddie county is the 1782 lists. Below is a chronological listing of all Kidds that appear on these lists from 1782 through 1858, the last year that we have examined to date.

Due to the dearth of surviving records for Dinwiddie County prior to 1865, these PPTLs take on added significance and importance to genealogical researchers.

Our Kidd ancestors lived in the western part of Dinwiddie county, along Namozine Creek, which is the boundary between Dinwiddie on the southeast, and Amelia county on the northwest side of this creek. They tended to move back and forth across the boundary, and thus are found alternating in one county or the other. Therefore, it is necessary to examine both counties' PPTLs when pursuing a specific individual. In addition, Nottoway county is just to the south of both Amelia and Dinwiddie, and several Kidd individuals ALSO appear there intermittently.

Below are the abstracted records of Kidds on the Dinwiddie county PPTLs from 1782-1858, listed in chronological order, along with the Family History Library (FHL) microfilm reel or Library of Virginia reel on which they can be found. The FHL reels are available online, via familysearch.org.

Dinwiddie Co., VA PPTLs, 1782-1799 (FHL #31112)

1782 – microfilmed pages very faint. No Kidds found

1783 – no Kidds in any of commissioners' lists.

1784 – no Kidds in any of commissioners' lists.

1785 – no Kidds in any of commissioners' lists.

1786 - no Kidds in any of commissioners' lists.

1787 - no Kidds in any of commissioners' lists.

1788 - no Kidds in any of commissioners' lists.

1789 - no Kidds in any of commissioners' lists.

1790 – Benjamin Kidd, in Wood Tucker's district. No slaves or horses. No tax.
(no other Kidds in this or other districts)

1791 – Wood Tucker's district
> Benjamin Kidd - No slaves, horses or tax.
> no other Kidds in this district.

> William Watts' district
> No Kidds in this district.

1792 –Braddock Godwin's district (evidently formerly Wood Tucker's district):
> Kid, Benjamin – no slaves, one horse
> No others

> William Watts' district:
> Kidd, Loddick – no slaves, one horse

1793 – Braddock Godwin's district:
> Kid, Benjamin – 1 slave over 16, 2 horses
> (no others)

> William Watts' district:
> No Kidds

1794 – 1799 – No Kidds in either district.

Dinwiddie Co., VA PPTLs, 1800-1819, FHL # 31113

1800-1801 No Kidd's listed

1802 – George Kidd. No personal property, horses or wheels. No tax

1803 – Laudwick Kidd. No property. No tax
        Leach, John. No property, no tax.
        (no George Kidd in either district)

1804 – Laudwick Kidd. No slaves; 3 horses.
        MANY Leaches

1805 – Ludwick Kidd. One slave >16, 2 horses.

1806 – George Kidd. No property, no tax.
        Laudwick Kidd. 1 slave over 16, 2 horses.

1807 – same as 1806

1808 – no tax list exists for this year

1809 – Ludwick Kidd. 2 slaves, 2 horses.
        Benjamin Kidd. 1 slave 12-15yo, 1 horse.
        George Kidd. No property, no tax.

1810 – Benjamin Kidd. 1 slave, 1 horse
        Ladwick Kidd. 1 slave, 2 horses.
        Thomas Kidd. No property, no tax.

1811 - Thomas Kidd. No property, no tax. (Scott's district)
        Ladwick Kidd. 1 slave, 3 horses. (Roper's district)
        Benjamin Kidd. 1 slave, 1 horse. "   "
        George Stell. 4 slaves, 3 horses   "   "

1812 – Ladwick Kidd. 1 slave, 3 horses
        Benjamin Kidd. 1 slave, 2 horses
        Thomas Kidd. No property, no tax. (all in Roper's dist.)

1813 – Lodwick Kidd **AND SON WILLIAM**. 1 slave, 3 horses.[540]
        Thomas Kidd
        Benjamin Kidd
        James Kidd

1814 – Lodwick Kidd and son. 2 slaves, 3 horses, 9 cows.
        Benjamin Kidd. No property, no tax.
        Thomas Kidd. No property, no tax.
        John Leach. 5 slaves, 2 horses.

1815 – Benjamin Kidd. 3 horses, 6 cattle
        Thomas Kidd. One slave 12-15.
        Lodwick & son William. 1 slave>16, 1 12-15, 1 9-11, 3 h, 9 cows.[541]

1816 – Kidd, Benjamin. 2 slaves, 5 horses.
        Ladwick & son. 3 slaves as above, 4 horses.
        Jasper Kidd. 1 horse (son of George Kidd Sr.)

---

[540] Scanned image available in Dinwiddie County file.
[541] Scanned image available in Dinwiddie County file.

1817 – Kidd, James 1WM>16 (nothing else) (Edw Scott's district)
      rest are in Peter Scott's district
      Kidd, Bartholomew 1WM>16
      William Kidd. 1 horse.
      Ladowick Kidd. 3 slaves, 2 horses.
      Jasper Kidd. 1 horse
      Thomas J. Kidd. 1 slave 12-15, no horses.
      Benjamin Kidd. 2 slaves, 4 horses.

1818 – William Kidd. 1 horse
      Ladowick Kidd. 3 slaves, 2 horses.
      Jasper Kidd. One horse.
      Thomas J. Kidd. 1 slave 12-15, 1 horse.
      Benjamin Kidd. 1 slave, 2 horses.
      James Kidd. 1 slave 12-15, 1 horse.
      ANOTHER James Kidd, in different dist. from those above).
            1 slave 12-15, 1 horse.

1819 – James Kidd. 1 slave, 1 carriage!
      Jasper Kidd. No property, no tax.
      Benjamin Kidd. TAXED FOR 2 WHITES (himself + one more) FOR THE FIRST TIME. 1 slave,
      4 horses.
      James Kidd. 1 carriage, no slaves.
      Ladowick Kidd. 3 slaves.
      William Kidd. No property, no tax.
      Thomas J. Kidd. 1 slave 12-15, 1 horse.

LDS Microfilm #0031114, Dinwiddie Co., VA PPTLs, 1820-1841
1820 – Peter Scott's list
      Kidd, Lodowick – 1WM>16, 2 slaves >16, 1 slave 12-16, 2 horses
      " , William – 1WM>16, no property
      " , James – 1WM>16, 1 horse, 1 carriage worth $30
      " , Benjamin – 1WM>16, 1 slave over 16, 5 horses, 1 carriage worth $20
      " , Thomas J. – 2WM>16, 1 slave 12-16, 1 horse, 1 carriage worth $40
      " , James Jr. – 1WM>16, 1 carryall worth $60

1821 – Peter Scott's list (this year's list doesn't list # of white males in HH)
      Kidd, Lodowick – 3 slaves over 12, 2 horses
      Kidd, James "(son Ben)" – 1 horse, 1 carriage worth $25
      Kidd, Benjamin – 1 slave over 12, 4 horses, 1 carriage worth $40
      Kidd, Thomas J. – 1 slave over 12, 1 horse
      Kidd, James – 1 carryall worth $50

1822 – Peter Scott's List
      Kidd, Lodowick – 3 slaves >12, 2 horses
      Kidd, James Jr. – 1 slave >12, one horse
      Kidd, Thomas J. – 1 slave >12, 1 horse
      Kidd, Mary – no slaves, 2 horses, 1 carriage worth $20
      Kidd, James Sr. – one carryall worth $40

1823 – Peter Scott's list
      Kidd, James Jr. – 1 slave over 12, 1 horse
      Kidd, James Sr. – no slaves or horses(!), 1 carriage worth $30
      Kidd, Mary – 2 horses, 1 carriage worth $20
      Kidd, Thomas J. – 1 slave over 12, 1 horse

1824 – Peter Scott's list
    Kidd, Mary – no slaves, two horses
    Kidd, James – 1 slave over 12, 1 horse
    Kidd, Thomas J. – 1 slave, no horses

1825 – Peter Scott's list
    Kidd, Mary – 1 slave over 12, 2 horses
    Kidd, James – 1 slave over 12, 1 horse

1826 – Peter Scott's list
    Kidd, Mary – no slaves, 1 horse
    Kidd, Thomas – 1 slave, no horses
    Kidd, William – no slaves or horses, 1 carryall worth $80

1827[542] – Lewis P. Lanier's list (took over Peter Scott's district)
    Kidd, James – 1WM>16, no property
    Kidd, Mary – no WM>16 or slaves, 3 horses
    Kidd, John – 1WM>16, no property
    Kidd, Jasper – 1WM>16, no property
    Kidd, William – 1WM>16, 1 slave over 12, no horses

1828 – Lewis P. Lanier's list
    Kidd, William – 1 slave over 12, 1 horse, 1 carryall worth $120
    Kidd, Mary – no slaves, 2 horses
    Kidd, Thomas J. – 1 slave over 12, no horses

1829 – Lewis P. Lanier's list
    Kidd, William – 1 slave over 12, 1 horse, 1 carryall or carriage worth $110
    Kidd, James – 1 slave over 12, no horse
    Kidd, Mary – no slaves, 2 horses

1830 – NO list for Lewis Lanier on microfilm – only the one list, below.
    BUT this PPTL IS found on FHL microfilm #29922, containing Dinwiddie Land Tax Lists.
    [543] Evidently the people making the microfilms grabbed the PPTLs of Lewis Lanier, along with his Land Tax ledger for this year.
    <u>**Lewis Lanier's list[544]**</u>
    Kidd, William - one slave over 12, 1 horse, 1 2wheel carriage worth $90
    Kidd, James - one slave over 12, nothing else
    Kidd, Mary - no slaves, 2 horses, mules or colts.

    Burwell T. Goodwin's list (took over Henry Young's district)
    No Kidds

1831 – NO list for Lewis Lanier on microfilm #0031114 – only the one list, below.
    BUT this PPTL IS found on FHL microfilm #29922, containing Dinwiddie Land Tax Lists. Evidently the people making the microfilms grabbed the PPTLs of Lewis Lanier, along with his Land Tax ledger for this year.
    Lewis P. Lanier's list[545]
    Mary Kidd – No slaves, two horses.   (No other Kidds on this list) [546]

---

[542] In 1827, the lists resumed listing the number (but not the names) of all white males over 16 in the HH.
[543] FHL # 29922, images 378-388, viewable online via familysearch.org (unrestricted access).
[544] Ibid, image 382.
[545] FHL #29922, images 482-494, viewable online via familysearch.org (unrestricted access).
[546] Ibid, image 487.

Burwell T. Goodwin's list (took over Henry Young's district)
No Kidds

1832 – Lewis P. Lanier's list
Kidd, William – no slaves, 2 horses
Kidd, William – 2 slaves over 12, 1 horse
Kidd, Mary – no slaves, 1 horse

1833 – Lewis P. Lanier's list
Kidd, John – one horse
Kidd, William Jr. – 2 slaves over 12, 1 horse, 1 carriage worth $30
Kidd, William – 1 slave over 12, 2 horses
(Mary Kidd disappears from the lists, and may have died, or moved away)

1834 – Lewis P. Lanier's list
Kidd, William Jr. – no slaves, 1 horse
Kidd, William Sr.[547] – 2 slaves over 12, 1 horse, 1 carriage worth $30
Kidd, Thomas J. – 1 slave over 12, 1 horse

1835 – Lewis P. Lanier's list
Kidd, Thomas J. – 1 horse
Kidd, William – 1 horse
Kidd, William – 1 slave over 12, 1 horse, 1 carriage worth $30

1836 – Lewis P. Lanier's list
Kidd, William – 1 horse
Kidd, William – 1 slave over 12, 1 horse, 1 carriage worth $40
Kidd, Thomas J. – 1 horse

1837 – Lewis P. Lanier's list
Kidd, William Jr. – 1 horse
Kidd, William Sr. – 1 horse, 1 carriage worth $40
Kidd, Thomas J. – 1 horse

1838 – Lewis P. Lanier's list
Kidd, William Jr. – 1 horse
Kidd, William – 1 horse, 1 carriage worth $30
Kidd, Thomas J. – 1 horse

1839 – Lewis P. Lanier's list
Kidd, William Jr. – 1 horse
Kidd, William – 1 horse, 1 carriage worth $30
Kidd, Thomas J. – 1 slave over 12, 1 horse

1840 – Lewis P. Lanier's list
Kidd, William Sr. – 2 horses
Kidd, Thomas J. – 1 horse

1841 – Lewis P. Lanier's list
Kidd, William Jr. – 1 horse

---

[547] The designations "Junior" and "Senior" don't necessarily imply son and father relationships in this era, and in this context; often they were used to distinguish "the younger" from "the elder," without implying a father-son relationship. That's likely the case here, where the older William was the son of Lodawick Kidd, and the younger William the son of James Kidd (son of Benjamin). At least, that's RK's working hypothesis as of May 2009.

Kidd, William Sr. – 2 horses
Kidd, Thomas J. – 1 slave over 12, 1 horse

FHL #31115, Dinwiddie PPTLs 1842-1852   [N. B. "i 43" = image 43 on this microfilm reel]

1842 – Lewis P. Lanier's list (starts on image 6)
William Kidd Sr. – no slaves >12, 2 horses (i 9)
Thomas J. Kidd – 1 slave over 12, 1 horse

1842 – Hubbard Wyatt's list (i 19)
No Kidds (i 25)

1843 – William Bishop's list (i 40)
James Kidd – 1 slave >12, no horses (i 46)
no others

1843 – Louis P. Lanier's list (i 68)
William Kidd Sr. – 0 slaves >12, 2 horses (i 75)
Thomas J. Kidd – 0 slaves >12, 1 horse

1844 – William Bishop's list (i 89) – new headings: WM >16/Slaves >12/Horses, etc.
James Kidd – 1/0/0 (i 96)
no others

1844 – Lewis P. Lanier's list (i 113)
William Kidd Sr. – 3/0/3 (i 122)
Thomas J. Kidd – 1/0/1
William Kidd – 1/0/1 (this is most likely William R. Kidd – see 1845, ff.)

1845 – William Bishop's list (i 138) new headings: WM >16/S >16/S 12-16/Horses
James Kidd – 1/0/0/1 (i 143)
No others

1845 – Lewis P. Lanier's list (i 157) – same headings as above
William Kidd Sr. – 3-0-0-3 (i 164)
William R. Kidd – 1/2/0/1 + 1 4-wheel carriage, valued at $50
Thomas J. Kidd – 1/0/0/0

1846 – William Bishop's List (i 182)) – no change in headings
James Kidd – 1/0/0/0 (i 187)
No others

1846 – Lewis P. Lanier's list (i 201)
Archibald Kidd – 1/0/0/0   (i 208)
William R. Kidd – 1/1/0/1
Thomas J. Kidd – 1/0/0/0
William Kidd – 3/0/0/2 (This is RK's William, aka William Sr.)

1847 – William Bishop's list (i 224)) – no change in headings
James Kidd – 1/1/0/1 (i 229)

1847 – Lewis P. Lanier's list (i 244)
Thomas J. Kidd – 2/0/0/0 (i 251)
William Kidd – 3/0/0/2
Francis Kidd – 1/0/0/0
William R. Kidd – 1/0/0/1

1848 – William Bishop's list (i 267) – no change in headings
James Kidd – 1/1/0/1   (i 272)

1848 – James Boisseau's list   (i 287)
William Kidd – 3/1/0/3 (William Sr., RK's ancestor) (i 294)
James Kidd – 1/5?/0/4
Archer Kidd – 1/0/0/0
Thomas J. Kidd – 2-0-0-1
Francis Kidd – 1/0/0/0
William R. Kidd – 1/0/0/1

1849 – William Bishop's list   (i 309) – Headings unchanged from 1848
James Kidd – 2-0-0-1   (i 314)

1849 – James Boisseau's list (329)
James Kidd – 1/4/4/4   (i 336)
William R. Kidd – 1-0-0-1
Thomas J. Kidd – 2/0/0/1
Stith J. Kidd – 1/0/0/0
Francis Kidd – 1/0/0/0

1850 – William Bishop's list (i 350) –New Column added
WM >16 / Free Negros >16 / Slaves >16 / Slaves 12-16 / horses, etc.
James Kidd – 1/0/0/0/1 (i 356)

1850 – James Boisseau's list (i 372)
Stanfield J. Kidd – 1-0-0-0-5 (i 380) (son of Thomas J.)
James Kidd – 1/0/4/4/4
Francis Kidd – 1/0/0/0/0 (i 381)
Thomas J. Kidd – 1/0/0/0/0
William R. Kidd – 1/0/1/1/1

1851 – William Bishop's list (i 398) - Column headings unchanged
James – 1/0/0/0/1 (i 407)

1851 – Robert G. Boisseau's list (i 424)
James Kidd – 1/0/4/4/3 (i 434)
William R. Kidd – 1/0/0/0/1
Robert S. T. Kidd – 1/0/0/0/1
Archibald J. Kidd – 1/0/0/0/0
Francis Kidd – 1/0/0/0/0
Thomas J. Kidd – 1/0/0/0/0

1852 – William Bishop's list (i 443) <u>HEADINGS REARRANGED this year</u>:
Free males >16/ slaves >16 / WM of 21 yr old/Male Free Negroes 21-55 /slaves above 12/ #
of horses, and value/ # of CSH[548], and value
James 1/0/1/0/0/1 - $40/23 - $108 (i 469)

1852 – Robert G. Boisseau's list (i 492) – column headings as above
Thomas J. Kidd – 1/0/0/0/0/0/0   (i 512)
Stanfield T. Kidd – 1/1/1/0/1/1, $5)/10, $19
Archer J. Kidd – 1/0/1/0/0/0/0
Francis Kidd – 1/0/1/0/0/0/0
James Kidd – 1/5/1/5/2 - $130/49 - $122
William R. Kidd – 1/0/1/0/0/2 - $60/16 - $54

---

[548] Cattle, sheep and hogs.

<u>FHL #31116, Dinwiddie Co., VA PPTLs, 1853-1858</u>

1853 – William Bishop's list (i 6) - Column headings unchanged
James Kidd – 2/0/1/0/0/1 - $40/32 - $128   (i 22, line 27)

1853 – Robert G. Boisseau's list (i 46)
Stanfield J. (sic) – 1/0/1/0/0/1 – $10/8 - $20   (i 66)
James Kidd Sr. – 1/5/1/0/2/2 - $120/67 - $185
William R. Kidd – 1/2/1/0/2/4 - $160/10 - $25
Francis Kidd – 1/0/1/0/0/0/0

1854 – William Bishop's list (i 96) – column headings unchanged
James Kidd – 2/1/5/1/0/1 - $50)/32 - $110   (i 114)

1854 – Robert G. Boisseau's list (i 137)
William R. Kidd – 1/5/1/0/6/4 -$160)/7 - $30
Francis Kidd – 1/0/1/0/0/0/0/0
James Kidd Sr. – 1/4/1/0/4/3 - $200/73 - $140
Archibald J. – 1/0/1/0/0/0/0/0

1855 – William Bishop's list (i 201) – no change in column headings
James Kidd – 1/0/1/0/0/1 - $40/35 - $130 (i 219)
Asa Kidd – 1/4/1/0/7/3 -200/0 plus 4 clocks

1855 – Robert Boisseau's list (i 242)
Francis Kidd – 1/0/1/0/0/0/0   (i 264)
Delitha A. Kidd 0/0/0/0/0/1 - $30/12 - $30

1856 – William Bishop's list (i 298)
James Kidd – 1/0/1/0/0/1 - $40/33 - $160 plus 1 4-wheel carriage
Asa Kidd – 1/5/1/0/8/3-$200/4 - $60   (i 316)

1856 – Robert G. Boisseau's list (i 339)
Francis Kidd – 1/0/0/   (i 363)
Archer J. Kidd – 1/0/0
No Delitha

1857 – Thomas Farley's list   (i 393)
James Kidd **Jr.** – 1/1/1/0/1/1 - $30/25 - $132   (i 411)
Asa Kidd – 1/5/1/0/8/3 - $200/15 - $70, plus 1 pleasure carriage (i 413)

1857 – William P. Spain's list (i 436)
Archiball (sic) Kidd – 1/0/0   (i 460)
Francis Kidd – 1/0/0

1858 – Thomas Farley's list   (i 498)
James Kidd Jr. – 1/1/1/0/1/1 - $30/37 - $75
Asa Kidd – 1/7/1/0/8/2 - $120/1- $50 plus 1 pleasure carriage

1858 – List of William P. Spain (i 542)
Archibald J. Kidd – 1/0/0/0
Francis Kidd – 1/0/0

DINWIDDIE COUNTY LTLs, 1814-1857, KIDD ENTRIES, BY GIVEN NAME

YEAR	LIST	NAME	Res.	Fee or Life	Acres	Description	from CH	rate per acre	Levy added, bldg, etc.	total value	tax	ALTERATIONS (and Comments)
1857	TF	Asa Kidd	Din	Fee	171	on Rohowick Swamp	11NE	$40	$1000	$6,800	$27.20	"Deeds from J. Dupuy" (FHL #29925, image 408)
	TF	Asa Kidd	Din	Fee	20	Lot 3, near Petersburg	14NE	$50		$1,000	$4.00	
1814	CR	Kidd, Benjamin	Din	Fee	218	on White Oak Cr.	13NW	7/7		$275.52	$2.34	"deed from H.B. Duvall"
1815	CR	Kidd, Benjamin	Din	Fee	218	on White Oak Cr.	13NW	7/7		$275.52	$2.34	
1816	CR	Kidd, Benjamin	Din	Fee	218	on White Oak Cr.	13NW	7/7		$275.52	$2.07	
1817	PS	Kidd, Benjamin	Din	Fee	218	on White Oak Cr.	13NW	7/7		$275.52	$2.07	
1818	PS	Kidd, Benjamin	Din	Fee	211	on White Oak Cr.	13NW	7/7		$266.69	$2.00	"7 ac. Transferred to Arrested Cassel's Flat"
1819	PS	Kidd, Benjamin	Din	Fee	211	on White Oak Cr.	13NW	7/7		$266.69	$2.00	
1820	PS	Kidd, Benjamin	Din	Fee	211	on White Oak Cr.	13NW	$5	$100	$1,055	$1.32	
1821	PS	Kidd, Benjamin	Din	Fee	211	on White Oak Cr.	13NW	$5	$100	$1,055	$0.95	
1856	RGB	Kidd, Delitha A	Din	Fee	25	On Kitt's branch	14NW	$2.50	$50	$67.50	$0.26	"from Prussian Fraser by; deed" (FHL #29925, image 268)
1857		Kidd, Delitha A	Din	Fee	25	On Kitt's branch	14NW	$5	$50	$125.00	$0.50	FHL #29925, image 382

DINWIDDIE COUNTY LTLs, 1814-1857, KIDD ENTRIES, BY GIVEN NAME

YEAR	LIST	NAME	Res.	Fee or Life	Acres	Description	from CH	rate per acre	Levy added, bldg, etc.	total value	tax	ALTERATIONS (and Comments)
1818	PS	Kidd, James	Din	Fee	110	branches of Bear Swamp	9NW	6/1		$111.53	$0.84	"deed from Elliot Young"
1819	PS	Kidd, James	Din	Fee	110	branches of Bear Swamp	9NW	6/1		$111.53	$0.84	
1820	PS	Kidd, James	Din	Fee	110	branches of Bear Swamp	9NW	$5	$200	$550	$0.69	
1821	PS	Kidd, James	Din	Fee	110	branches of Bear Swamp	9NW	$5	$200	$550	$0.50	
1822	PS	Kidd, James	Din	Fee	110	branches of Bear Swamp	9NW	$5	$200	$550	$0.50	
1823	PS	Kidd, James	Din	Fee	110	near Bear Swamp	9NW	$5	$200	$550	$0.44	
1828	LPL	Kidd, James	Din	Fee	60	on George's branch	17NW	$5	$0.00	$301.20	$0.25	by deed from Wm E & Hannah Hardaway (#29922, image 315)
1829	LPL	Kidd, James	Din	Fee	60	on George's branch	17NW	$5	$0.00	$301.20	$0.25	
1830	LPL	Kidd, James	Din	Fee	60	on George's branch	17NW	$5	$0.00	$301.20	$0.25	
1831	LPL	Kidd, James	Din	Fee	60	on George's branch	17NW	$5	$0.00	$301.20	$0.25	
1832	LPL	Kidd, James	Din	Fee	60	on George's branch	17NW	$5	$0.00	$301.20	$0.25	
1833	LPL	Kidd, James	Din	Fee	60	on George's branch	17NW	$5	$0.00	$301.20	$0.25	
1834	LPL	Kidd, James	Din	Fee	60	on George's branch	17NW	$5	$0.00	$301.20	$0.25	
1835	LPL	Kidd, James	Din	Fee	60	on George's branch	17NW	$5	$0.00	$301.20	$0.25	
1836	LPL	Kidd, James	Din	Fee	60	on George's Branch	17NW	$5	$0.00	301	$0.25	
1837	LPL	Kidd, James	Din	Fee	60	on George's Branch	17NW	$5	$0.00	$301	$0.25	

YEAR	LIST	NAME	Res.	Fee or Life	Acres	Description	from CH	rate per acre	Levy added, bldg, etc.	total value	tax	ALTERATIONS (and Comments)
1838	LPL	Kidd, James	Din	Fee	60	on George's Branch	17NW	$5	$0.00	$301	$0.31	
1839	LPL	Kidd, James	Din	Fee	60	on George's Branch	17NW	$5	$0.00	$301	$0.31	
1848	JB	Kidd, James & wife	Din	Fee	425½	on the Great Branch	5NW	$3.25	$500.00	$1,382	$1.40	"deed from Ann M. Thweat"
	JB	Kidd, James & wife	Din	Fee	4½	on the Great Branch	5NW	$2.50	$0.00	$11	in above	
1849	JB	Kidd, James	Din	Fee	430	on the Great Branch	5NW	$3.25	$500.00	$1,397	$1.40	"from Jas. Kidd & wife to James (?) Boisseau by deed; from Jas. Boisseau to Jas. Kidd by deed."
1850	JB	Kidd, James	Din	Fee	430	on the Great Branch	5NW	$3.25	$500.00	$1,397	$1.40	
1851	RGB	Kidd, James	Din	Fee	430	on the Great Branch	5NW	$3.00	$590.00	$1,280.00	$1.55	FHL#29925, image 22
1852	RGB	Kidd, James	Din	Fee	430	on the Great Branch	5NW	$3.00	$590.00	$1,290.00	$2.33	FHL#29925, image 70
1853	RGB	Kidd, James	Din	Fee	430	on the Great Branch	5NW	$3.00	$590.00	$1,290.00	$2.58	FHL#29925, image 116
1854	RGB	Kidd, James	Din	Fee	430	on the Great Branch	5NW	$3.00	$590.00	$1,290.00	$2.58	
1850	WB	Kidd, James	Din	Fee	123	on Vaughan's Rd.	2_E	$3	$200.00	$369	$0.37	deed from (faint writing) John P. Crump(?)
1851	WB	Kidd, James	Din	fee	123	on Vaughans Road	2E	$3	$200.00	$369	$0.45	FHL #29925, image 48
1852	WB	Kidd, James	Din	fee	123	on Vaughans Road	2E	$3	$200.00	$369	$0.67	ibid, image 92
1853	WB	Kidd, James	Din	fee	123	on Vaughans Road	2E	$3	$200.00	$369	$0.74	ibid, image 140

DINWIDDIE COUNTY LTLs, 1814-1857, KIDD ENTRIES, BY GIVEN NAME

YEAR	LIST	NAME	Res.	Fee or Life	Acres	Description	from CH	rate per acre	Levy added, bldg, etc.	total value	tax	ALTERATIONS (and Comments)
1854	WB	Kidd, James	Din	fee	123	on Vaughans Road	2E	$3	$200.00	$369	$0.74	ibid, image 189
1855	WB	Kidd, James	Din	fee	123	on Vaughans Road	2E	$3	$200.00	$369	$0.74	ibid, image 241
1856	WB	Kidd, James	Din	fee	123	on Vaughans Road	2E	$3	$200.00	$369	$1.48	ibid, image 355
1857	TF	Kidd, James Jr.	Din	fee	123	on Vaughans Road	2E	$10	$600.00	$1,230	$4.92	ibid, image 409
1817	PS	Kidd, Jasper	Din	Fee	70	on Cox Rd.	14NW	8/1		$94.31	$0.71	"land from Joel Walker"
1818	PS	Kidd, Jasper	Din	Fee	70	on Cox Rd.	14NW	8/1		$94.31	$0.71	
1819	PS	Kidd, Jasper	Din	Fee	70	on Cox Rd.	14NW	8/1		$94.31	$0.71	
1820	PS	Kidd, Jasper	Din	fee	70	on Cox Rd.	14NW	$5	$100	$350	$0.44	
1814	CR	Kidd, Lodwick	Din	Fee	152	on Bowens Branch	12NW	6/1		$154.12	$0.73	
1815	CR	Kidd, Lodwick	Din	Fee	152	on Bowen Branch	12NW	6/1		$154.12	$1.30	
1816	CR	Kidd, Lodwick	Din	Fee	152	on Bowen Branch	12NW	6/1		$154.12	$1.16	
1817	PS	Kidd, Lodwick	Din	Fee	152	on Bowen Branch	12NW	6/1		$154.12	$1.16	
1818	PS	Kidd, Lodwick	Din	Fee	152	on Bowen Branch	12NW	6/1		$154.12	$1.30	
1819	PS	Kidd, Lodwick	Din	Fee	152	on Bowen Branch	12NW	6/1		$154.12	$1.30	
1820	PS	Kidd, Lodowick	Din	Fee	152	on Bowen Branch	12NW	$5	$140	$760	$0.50	

DINWIDDIE COUNTY LTLs, 1814-1857, KIDD ENTRIES, BY GIVEN NAME

YEAR	LIST	NAME	Res.	Fee or Life	Acres	Description	from CH	rate per acre	Levy added, bldg, etc.	total value	tax	ALTERATIONS (and Comments)
1821	PS	Kidd, Lodowick	Din	Fee	152	on Bowen Branch	12NW	$5	$140	$760	$0.69	
1822	PS	Kidd, Lodowick	Din	Fee	152	on Bowen Branch	12NW	$5	$140	$760	$0.69	
1822	PS	Kidd, Mary	Din	Fee	211	on White Oak Cr.	13NW	$5	$100	$1,055	$0.95	"by way of Benjamin Kidd"
1823	PS	Kidd, Mary	Din	Life	211	on Whiteoak Creek	13NW	$5	$100	$1,055	$0.85	
1824	PS	Kidd, Mary	Din	Life	211	on Whiteoak Creek	13NW	$5	$100	$1,055	$0.85	
1825	PS	Kidd, Mary	Din	Life	211	on Whiteoak Creek	13NW	$5	$100	$1,055	$0.85	
1826	PS	Kidd, Mary	Din	Life	211	on Whiteoak Creek	13NW	$5	$100	$1,055	$0.85	
1827	LPL	Kidd, Mary	Din	Life	211	on Whiteoak Creek	13NW	$5	$100	$1,055	$0.85	
1828	LPL	Kidd, Mary	Din	Life	211	on Whiteoak Creek	13NW	$5	$100	$1,055	$0.85	
1829	LPL	Kidd, Mary	Din	Life	211	on Whiteoak Creek	13NW	$5	$100	$1,055	$0.85	
1830	LPL	Kidd, Mary	Din	Life	211	on Whiteoak Creek	13NW	$5	$100	$1,055	$0.85	
1831	LPL	Kidd, Mary	Din	Life	211	on Whiteoak Creek	13NW	$5	$100	$1,055	$0.85	
1832	LPL	Kidd, Mary	Din	Life	211	on Whiteoak Creek	13NW	$5	$100	$1,055	$0.85	
1833	LPL	Kidd, Mary	Din	Life	211	on Whiteoak Creek	13NW	$5	$100	$1,055	$0.85	
1834	LPL	Kidd, Mary	Din	Life	211	on Whiteoak Creek	13NW	$5	$100	$1,055	$0.85	
1835	LPL	Kidd, Mary	Din	Life	211	on Whiteoak Creek	13NW	$5	$100	$1,055	$0.85	
1836	LPL	Kidd, Mary	Din	Life	211	on White Oak Creek	13NW	$5	$100	$1,055	$0.85	

DINWIDDIE COUNTY LTLs, 1814-1857, KIDD ENTRIES, BY GIVEN NAME

YEAR	LIST	NAME	Res.	Fee or Life	Acres	Description	from CH	rate per acre	Levy added, bldg, etc.	total value	tax	ALTERATIONS (and Comments)
1837	LPL	Kidd, Mary	Din	Life	211	on White Oak Creek	13NW	$5	$100	$1,055	$0.85	
1838	LPL	Kidd, Mary	Din	Life	211	on White Oak Creek	13NW	$5	$100	$1,055	$1.06	
1839	LPL	Kidd, Mary	Din	Life	211	on White Oak Creek	13NW	$5	$100	$1,055	$1.06	.
1840	LPL	Kidd, Mary	Din	Life	211	on White Oak Creek	13NW	$2	$100	$422	$0.43	
1841	LPL	Kidd, Mary	Din	Life	211	on White Oak Creek	13NW	$2	$0	$422	$0.53	
1842	LPL	Kidd, Mary	Din	Life	211	on White Oak Creek	13NW	$2	$0	$422	$0.53	
1843	LPL	Kidd, Mary	Din	Life	211	on White Oak Creek	13NW	$2	$0	$422	$0.64	
1836	LPL	Kidd, Thomas J.	Din	Fee	143⅓	on Butterwood Road	16SW	$5				"less $120,buildings old and decayed"
1838	LPL	Kidd, Thomas J. & wife	Din	Fee	143⅓	on Butterwood Road	16SW	$5	$700	$716	$0.72	"deed from A.H. Reamus (=sp?)"
1839	LPL	Kidd, Thomas J. & wife	Din	Fee	71⅓	on Butterwood Road	16SW	$5	$0	$356	$0.36	"72 acres deeded to Sally & Gemima Whitmore; bldgs improperly chgd. Heretofore"
1840	LPL	Kidd, Thomas J.	Din	Fee	71⅓	on Butterwood Road	16SW	$2	$120	$143	$0.31	
1840	LPL	Kidd, Thomas J.	Din	Fee	81	on Butterwood Road	16SW	$2	$0	$162	in above	"deed from Sally & Gemima Whitmore."
1841	LPL	Kidd, Thomas J.	Din	Fee	152⅓	on Butterwood Road	16SW	$2.00	$120	$305	$0.39	

DINWIDDIE COUNTY LTLs, 1814-1857, KIDD ENTRIES, BY GIVEN NAME

YEAR	LIST	NAME	Res.	Fee or Life	Acres	Description	from CH	rate per acre	Levy added, bldg, etc.	total value	tax	ALTERATIONS (and Comments)
1842	LPL	Kidd, Thomas J.	Din	Fee	152⅓	on Butterwood Road	16SW	$2	$120	$305	$0.39	
1843	LPL	Kidd, Thomas J.	Din	Fee	152½	on Butterwood Road	16SW	$2	$120	$305	$0.46	
1845	LPL	Kidd, Thomas J.	Din	Fee	20	Near Butterwood Road	16W	$1.50	$0	$30	$0.03	Deed from P.W. Harper
1846	LPL	Kidd, Thomas J.	Din	Fee	20	Near Butterwood Road	16W	$1.50	$0	$30	$0.03	
1847	LPL	Kidd, Thomas J.	Din	Fee	20	Near Butterwood Road	16W	$1.50	$0	$30	$0.03	
1848	JB	Kidd, Thomas J.	Din	Fee	20	Near Butterwood Road	16W	$1.50	$0	$30	$0.03	
1849	JB	Kidd, Thomas J.	Din	Fee	20	Near Butterwood Road	16W	$1.50	$0	$30	$0.03	
1850	JB	Kidd, Thomas J.	Din	Fee	20	Near Butterwood Road	16W	$1.50	$0	$30	$0.03	
1851	RGB	Kidd, Thomas J.	Din	Fee	20	Near Butterwood Road	16W	$3		$180	$0.22	FHL #29925, image 22
1852	RGB	Kidd, Thomas J.	Din	Fee	20	Near Butterwood Road	16W	$2.50		$50	$0.09	FHL #29925, image 70
1823	PS	Kidd, William	Din	Fee	62	on Bowan's branch	12NW	$5	$120	$310	$0.25	by deed from Lodowick Kidd
1824	PS	Kidd, William	Din	Fee	62	on Bowan's branch	12NW	$5	$120	$310	$0.25	
1825	PS	Kidd, William	Din	Fee	62	on Bowan's branch	12NW	$5	$120	$310	$0.25	
1826	PS	Kidd, William	Din	Fee	62	on Bowan's branch	12NW	$5	$120	$310	$0.25	

DINWIDDIE COUNTY LTLs, 1814-1857, KIDD ENTRIES, BY GIVEN NAME

YEAR	LIST	NAME	Res.	Fee or Life	Acres	Description	from CH	rate per acre	Levy added, bldg, etc.	total value	tax	ALTERATIONS (and Comments)
1827	LPL	Kidd, William	Din	Fee	62	on Bowan's branch	12NW	$5	$120	$310	$0.25	
1828	LPL	Kidd, William	Din	Fee	62	on Bowan's branch	12NW	$5	$120	$310	$0.25	
1829	LPL	Kidd, William	Din	Fee	62	on Bowan's branch	12NW	$5	$120	$310	$0.25	
1830	LPL	Kidd, William	Din	Fee	62	on Bowan's branch	12NW	$5	$120	$310	$0.25	
1831	LPL	Kidd, William	Din	Fee	62	on Bowan's branch	12NW	$5	$120	$310	$0.25	
1832	LPL	Kidd, William	Din	Fee	62	on Bowan's branch	12NW	$5	$120	$310	$0.25	
1833	LPL	Kidd, William	Din	Fee	62	on Bowan's branch	12NW	$5	$120	$310	$0.25	
1834	LPL	Kidd, William	Din	Fee	62	on Bowan's branch	12NW	$5	$120	$310	$0.25	
1835	LPL	Kidd, William	Din	Fee	62	on Bowan's branch	12NW	$5	$120	$310	$0.25	
1836	LPL	Kidd, William	Din	Fee	62	on Bowen's branch	12NW	$5	$0.00	$310	$0.25	
1837	LPL	Kidd, William	Din	Fee	62	on Bowen's branch	12NW	$5	$120	$310	$0.25	
1838	LPL	Kidd, William	Din	Fee	62	on Bowen's branch	12NW	$5	$120	$310	$0.31	
1839	LPL	Kidd, William	Din	Fee	62	on Bowan's branch	12NW	$5	$120	$310	$0.31	
1840	LPL	Kidd, William	Din	Fee	62	on Bowan's branch	12NW	$4.50	$120	$279	$0.28	

DINWIDDIE COUNTY LTLs, 1814-1857, KIDD ENTRIES, BY GIVEN NAME

YEAR	LIST	NAME	Res.	Fee or Life	Acres	Description	from CH	rate per acre	Levy added, bldg, etc.	total value	tax	ALTERATIONS (and Comments)
1841	LPL	Kidd, William	Din	Fee	62	on Bowan's branch	12NW	$4.50	$120	$279	$0.35	
1842	LPL	Kidd, William	Din	Fee	62	on Bowan's branch	12NW	$4.50	$120	$279	$0.35	
1843	LPL	Kidd, William Sr.	Din	Fee	62	on Bowan's branch	12NW	$4.50	$120	$279	$0.42	
1844	LPL	Kidd, William Sr.	Din	Fee	62	on Bowan's branch	12NW	$4.50	$120	$279	$0.41	
	LPL	Kidd, William Sr.	Din	Fee	14	adjoining the above	12NW	$3.50	$0	$49	in above	"deed from Archer J. Bevill & wife"
1845	LPL	Kidd, William Sr	Din	Fee	62	on Bowan's branch	12NW	$4.50	$120	$279	$0.33	
	LPL	Kidd, William Sr.	Din	Fee	14	adjoining the above	12NW	$3.50	$0	$49	in above	
1846	LPL	Kidd, William Sr.	Din	Fee	62	on Bowan's Branch	12NW	$4.50	$120	$279	0.33	
	LPL	Kidd, William Sr.	Din	Fee	14	adjoining the above	12NW	$3.50	$0	$49	in above	
1847	LPL	Kidd, William Sr.	Din	Fee	62	on Bowan's Branch	12NW	$4.50	$120	$279	0.33	
	LPL	Kidd, William Sr.	Din	Fee	14	adjoining the above	12NW	$3.50	$0	$49	in above	
1848	JB	Kidd, William Sr.	Din	Fee	62	on Bowan's Branch	12NW	$4.50	$120	$279	0.33	
	JB	Kidd, William Sr.	Din	Fee	14	adjoining the above	12NW	$3.50	$0	$49	in above	

DINWIDDIE COUNTY LTLs, 1814-1857, KIDD ENTRIES, BY GIVEN NAME

YEAR	LIST	NAME	Res.	Fee or Life	Acres	Description	from CH	rate per acre	Levy added, bldg, etc.	total value	tax	ALTERATIONS (and Comments)
1835	LPL	Kidd, William & wife	Din	blank	60	on Cox Rd.	13NW	$5	$0	$300.00	$0.24	"heretofore charged to Matilda W. Wells" (FHL #29922, i 744)
1836	LPL	Kidd, William & wife	Din	Fee	60	on Cox's Road	13NW	$5	$0	$300	$0.24	FHL #29923, image 60
1837	LPL	Kidd, William & wife	Din	blank	60	on Cox's Road	13NW	$5	$0	$300	$0.24	ibid, image 86
1838	LPL	Kidd, William & wife	Din	blank	60	on Cox's Road	13NW	$5	$0	$300	$0.30	ibid, image 219
1839	LPL	Kidd, William & wife	Din	blank	60	on Cox's Road	13NW	$5	$0	$300	$0.30	ibid, image 232
1840	LPL	Kidd, William & wife	Din	blank	60	on Cox's Road	13NW	$3	$0	$180	$0.18	ibid, image 327
1841	LPL	Kidd, William & wife	Din	Fee	60	on Cox's Road	13NW	$3	$0	$180	$0.23	FHL #29924, image 55
1842	LPL	Kidd, William & wife	Din	Fee	60	on Cox's Road	13NW	$3	$0	$180	$0.23	ibid, image 149
1843	LPL	Kidd, William & wife	Din	Fee	60	on Cox's Road	13NW	$3	$0	$180	$0.26	ibid, image 166
1844	LPL	Kidd, William & wife	Din	Fee	60	on Cox's Road	13NW	$3	$0	$180	$0.23	ibid, image 202

DINWIDDIE COUNTY LTLs, 1814-1857, KIDD ENTRIES, BY GIVEN NAME

YEAR	LIST	NAME	Res.	Fee or Life	Acres	Description	from CH	rate per acre	Levy added, bldg, etc.	total value	tax	ALTERATIONS (and Comments)
1845	LPL	Kidd, William & wife	Din	Fee	60	on Cox's Road	13NW	$3	$0	$180	$0.18	ibid, image 240
1846	LPL	Kidd, William & wife	Din	Fee	60	on Cox's Road	13NW	$3.00	$0	$180	$0.18	ibid, image 306
1847	LPL	Kidd, William & wife	Din	Fee	60	on Cox's Road	13NW	$3.00	$0	$180	$0.18	ibid, image 348
1848	JB	Kidd, William & wife	Din	blank	60	on Cox's Road	13NW	$3.00	$0	$180	$0.18	FHL #29924, image 390
1849	JB	Kidd, William & wife	Din	blank	60	on Cox's Road	13NW	$3	$0	$180	$0.18	FHL #29924, image 437
1850	JB	Kidd, William & wife	Din	blank	60	on Cox's Road	13NW	$3	$0	$180	$0.18	FHL #29924, image 463
1851	JB	Kidd, William & wife	Din	blank	60	on Cox's Road	13NW	$3	$0	$180	$0.22	FHL #29925, image 22
1852	RGB	Kidd, William & wife	Din	blank	60	on Cox's Road	13NW	$3	$0	$180	$0.33	FHL #29925, image 70
1853	RGB	Kidd, William & wife	Din	blank	60	on Cox's Road	13NW	$3	$0	$180	$0.36	FHL #29925, image 116
1854	RGB	Kidd, William & wife	Din	blank	60	on Cox's Road	13NW	$3	$0	$180	$0.36	FHL #29925, image 163

DINWIDDIE COUNTY LTLs, 1814-1857, KIDD ENTRIES, BY GIVEN NAME

YEAR	LIST	NAME	Res.	Fee or Life	Acres	Description	from CH	rate per acre	Levy added, bldg. etc.	total value	tax	ALTERATIONS (and Comments)
1855	RGB	Kidd, William & wife	Din	blank	60	on Cox's Road	13NW	$3	$0	$180	$0.36	FHL #29925, image 216
1856	RGB	Kidd, William & wife	Din	blank	60	On S. S. R. Road	13NW	$3	$0	$180	$0.72	ibid, image 268
1857	WS	Kidd, William & wife	Amelia	Life	61	On S. S. R. Road	13NW	$6	$0	$360	$1.44	FHL #29925, image 382